The Sweet Second Summer
of Kitty Malone

MATT COHEN

The Sweet Second Summer of Kitty Malone

McCLELLAND AND STEWART

The Canadian Publishers
McClelland and Stewart Limited
25 Hollinger Road
Toronto M4B 3G2

CANADIAN CATALOGUING IN PUBLICATION DATA

Cohen, Matt, 1942-
  The sweet second summer of Kitty Malone

ISBN 0-7710-2221-2

I. Title

PS8555.038S94   C813'.5'4   C79-094035-3
PR9199.3.C63S94

The author is grateful to The Canada Council for
support during the writing of this book.

Brief excerpts first appeared in *Aurora* and *The
Sewanee Review.*

Printed and bound in Canada
by John Deyell Company

The Sweet Second Summer of Kitty Malone

One

Friday. And it was late.

Through the screen window Pat Frank could feel the June air breathing, rubbing cool against his face and neck, bringing into the room the sweet heavy fragrance of lilacs, the promise of the summer ahead. He could feel the June air breathing, and he was right in the centre of himself breathing with it, measured and slow; and as he breathed he could feel himself moving into this new season, sliding sideways like a happy cunning crab, edging into the coming warmth.

He was a skinny, long-boned man, Pat Frank, who measured six foot three when he straightened up. But right now he was bent, almost huddled, sitting on the bed in the attic room of the house that Kitty Malone's grandfather had built. With him was his inevitable Friday night companion, a bottle of Barclay Five Star Brandy. Reminded by a gentle stirring of the air that he was in fact awake, he pulled the bottle to his mouth and drank from it so slowly, so thoughtfully, that he almost laughed with the idea that he might have done different.

Different? No. Everything had to be as it was. Because, as of this happy huddled moment, with a cigarette in one hand and the brandy in the other, Pat Frank was perfectly in the centre of himself. The brandy he had drunk burned in his chest.

He dropped the cigarette to the pine floor and ground it out carefully.

Sometimes he drank to be social.

Sometimes he drank to keep his anger down.

But tonight he was alone. He had no one to be drinking with, no one to be angry at. He was only drinking to keep himself company. He was only drinking because he had to.

He looked at the bottle glinting in the moon's light, looked at the hands that held it.

Like the rest of him they had started off long and thin. Lying curled in his mother's belly, his fingers had been long starfish tendrils, swimming in the womb's warm fluid, seeking nothing but the soft perpetual baby's ride to nowhere.

Now his hands were grown up. Forty-nine years' exposure to water and snow had taken the skin from a soft baby's pink to a calloused and abrasive hide. Accidents long forgotten had mashed and thickened the knuckles and bones, making the fingers as knobbly and swollen as old birds' legs. His palms had been shaped by the wooden handles of tools—axes, saws, shovels, hoes had first pushed them wide, then finally cupped them to their own curve, the compliant human bones forced to receive the yellowed hickory shafts.

Sitting in the attic room with the moon and the sweet June air, he was not exactly drunk. But he was at that stage when he knew he could betray himself. So as he tired of the sight of his hands wrapped around the bottle, and reached down to return it to the floor, he directed his body carefully, as if it were a car that he was driving.

Earlier that same night he had been lying beside Kitty Malone, in her downstairs bedroom double bed. And then, at three o'clock in the morning, tired of lying on his back and waiting for his dreams, but not tired enough to sleep, he had dressed again and, with his bottle accompanying him more faithful than any dog, he had climbed the stairs to the attic.

Outside there was a moon which was waxing full. Low in the sky, its light spotted through the trees near the house, scattered through the awkward attic room; and as the breeze made the branches sway, the light moved too, a magic cloak swinging through the angled spaces.

He breathed, and he could feel the night breathe with him.

It seemed that he never slept any more. Ever since the winter had started to melt into spring he had been waking in the middle of the night to discover himself breathing the dark air, slow and careful, drawing it through places in his body that had slept for decades. The air sifted through him until it turned his life transparent, until he felt himself turned into the boy he had once been, felt his whole young body green and reedy, the force of the spring earth pushing through it, making him tingle like a seed ready to explode.

Sometimes, lying in bed and breathing his boy's breath, dreaming his boy's dreams of iced spring water running through the creases of the land, he would forget himself, his age, everything that had disappointed, and breathing the cool dark air he would believe he had found his boy's body again, believe that his bones were soft and unmarked, his skin tense and white, his hands smooth and supple as his boy's hands had been, as was this hand he now held between his older rougher ones, the hand of Lynn Malone.

The moon had sunk so low now that the light from the window shone directly on her head, showing the dark hair curled protectively around her face. And in the pale glow Pat could see the perfect fan of her eyelashes on her cheeks: so innocent he could feel his own eyes quiver and his heart clench in his chest. As if his tears for Lynn asleep could make up for what she missed awake.

Her fingers curled in his hand, trusting. She was seven years old now, a surprise souvenir from a week one winter when he and Kitty had tried for the tenth, or was it the fiftieth, time to reconcile themselves to the love they couldn't shake. Or at least, the grip on each other's lives they couldn't let go.

She shifted now, as if conscious of the light on her face. He felt her hand tighten in his, then travel over it, her fingers tracing their way along his broad palms, then wriggling into the spaces between his fingers.

"Pat, you come to see me?"

"Just came up to say goodnight." He whispered, conscious of the rasping adult sound of his voice in Lynn's room. "Don't you wake up now, it's late."

"I was awake," Lynn said. "I haven't fallen asleep yet." She rubbed her eyes and sat up. She was wearing one of Kitty's nightgowns—her own were at Charlie's house where she usually stayed—and in it she looked so tiny and forlorn that for a moment Pat wanted to bend over her, for once to break his reserve and wrap her up in his long drunken arms.

"You're sleepy," Pat said. "You're asleep right now." His big hands more than covered her shoulders as he pushed her back down, arranged the blankets, as Lynn, giggling, struggled and then bit into his wrist.

Like a boy. After forty-nine years of trying to grow up it seemed that he had now collapsed, that he now wanted to cry every time someone smiled at him, wanted to explode with love and tenderness as if these long waking nights were making him soft in the head. And now, letting Lynn go and reaching into the breast pocket of his denim jacket for rolling tobacco and papers, the thought of his head stayed with him. His bony balding head, his hands, the colour of his eyes and the forced curvings of his bones—this year his body had become an obsession. Even his brain had been discovered: because he had read an article in the Reader's Digest that said alcohol killed the outside cells of the brain and then made it shrink.

"Pat."

"Ain't you asleep?"

He had his cigarette rolled now, and in the flare of the match he could see Lynn smiling and settling into the pillow.

"I'll just finish this," he said. "And then I'll go downstairs."

"All right." In the day her eyes were round and brown, but in this broken light of the moon they glowed like an animal's; and looking closely at them Pat saw not the sad and comfortably known eyes of Lynn Malone but tiny points of reflected amber and glass.

"Pat, can I ask you something?"

"Sure."

"Is my mother going to die?"

Her question startled him so much that he forgot where he was and tried to jerk to his feet. His head bumped against the slanted ceiling and he sank down again onto the bed. "Where'd you get that idea?"

"I don't know," Lynn said. "Kitty told me she was going to the hospital—" Lynn's voice sounded amazingly adult for a moment, then collapsed–"Pat, you . . . a few days, she said."

His heart felt as if it had suddenly grown in his chest, as if it could batter down the walls of his body and pour love right out into the room, into Lynn's heart, into her eyes that now shone blank and fearful. "Lynn. It isn't—"

"And then you came up tonight, and sat on my bed. I thought you'd come to tell me something." Now she was crying and finally Pat reached out for her, took her in his arms and, wrapping the nightgown around her like a blanket around a doll, lifted her out of the bed and into his lap.

"You crazy girl."

"Am I crazy?" Her face was so open.

"Sure," Pat said. "Everyone around here is crazy." He rubbed at her cheeks with his fingers, rubbing them dry, and felt for a moment the total unexpected softness of her, so trusting and compliant she might have been warm clay. "You're crazy to think Kitty's going to die when she's hardly even sick. Kitty's crazy to be asleep when she could be up here having fun with us and I'm crazy to be sitting here dry as the goddamn Arabian desert."

"You better have a drink."

"A gentleman doesn't drink in the room of a lady."

"Go on."

His head still hurt from its collision with the eaves, and he could imagine his poor brain caroming inside his skull like a bruised orange. He lifted the bottle to his mouth. The familiar warmth glowed briefly in his throat, then ran down inside his chest, past his aching heart to his stomach. Kitty, Kitty dying. It was more than twenty years since the summer he and Kitty had met, or at least the summer they had first slept together, the summer she had chased him around the township like a cat in heat until one night they'd found each other in a field. That night and every night thereafter through the whole lazy summer until finally he had told her that he was too old for her, that he wouldn't see her any more. Too old was what he had said, but the truth was worse than that. The truth was that he had lost whatever propelled lives forward, but Kitty's life still lay ahead. The truth was that there was something wrong with him, something missing. That where others conserved their energy and aimed some place in the future—even Mark's wrecked cars and Charlie's shambling farm were something—he had nothing to do with his life but consume it in endless seasons of drinking and fighting and loving, and paying the price with his body when he had to.

Lynn, reassured, had fallen asleep in his arms. For a moment he sat still, his surprise love for her caught like a wedge in his throat. Then, very slowly, he began to rock back and forth. With his eyes closed he was rocking her, rocking her and singing a song of held-back love and Barclay Five Star Brandy; he cradled her in the night, protecting her from the darkness, from the mysterious shadows, from the whispers she had heard, until finally, afraid she would be woken by the violent uncontrollable beating of his own heart, he carefully lowered her down to the pillow and smoothed the covers over her. Bottle still firmly grasped in one hand, letting his feet patiently search out the quiet boards, he stepped out of Lynn's room and down the stairs from the attic.

Outside the breeze had cooled. Standing in the yard of the house Kitty's grandfather had built, Pat Frank buttoned his denim jacket and then, without thinking, began to roll himself another cigarette. Early June. The smell of lilacs that had been resonant in Lynn's room was here heavy and almost overpowering.

He lit his cigarette, then dug his hands into his back and stretched. Sometimes these days he hardly recognized himself: working steady hours, getting up every morning and eating breakfast, he had even caught himself trying to drink less, as if, after all these years, his body was ready to sue for peace.

And not only his body, but his feelings too. Because ever since he had started working again at the Salem Garage And General Repair, he had been seeing Kitty again, on week-ends.

Natural as anything, Charlie Malone would come by the shop late Friday night. Standing in the bare front office, looking out the big picture window to the dirt yard where the gas pumps sat, flooded by white neon lights, they would pass the brandy back and forth. And gradually, to the rhythm of the bottle slapping down on the arborite counter, the working days would drain away; until after a few drinks they might even make a trip to the No-Tell Motel to view the spring's entertainment sensation—a green bosomed singer in a plastic green grass skirt. On the way home Charlie, without asking, would let Pat off at the place where his own driveway branched into the trail that led to his sister's house.

"Son of a bitch," Charlie Malone would say, "here we are." And would punch Pat on the shoulder, his stubby farmer's weight sometimes forcing Pat right out the door. And Pat, drunk or sober, would regain his footing and, slapping the door of the truck as if it were Charlie's back, wave goodnight. Listen to the slow rattling progress of the truck. And then begin his own erratic march down the trail to Kitty's house.

The lower edge of the moon was touching the horizon now; soon it would be hidden behind the ridges of maple and oak that surrounded the Malone farm. With his jacket buttoned tight and his hands stuffed deep in his pockets, Pat Frank paced about the yard of the house, so exhausted with these sleepless nights he could hardly move, but still propelled by nervous energy, by the brandy in his belly and the sweet breeze blowing across the land. This was his time of night; the hours before sunrise when his body went sullen and stunned, his mind suddenly glowed alive, flaming itself away like the last burst of an old log before it crumbled.

Dizzy with his own speeding thoughts, he turned to look at the house Kitty's grandfather had built. Set on a foundation that had long since rotted into the earth, it rose only a brief storey and a half before being capped by a panoramic tin roof that stretched well out from the walls to enclose a spacious porch. It was a small house, with a kitchen and a bedroom downstairs, and one bedroom up; and with the circling porch and the all-encompassing roof, it looked like a small head drowned by an enormous wide-brimmed hat.

And in fact the porch, with its extravagant maple floor and oaken railing, was the best part of the house. On that porch he and Kitty used to meet each other early in their courtship, and it was to those familiar shadows that he now retreated. After standing there briefly, comforted by its hat as if it were his own, he picked up the bottle from one of the posts and sat down slowly, stretching his legs and sighing.

Now the brandy was like a river in his throat, the heat burning his mouth, forcing open his chest so he could breathe. Calm again, nursing the remembered weight of Lynn in his arms, he was once more suddenly at home in himself. Ghosts past and present moved through the dark air. After all these years of sober drinking something had finally given way and he was haunted; not only by the ghosts of those dead, or of those still living, but haunted by the boy he had been; haunted by memories he had long ago discarded, by sounds and smells brought to him by the wind. He could feel his brain burning worse than any Reader's Digest could suspect, burning itself to oblivion while the summer night tunnelled deep into its centre, making the wind sweet in a way it hadn't been for forty years, so sharp and poignant he wanted to cry with the pain of it, with this whole long gentle spring that had somehow eaten into his nerves and was making him young again. And sitting on the comfortable old porch in the dark, dizzy from the brandy and his own frightened thoughts, it seemed suddenly that the whole universe was fragile, that the comfortable old wood supporting him, the familiar June wind that washed his face and neck, were suddenly in danger of disappearing, leaving him stranded in the centre of a black markless night, leaving him the lone survivor with his life torn open, pouring love and regret into the cold air.

When he woke the sky was a glassy blue, the stars a bright electric white. Pat, stiff and sleepy, still holding the bottle, stood up and stumbled through the house to Kitty's bedroom. There he stripped off his clothes, looked briefly at his gaunt scarecrow body, then slid carefully into the sheets, trying to spoon Kitty's sleeping body into his own. Her back was absolutely stiff. Then she jerked away and the light snapped on.

"Where were you?"

"Outside."

"I thought you'd gone home."

"No. I couldn't sleep."

"You'd sleep better if you'd stay in bed."

"Sorry," Pat said. Up on one elbow, thinking that he *was* sorry, sorry that he hadn't walked home through the bush instead of getting into another fight with Kitty. He rubbed his eyes and squinted through the lamplight at Kitty. She was lying on her back, her head propped up on the two pillows she always used, her blue eyes open wide. She looked like she had been awake for hours.

"How are you feeling?"

"Sick," Kitty whispered. "It hurts."

Like Pat's, Kitty's face was strong-boned and wide. But whereas Pat's flesh was fallen away from drinking, so that even in this bright light his face was all hollows and shadows, Kitty's skin was still young and full, and her white-blond hair gave her a curiously ageless look.

"I don't know what's wrong," Kitty said. "It's not supposed to hurt." She brushed her wispy hair away from her forehead; and her eyes, which had briefly looked into his, shifted away now too. Pat, levering himself up, followed the movement of her eyes; he was so attuned to that movement, to that shifting away, that it sometimes seemed to him that everything that had gone wrong for them in the past twenty years could be summed up in that one gesture, in the way she focussed on him briefly and then shifted away, preferring her own private world to anything that could be shared.

"You want a pill?"

"An aspirin, I'll get it."

"No, I will." Pat got out of bed and started for the kitchen. Then, remembering Lynn, wrapped a towel around his waist. When he returned with the water and pill Kitty was sitting up and smoking.

"This okay? I got some brandy left."

"No. Just water." She swallowed it down, making a face. "I wish they wouldn't have put off the operation."

"Well," Pat said, "we're going to the hospital today. They'll make you better there."

"I know." Kitty stubbed out her cigarette and turned off the light.

"I'm cold," Kitty said.

"I could make a fire."

"Don't bother now." She reached down to the foot of the bed for the quilt, pulled it up over them. Pat, liking its weight, slid deeper under the covers. Then felt Kitty take his hand, guide it slowly to her belly.

"Do you think it's getting bigger?"

The heat of her skin flooded into his palm. He pressed down. Nothing, he could feel nothing at all but Kitty's familiar belly. He realized she was holding her breath and he let his hand move away.

"Well?"

"No," Pat said. "I guess it's about the same."

A cyst, the doctor had said, an ovarian cyst. Kitty had never felt it herself until she had gone to the doctor, because she was three months late. And when she had told Pat about it, she had been so long and twisted in the telling that for a moment he had thought she was pregnant again. But she wasn't. And when they took the cyst out they were going to pinch her tubes. So she wouldn't be. The skin beneath his hand was damp with sweat. Kitty, since seeing the doctor, had claimed she could feel it, that it was as big as a grapefruit. Pat caressed her stomach slowly, so tired now his mind was filled only with images of himself sleeping, of his head buried in the pillow and his eyes sealed shut; and he could feel his own weight pulling him down into the mattress, his bones buzzing warm and contented, his whole night's worrying and dreaming over now, nothing left for him but pure deep sleep.

"I was thinking about making a will."

"What for?"

"I've got to leave Randy and Lynn provided for."

"Randy. You don't have to worry about Randy, he's looked after already."

"He's my son."

"That's right," Pat said. "I never said he was mine." He reached his hand down to the floor and felt around until he found the bottle, opened it, then pulled it up to his mouth. Swallowing lying down made him cough, but at least it woke him and he sat up shaking his head. The night was over now, the dark suddenly gone; and now the room was filled with the first gold washings of day. Kitty, propped by her pillows, looked absurdly beautiful in this light, looked younger and more desirable than she had ever been before, her wispy hair curling gold on her bare shoulders, her eyes so blue and cold he wanted to kiss them.

"What are you thinking?"

"I don't know," Pat said. "Maybe I was thinking that if you're wanting to make a will you must be pretty worried."

"I know it's stupid. But what if something happens?"

"For Christ's sake." She had a familiar stubbornness in her voice, an insistent braying note that sometimes reminded him of a mule insisting its way into the garbage. Here it was morning and he still hadn't slept, morning and just because she was looking for a fight and he had promised to drive her to the hospital, he couldn't swing up out of bed and start the long walk to where he belonged, his own house where he breathed his own breath, thought his own thoughts, got his whisky stolen by his own brother, and didn't get woken up in the middle of the night by someone who wasn't even sick wanting to write their will.

"Go back to sleep."

"I'm up now." He reached for his tobacco and started to roll a cigarette. "Anyway, what do you need a will for? You don't have anything that people are going to fight over."

"Lynn."

"What about her?"

"Who's going to look after Lynn?"

"I will."

"Don't be crazy."

"I'm not." And, in fact, as he licked the newly rolled cigarette, he felt a sudden and perfect confidence. Look after Lynn? Of course he could. Still drunk enough to be monitoring his body, which he did without even thinking, the long-developed drinker's cunning taking him through another night, he reached carefully down to the floor for his pants, searched the pockets for matches.

"Don't you think I could do it?"

"I don't know. You never wanted to."

Lynn? Yes, of course he could take care of Lynn. The idea of Kitty's death had never occurred to him before tonight, but now that she had made the challenge, he immediately imagined himself meeting it. Permanently sober, in mourning, he would finally shoulder his responsibilities, live in this house and take close and sober care of Lynn to the sacred tune of Kitty's memory. And the more he thought about it, the more he realized that this coming task was the meaning of the whole drunken night he had had, the whole long drunken spring that was tearing apart his nerves and body. Lynn? Yes, of course. He lit his cigarette, and as he did the light of the match caught so strangely in his eye that he lurched, almost fell to the floor. Dizzy and excited he swung out of bed, promising himself as his feet wavered downward to stop drinking, to stop drinking absolutely.

"Pat."

"I could do it," he insisted. He would even take care of her garden, growing weedless and straight the hopeless mixture of vegetables and weeds she let rise every summer. He swung round to face Kitty for confirmation.

She was bent over double, her face in the pillow.

"It's not funny, for Christ's sake." He could feel his temper starting, shooting through him in an unwelcome, sobering flame, and it was only as he strode towards the bed, his long arm reaching out to grab her shoulder, that he realized she was crying.

"What's wrong now?"

"You bastard," she choked out, "you want me to die."

"Oh no, have a drink."

"I don't want a drink."

He lay down beside her and pulled her head into his chest.

"Kitty," he whispered, "now Kitty, now Kitty. It's going to be all right. You know it's going to be all right."

Lynn woke to the sounds of the bed springs creaking and whispers from the downstairs bedroom. It used to be that when the bed creaked there were no whispers, only groans and cries. When Charlie and Sadie made the bed creak that was the only sound there was, long lingering complaints of springs and wood. And when the noise of the bed stopped so did everything else. Silence. With Pat and Kitty there was not much of silence. Even after the bed gave up, Pat and Kitty kept whispering, whispering and sometimes even talking. But they never talked clearly enough for her to hear, and sometimes she wondered if they wanted it that way, wanted to have secrets from her just so she could guess them.

Holding Kitty's nightgown up, she crossed the floor, tiptoeing so they wouldn't know she was up. The sun was rising now, its big yellow edge was poking over the hill and soon its whole face would show. Except that no one would see it, it would be too bright to see, too bright to see the face purse its lips, take one deep scalding breath, and blow the mist right off the fields.

Looking at the sun now, wondering if staring at it would blow the eyes right out of her head, she remembered waking in the night. Pat had been sitting on the bed and he had told her that Kitty was going to live. He was a drunk, Pat Frank, everyone knew that he was a crazy fool of a drunk and that Kitty Malone had lost her heart over him and ruined her life. At least that's what Ellen—Kitty's mother and Lynn's grandmother—had said. Which reminded her of the taste of Pat Frank's wrist in her mouth, hairy and sour, that crazy drunk who had ruined her mother's life, he was lucky she liked him. He was lucky she hadn't bitten his arm in two.

There was an apple on the dresser she had started the night before. Now, as she dressed, she continued it, like an unfinished chapter of a book, and when she was done she walked slowly downstairs, her small feet carefully searching for the same solid boards Pat Frank's had; and when she got downstairs she stood for a moment outside Kitty's bedroom. Saw Kitty, asleep, and

Pat asleep beside her; and she was still thinking about that quiet sight, and wondering how one person could ruin another person's life, when she heard the unmuffled growl of Randy's truck coming up the lane.

Two

With Kitty there were things so bad she wanted to stay away from them forever.

Worst of all was her father's death. She was fifteen years old when her father, riding in a car driven by his friend and neighbour Stanley Kincaid, slammed into the rock cliff that marked the turn to the Catholic Church.

No loss or betrayal ever shook her as much again, but there were two events that came very close. One was the way Pat Frank had looked her straight in the eye as if he had never seen her before except across a big room. And had said good-bye. Had said he was too old, too ruined, too crazy, too drunk. That night she had, as she sometimes said to herself, forgotten but not forgiven.

The second was her marriage to Randy Blair.

She managed to forget, most of the time, what the marriage had been like, but the memory of leaving him stayed close to the surface.

It had happened on her twenty-second birthday, on August the third of 1958.

As noon came around, the actual hour of her birth, she was

standing in Union Station in Toronto, as hot and muggy as the day. It smelled, she thought, like everything else she was growing to hate about Toronto in the summer: deodorized perspiration from thousands of bodies, exhaust fumes, instant food factories, stale fish-tainted air from the lake. Attached to her hand was her first child, Randy Blair Junior, and in her belly was the beginning of a second, which she hoped her girdle would hide. But her dress was pushed up by it and rode awkwardly on the elastic, only making her feel that much more uncomfortable and conspicuous.

Even at twenty-two her face was too strong-boned to be pretty. Her straw-blond hair revealed a high wide forehead, and her blue eyes seemed too large and were always shifting away. Now, however, they were fastened to the clock in the centre of the station, waiting for the time when she could board the train to Brockville.

To everything that came into her own mind, and to everything her son said, she mumbled, "Not now." *Not now, not now*; the words spun round in her mind, a litany with no purpose except blocking out everything else. In order to keep him quiet she had given Randy Junior a cookie and, because with him and the suitcases it was too awkward to struggle with getting and lighting a cigarette, she was eating a cookie too, reminding herself of a neurotic cow, chewing away so hard her cheeks ached.

Randy, whom she had spanked three times in the last hour, was finally calm. His cheeks were red and swollen with tears, his eyes, round and brown exactly like his father's, were fixed on the swirling crowds. Despite the heat, the hours of discomfort she knew were ahead, Randy's temperamental behaviour, and her own ridiculous and slightly nauseated condition, she was just beginning to feel peaceful when Randy Blair came storming towards her with such fury that even his son shrank into her.

"And where in the hell do you think you're going?" Randy Blair was a tall, florid man, with strawberry blond hair that was greased straight back and a pugged, lifted-up nose that looked surgically created. In this weather, as in all weather, he was wearing his only and favourite coat, a black leather bomber jacket with sheepskin lining and silver zippers everywhere.

"I'm going home," Kitty said. "And don't shout."

"You think you're walking out on me?"

"I'm not walking out on you," Kitty said, in the patient voice she had learned to use for him. "I'm leaving. And you are the one that drove me here, only twenty minutes ago."

"Don't give me that bullshit."

"All right," Kitty said. And turned away, giving her husband her broad and sweatered back. Which he grabbed as he pulled her around.

"Please," said Kitty.

"*Please.*" His face squinched up and his eyes screwed down tiny as chicken's eyes. "Jesus Christ, Kitty," he said, his voice pleading, "won't you come back?"

"No."

"Don't tell me no." His voice was down to a whisper but she was familiar with this tactic. It led to tears, hers, a frantic hour in bed, and then everything reverted to normal: a one-bedroom apartment above a grocery store where she spent twenty-four hours a day minding his kid while he drove his taxi and stood around the racetrack, waiting for his horse to come in.

"Okay," she said. "I won't tell you anything." He had let his eyes fall open again and they were now round and ready to cry. Actual tears began to slide out the corners, and Kitty was so startled she didn't know whether to join him, give in, or finally do what she had wanted to the whole endless morning of this fight: step back and deliver to him the famous Malone round-house uppercut and lay him out—round baby eyes and all—on the marble floor of this train station.

"Daddy," Randy Junior said.

Randy Senior looked down at his son with an expression of amazement, of surprise that *he* should be here, the same surprise and resentment he showed when Kitty wouldn't make love in the morning after Randy was already running restlessly about the apartment. Instinctively she put her hand to her flattened belly: a secret of course, he would never let her go if he had *that* on her too.

"You don't want to leave me, do you son?"

Randy Junior, who was not quite two and understood only

selectively, looked up to Kitty for instruction.

"It's all right," Kitty said. "We're only going for a holiday."

"Some holiday."

"That's right," Kitty said. "Some goddamned holiday." And all of a sudden she thought she was going to scream out to the whole station that this crazy florid taxi driver had filled her guts with kids and then left her in an apartment that was hotter than a tin-roofed henhouse and only wanted to come home to get food and loving as if he had invented the whole world by picking her up in a bar three years ago.

"You know what?" Kitty asked.

"What?"

"It's my birthday." And one last time her eyes jumped to his. "Not now," she said. "Don't cry now."

The train finally left. She was installed on a big set of double facing seats with Randy, and while he lay down to sleep she stretched out her legs and read the paper. The train moved slowly, sliding through the railyards and stopping at every crossing, but Kitty didn't care, she felt free at last; and looking out the window for the first sign of fields it occurred to her that Randy Blair in his bomber jacket had never been to Salem, or her farm. Which was consoling because in all the time she had considered leaving him, the one event she had dreaded was that some night she would be lying in her old room at the farm with the dark air breathing over her, and suddenly he would jump through the window, crazy and red-faced and wanting to start an argument. And she knew if he ever attacked her on her own ground she would have no defence left at all, she would just die and crumple up like another wrapper to be stuffed in his silver-zippered pockets.

Randy groaned in his sleep. She picked him up and laid him across her lap. His face landed on her bare arm; his wet breath on her skin unnerved her; and she finally began to cry as the train crawled through Toronto's outskirts of warehouses and flat-topped factories.

At Brockville she changed trains and got on the small branch line that still ran twice daily to Salem. Her last visit home had been at Christmas, when Randy was still an infant. But the gap seemed larger than a few months. It could have been forever, because then she had been returning as a married woman with a child, as Kitty Malone Blair who had left Salem and made a life for herself in the big city, home to visit with trinkets, magazines, and most of all, exotic stories of life in the metropolis; but now she was coming back alone and defeated, Kitty Malone, preceded only by a short telephone call to the post office to leave a message for her brother.

Kitty Malone Blair she had been and now that she was away from him and once more Kitty Malone, she couldn't hate him any more. As the train moved slowly north, the green and yellow fields began to sprout rocks, patches of bush, and finally small hills. With this before her eyes, clear and familiar even through the smogged-up windows of the ancient coach, she couldn't feel anything except relief at being away—from her husband, from their crazy fights, from the city where she could find no live place in herself that knew how to respond.

When they left Brockville it was six in the evening. She and Randy had eaten nothing all day except cookies, some doughnuts, and stale-tasting milk from the dining-car on the first train. Now Randy began to get cranky; the sun was lengthening on the fields and the train was losing its novelty. Kitty changed him, then sat him on her knee and wrapped her arms around him. His hair was still silky baby's hair, white blond and so fine she could blow into it and make it spray out like milkweed. She held him close and rocked him back and forth, trying to time her rocking to the slow swaying of the train. The country was getting rougher and more choppy; there were places where the track sliced its way through rocky embrasures, steep cliffs that cut away into valleys with huge trees so inaccessible they had never been logged.

"You know what?" she said to Randy, who at eighteen months had only a few words but liked being talked to. "You know where we're going to live? In the house your great-grandfather built. A white house with glass windows and stairs that go from the bottom to the top."

Kitty Malone she had been; Kitty Malone Blair she had become. In a stone church in Toronto, with only her mother and her brother to see her off, she had wed Randy Blair as soon as she found out she was pregnant. There was nothing wrong with getting married that way, everyone did, and at the sight of him in his blue serge suit, slicked-back strawberry hair cut so short the nape of his neck was striped red and white, she had almost believed it would work. That night they had gone home to the apartment where they already lived, and with Charlie and her mother killed two bottles of rye. Then Charlie had insisted on setting out for Salem, even though it was close to midnight.

"Can't drive this late," Kitty insisted.

"Of course I can," Charlie said. "Can't spoil the honeymoon."

"That's right, honey," Randy had laughed, by then unjacketed and his white shirt stained with ginger ale and sweat. "He can do it."

So she had gone to bed angry, ready to blame him for the gory accident she was almost sober enough to imagine. But because it was their wedding night and they were both drunk and she didn't want to start wrong, she had pretended to be pleased. Ten minutes later he was lying beside her, asleep, curled tight as a plump snail. That was the night she had become Kitty Malone Blair; *Blair* she had said to herself, loving him then, needing his smell, the surprising whiteness of his skin, the smooth layers of fat that ran like sand rivers over his hips and back. *Blair* she had said to herself, curling into him, closing her eyes, letting her hand slide round to his chest and the feel of his sleeping breath against her fingers.

It was Charlie who met them at the station.

Kitty reached up to Randy and swung him down the iron steps. Then she stood back on the platform while the conductor helped her out with her bags.

"Look at him," Charlie said, crouching down to be at Randy's height. Randy shrunk away but Charlie snaked out his hand and had it flat on Randy's stomach. "Quite a belly you got there, boy."

"It's your Uncle Charlie," Kitty said.

Charlie took his hand away, then brought it back, filled with a package of gum. "Care for a stick?"

Randy hesitantly reached out, then, taking both hands away from Kitty, grabbed at the package.

"That's better," said Charlie. "A man got to have a chew." Kneeling down on the station platform, his head half-bald and peeling scarlet, his large greasy hands filled with tinfoil and wrapping that Randy was slowly shredding, Charlie looked to his sister like a benevolent gnome. Then he stood up.

"How's my kid sister?" he asked.

"I'm okay."

"You look awful." They both had the same high-domed forehead and light wispy hair. But whereas the years were making Charlie have more scalp and less hair, pregnancy was having the opposite effect on Kitty, growing her hair thick and coarse, and as she brushed it away from her eyes she felt he must be telling the truth.

"We want you to live with us," Charlie said. "Sadie wants you to have the bedroom with the flowers, and she wants Randy to take the one at the end of the hall."

"She won't like having a child in the house."

"Oh no, Kitty, that's not true." And for just one moment Charlie's usual rye-drinker's schoolboy face fell away and Kitty saw him as a grown man, no longer just her brother, a husband in a marriage that had borne nothing but rabbits and cats.

"All right," Kitty said. "But after a while I'm going to move to Grandpa's house."

All this time Charlie had been helping Randy unwrap the gum and get it into his mouth. Now Charlie hoisted him up so he sat in the crook of his arm.

"Maybe you look okay," he said.

"Jesus," Kitty said. "It's good to be back." Then she looked at her son who was solemnly chewing away at the whole package of gum, unable to keep his lips closed, chewing with excruciating slowness, happily drooling with every movement of his jaws.

"Oh no, he'll choke on that." And to a new set of tears and wails she set about extracting the gum from Randy's mouth.

"Pat Frank was going to come," Charlie said. "But he's working this weekend at the General Repair."

"Pat?"

"Yeah. Pat Frank. You remember him." He had started walking down the platform, Randy in one arm and the heaviest suitcase hanging from the other. The day was turning into evening, and although in Toronto it had been hot and stale, here the air was growing cool, and she felt suddenly that her pores and lungs were so jammed up with the city that her skin couldn't breathe. She spat her gum out onto the tracks and tried to search her mouth clean with her tongue. With the mention of Pat's name it seemed her old self had jumped out, like filings to a magnet, and she realized he had been in and out of her mind almost every day for three years, though she hardly ever noticed it, and she never would have admitted that she had missed him.

Charlie's truck was new: or at least it was nothing less than new. It had been constructed, as were all his trucks, from a dozen rejects bolted and welded together; and to make them into one unified vehicle he had coated everything with thick black enamel from which streaks and dribbles stood out like cold treacle on one of Charlie's famous iron flapjacks.

"Nice, eh?" said Charlie, smacking the hood. The flat of his hand made a hard sharp noise. Randy Blair's palms were quilted and soft, like yellow-pink muffins, and one happy night she had told him they felt on her skin like the insides of pillows.

They drove through Salem slowly in the truck and, sitting in Charlie's truck window with the baby on her knee, Kitty felt on exhibit. Home after three years with one baby born and the next one soon to be showing: *Didn't waste any time*, they would say; and now she was starting to cry and couldn't stop, her tears sliding in sheets down her cheeks. Past the hotel and the tavern where she had once worked as a waitress, past the Salem General Repair where Pat Frank was working and too lazy to come meet her, past the liquor store, the beer store, the vegetable market where the paved road gave way to gravel and the noise of the stones against the jigsaw body of the truck was so loud she could cry without having to hear herself. Randy Junior joined in, at first just sniffling along, then outright wailing until she couldn't ignore him, and looked down to see his eyes screwed shut like his father's, his mouth wide open in a great round O. Charlie had stopped the truck. Randy's wail was so completely meaningless, so completely unanswered as it passed through the open windows into the gathering evening, that she and Charlie began to laugh, her laughing so hard she started crying again and found herself alternating back and forth, laughing and crying, until she was exhausted.

"Christ," Charlie said, grinning, "you're just as bad as ever."

"Well, look where you've brought me." And in fact they were parked by the black ironwork gate that marked the entrance to the Salem Burial Grounds. In that place all four of their grandparents now resided. And in that place their father was buried, too. At his funeral Kitty had suddenly given way to convulsions of uncontrollable tears, crying and whooping so loudly that Charlie had had to lead her away from the grave so the rest could hear the service. He had taken her to where he was walking her now, to the edge of the cemetery where a cliff fell away to a railway line, and they had sat at the top of the hill while she cried, and then kneeled forward and was sick until it seemed her whole insides had come out, there was no stop, and looking down that hill through her tears she had seen not the railway line, nor any bottom at all, but only a complete gap in herself that could never be closed.

Her mother had shrunk even further. She was sitting beside the stove waiting, but as Kitty came in the door she pushed herself up out of her chair and approached, her marvellous false teeth shining like silver in the electric light.

"You're pregnant again."

"That's right."

"They're always pregnant these days, ain't that right, Charlie? Look at her, keeping her belly in like that. No one even knows how to have a baby now." She had her arm woven into Kitty's for support. "You can't let them be putting it to you all the time; Christ child, learn to keep your feet. Ain't that right, Charlie?"

"All right," Charlie said. "She just came in on the train. Don't you want to say hello to Randy?" He lifted up the boy, who had been cowering by the door, and brought him forward. "Now just say hello nice," Charlie said. "You don't want to scare him."

derworlds and the cowboys and Indians all mashed together in a million technicolour scenes. Now, lying on this bed, she felt as if she were back in that old theatre, her mind running its life to itself, she the only spectator, sitting in the torn plush seats with her feet up watching over and over as the reels whizzed by. And, as with all her dreams, she couldn't remember it even while she was dreaming it, so finally she found herself awake, sitting on the edge of the bed, her feet reaching blindly for the floor and her skin covered in a panic of sweat and confusion. At first she thought she was still in Toronto, and looked for Randy, but as quickly as her arms stretched out she knew, and was suddenly relieved: a long sigh escaped as if she had been holding her breath this whole time.

She stood up and went to the window. The boxy shapes of the barns loomed close, their tin roofs gleaming with the light of the moon. In the city at night the rows of yellow lights wiped out all awareness of the sky, and she could never know if it was new moon or full. But now she saw the moon almost round. The window was jammed open with a flowerpot, and the air that settled around her was cool but not cold; it promised wet grass outside. And feeling wonderfully and extravagantly alone, she picked up her shoes and went out of her room, tiptoeing down the stairs the way she used to, remembering everything now: which stairs creaked, where it was safe to put her whole weight and where she had to use the banister to lift herself over the dangerous parts.

"Kitty."

The voice just inches away from her as she stood at the bottom landing. It was like a finger touching the basebone of her spine.

"Ellen?"

"I was just sitting here, Kitty." Her mother was in the wicker chair, blanketed in the shadow of the woodstove.

"You scared me."

"You got a cigarette, Kitty?"

"I'll look."

Without turning on the light she stepped into the centre of the kitchen. The moon had laid a silver pane in the middle of the room, and it had settled with wavy edges almost exactly on top of the great square table her grandfather had made. That was where she looked first, the table, and then when she saw nothing there, she moved to the counters. That was all there was to the kitchen: a woodstove near the base of the stairs, with its wicker chair for Ellen; a square table with eight square-backed chairs in the centre of the room; and two walls of counters, one with a metal sink and the other lined with tins of staples. Beside the sink, sitting neatly in an ashtray, she found her own package of Player's. The whole room was black and grey and silver, in the light of the moon; and when she opened her mouth to take the cigarette, Ellen's teeth shone silver too.

"You know——" began Ellen, but nothing followed. She smoked awkwardly at her cigarette, using her fingers as if they were tweezers, sucking it in sporadically, then letting it burn until the ash fell off onto her own skirt.

"I was going to go out," Kitty said.

"For a walk?"

"That's right." She sat in one of the straight-backed chairs and watched her mother smoke. She could feel it all coming back to her, the webs and scrambled words and long senile excursions that could set out in any direction.

"You know," Ellen said. "I think the boy liked me."

"He did."

"It's good you finally came home, Kitty. We been expecting you." She tried to put her cigarette out on the stove, but it fell to the floor, still glowing, illuminating a small circle of linoleum around itself. Kitty bent down and picked it up, threw it in the grate. "Aren't you going to kiss me?"

Kitty put her hands on her mother's shoulders; they were so bony, the skin so loose they felt like birds' bones and silky feathers. She leaned over and pressed her lips against her mother's lips: they were tart and rubbery, dried out black olives. She almost drew away but then stopped. And in that instant the taste grew stronger, almost overwhelming. Birds' bones and strong black olives: the sensations rushed into her, and in that place she had found empty when she cried for her father when Charlie had touched her this afternoon, she felt her mother's presence growing again, this crazy half-bald lady's love filling

33

her up like a well rising with water. And then losing control she dropped down and buried her head in her mother's sharp knees, hugging and squeezing them together until she heard Ellen whimper with love and pain.

"That's right," Ellen said, as Kitty stood up. "We've been expecting you all this time."

The moon was so bright Kitty could see her mother's eyes; they seemed all right, saner than sane. Even as a child she had wondered about Ellen and her sudden outbursts, and even then she had always reassured herself by looking at Ellen's eyes, buried in the dead skin of her face like open wet oysters in sand.

"Eh Kittens," Ellen said, the name they used to call her, "you better be going now." And as she said these words Kitty was on her feet and swinging through the screen door into the night.

In the kitchen the moon had been bright enough to lay its shadows across the room, but outside it was brighter yet. Everything that was new assaulted her at once: the night smell of the farm, the sound of wind moving slowly through the leaves, the long dark tunnel of the lane. As she walked her ankles kept twisting on her narrow city heels so finally she took the shoes off and carried them, placing each naked foot down slowly, tender to the pebbles and the cold.

When she came to the trail to her grandfather's farm, dirt and pebbles gave way to grass, and the walking was easier. She had no idea of the time, there were traces of neither evening nor dawn in the sky, and for the first time in years it seemed her mind had gone peacefully blank, ready to receive the summer. Twice she stopped: once to put her shoes on again when finally her feet got too cold; and a second time to sit at the side of the trail and smoke a cigarette.

Quiet, it was quiet here. Not silent, because actually the night was layered with the noises of wind, crickets, frogs grinding out their single message, loons calling from the lakes that were scattered around: but quiet in that between and through these signs of life no machines were woven. And then, as it seemed to a hundred times every day and night, a shadow of sensation passed through her belly and she was reminded that she was pregnant, that there was still this last souvenir to be dealt.

She got up, still smoking, and began to walk again, slowly, rocking her body with each step, letting herself feel her own weight being received by the ground. Kitty Malone she had been. Kitty Malone Blair she had become. And now she was going to be Kitty Malone again. With every step she increased her distance from Randy Blair and his soft hands and peachy skin, from his taxi and the plastic-wrapped picture he had of himself on the seat: Randy Blair—6′-1″, 195 lbs., 28 years old. But though the night was waiting and it was her own name she was trying to come to, she knew she would never meet her old self again. Every step that carried her away from Randy Blair was carrying her away from the smooth continuous line that had been her life for twenty-two years. And here on the trail that led to her grandfather's house she felt further from her past than she had ever been.

Kitty brushed her hair back from her forehead; her eyes shifted through the trees and saw, ahead, the place where the light was broken by the low winged shape of her grandfather's house. It was the whole three years of her marriage since she had walked here, but every step of the way was as familiar as her own body and as she came up to the deserted yard around the house there was something else that was familiar too, the feeling of Pat Frank's presence.

She stopped at the gate, her hand resting on the rusted iron latch. This seemed different; so much more paint had worn itself away in the rain, and the metal had grown thicker and rougher to the touch. And while she held the latch, almost caressed it, she searched the shadows of the porch, all of her strained and alert, unwilling to believe he was there, unwilling to believe he wouldn't be. Then there was the scrape and flare of a match and she saw him sitting where he always used to, on the porch, his back shoved up against the front door.

She pushed open the gate and started to walk through the yard. Here, in the place protected from the cows, thistles were growing up, and even by their touch she suddenly remembered them, purple spiked flowers that hung pendulously at the end of long green stems. Then she was up on the porch and, as she always used to, lowered herself down without speaking, stretching out her legs so they rested flat against the wood. All the sounds of the night seemed to have grown sharper, and as she accepted a cigarette from Pat Frank she found herself listening to the short high-pitched screech of a hunting owl.

"I had to come back," Kitty said. The owl screeched again, louder and longer. "They're killing each other out there."

"Just playing," said Pat Frank. She hadn't remembered his voice, but now that she heard it, it seemed the most intimate sound in the world, so close to her she could have spoken it herself.

"It wasn't him," Kitty said. "I didn't want to leave him, but I needed to be here."

"It grows on you," Pat said. In his tone was the twist he used to have, the voice he put on for customers and tourists.

"Don't laugh at me."

"No."

She felt like a double image: every gesture she made imposed almost exactly on the gestures she used to make—leaning forward to scratch her calves, the adjustment she made of her dress over her legs, wriggling herself comfortable against the warped boards of the porch floor. His voice was warm, but when she finally caught his face in the moonlight it was like a mask, cold and carved out of stone.

"Please sit closer," she said. And when he did Kitty Malone took his hand and put it on her belly, so he would know how it was.

"Ahh Kitty," Pat Frank said.

"Just three months."

"I never should have let you go."

"It was me that went, not you that made me."

And that was how it was that night, August third, 1958: the birthday she remembered: the night Kitty Malone came home to Salem. The moon set and left them in darkness. Then the sun began to rise and found them sitting still, awake, silent, smoking their cigarettes, breathing in the new day, waiting.

Pat shifted in his sleep. The long nights were harder on him now, and in the new morning sun his face was getting old, seamed and punched in by the weather. Kitty, sitting awake in the bed, watching Pat and remembering the night she came home to Salem, took his sleeping hand the way she had taken it then. Through the half-open door she could hear Lynn and Randy moving about the kitchen, arguing, starting water to boil. *I never should have left you.* Pat.

Three

Friday night had passed, and Saturday morning begun.

Mark Frank was seated in an old wooden rowboat, like a bull's-eye ensconced in the centre of a glass-calm lake. It was one of those shallow mud-bottomed lakes that dot the country north of Kingston, its banks thick with cedar and birch. At this early hour the trees blurred together like so many bruised fingers, and their colour leaked out into the water, purple-blue, just beginning to lighten with the rising sun. From the trees at the shore could be heard the sounds of small birds, but it was the time of day when the giant herons owned the water, big birds with wings that sounded across the whole lake as they flew.

As the sun's rays poked up into the sky, Mark Frank followed his daily habit by taking out his glass eye, inspecting it, then wiping it clean.

That glass eye was the first thing anyone would notice about Mark Frank: like his other eye it had been born brown, but because it had been a bargain twenty-five years ago, the white had aged into a porcelain yellow, and the brown turned beige with the sun. He had a square muscular face, his love of order showing through the square set of his bones, and meeting him for the first time it was hard to know which eye suited him better — the dry light one that stared at you without moving, or the moist dark one that kept blinking, too nervous for the man who carried it.

He was a short stocky man with a wide back and long thick arms that hung down from his shoulders with the look ex-athletes sometimes have, the look of heavy muscles running to fat. But Mark Frank was a welder by trade, and though his muscles ran heavy and his gut hung out over his wide leather belt, he was still strong enough. Strong enough, for example, so that when he fished he seemed like a giant overwhelming a child's toys. He had a small casting rod, which looked infantile in his huge hand, and to use it he simply flicked his massive wrist, sending the bait out in a straight screaming line until it was over the desired spot, where he jerked it to a stop and let it fall. From one oarlock dangled a long stringer; attached to it were six small-mouthed bass, all still alive and swimming by the boat.

Mark Frank believed it was useless to fish once the sun was fully in the sky. For his last cast, which he made as the sun put its first edge up over the horizon, Mark had used his final worm. His method was to use a Daredevil silver spoon and a worm at the same time, thus, he reasoned, getting twice the attraction for the same amount of work.

He had woken up in the middle of the night, and before setting out he had looked in his brother's room and seen it empty. This he noted carefully, in an orange scribbler he had begun to use for such things. He had purchased six of them at the Salem drugstore and he kept them hidden in his closet; the first was almost half filled. The idea of keeping a record had occurred when the widow Kincaid told him about finding her daughter's diaries; now, patiently worrying the lure through the shallow reeds, he thought warmly of his own, and their subject, which was the growing craziness of his twin brother. His most recent entry had been almost despairing:

> *Tonight I saw him spend five minutes staring at a potato. Ever since he got that job he doesn't eat right. He told me he thinks his brain is shrinking and I also say it is. After he finished looking at his potato*

he said he couldn't eat it. I ate it for him. He spent the whole night trying to tell me about his brain. I told him to go to a doctor but he said it wouldn't help. He has a map of the brain on the wall of his room but I say he won't find himself there.

Not a man ordinarily given to writing, Mark Frank had spent most of an hour in this composition. And, once contemplated and committed to paper, it remained in his mind so that now, as he cleared the lure from the reeds and watched the heightening sun, he began to wonder about the justice of one of his own remarks—"I also say it is." Although his brother thought his brain was shrinking perhaps it was in reality staying the same—only thinking it was shrinking was making him more stupid anyway, as a man can become a coward from fearing it. And in fact it seemed impossible to Mark Frank that a person's brain would actually get smaller, because it would be unnatural to have an empty space inside a person's head. For example he knew he would find the heads of his six small-mouthed bass filled to their tiny utmost with grey pearly brain; and thinking he must give this information to Pat, Mark took one last look at the sun, which was now fully riding the horizon, and began seriously to reel in his line. As he did, he flicked his wrist every few seconds, trying to make his lure seem more attractive. But it was only when he was ready to forget about it that the fish struck.

It was a large pike; and in unusual display its body rose right out of the water in a long yellow-silver arch. In the moment it hung there, before he could react, Mark Frank was fixed by the sight of the silver beads of water streaming off the scales in tiny chains to the lake. Then, with a blunt and practised movement, he jerked the rod back, putting to it the whole force of his massive arms, and the hooked pike flew straight towards him. Instantly he had one hand out, to knock it down into the boat, and just as soon as it had hit the floor he had set his rod on the seat and broken the fish's neck between his thumbs. It lay across the floor, still flapping, almost two feet long. "At least you didn't get caught by a tourist," Mark Frank said. The bass on the stringer had all somehow scented this death and were thrashing wildly beside the boat. When he had put away his tackle and wound in his line, Mark Frank reached into the water and killed them too.

Back at the house Mark cleaned the fish and started them frying, then went to the shelf and took down a tin of apricots. These days apricots were a specialty. Reading one of the medical texts his brother had taken to borrowing from the Salem Public Library, he had encountered the information that "apricots are an indisputable source of vitamin B, contributing to hair growth, longevity and virility." Just after he had read this there had been a sale of the tinned fruit at the general store and, proud of himself because for once he had taken advantage of a bargain, Mark Frank had bought a whole case.

He was, to be exact, up to his ninth can. He opened it and set it on the oilcloth-covered table, and with a long sundae spoon began to eat the fruit directly out of the tin. To accompany this, he switched on the radio and set last night's coffee to reheat on the stove. The sugary taste of the syrup helped wake him up, and the rusty orange colour of the apricots—stranded half-way between peaches and squash—intrigued him; but what had addicted him to this breakfast was the dense taste of the fruit itself, a musty nostalgic taste that confirmed its every medical claim and sometimes made him stop right in the middle of a bite, clear out his mind, and try to think what it reminded him of. Which he never could remember.

While he finished the apricots he stood at the counter and turned the fish in the pan. The pike jumping so unexpectedly had touched him; even while he had scraped the skin clean the sun had been strangely held by the scales, as if this fish, caught easily enough, had been a king in its own world. "Well," Mark Frank said to himself, "that's the way it goes." And he began to make the slices of toast that were to be the rest of his breakfast. An endless series of miscues with the welding torch had covered his thick hands with layers of scars and callouses, so he manipulated the toast and its buttering with all the grace of a man wearing stiff leather mitts. As each piece was readied, charred and mashed into near shapelessness, it was set on top of his coffee where, in order of appearance, it stayed steamy and warm until the pile threatened to topple and Mark Frank began to eat.

When he had been fortified by his ninth tin of apricots, two pike fillets, two bass fillets, six pieces of toast, and one cup of coffee, Mark re-filled his cup with dregs, added condensed milk until it turned the creamy beige of his glass eye, looked one last time at the pike's severed head, and stepped outside to survey his own domain.

In the time of his father's ascendancy there had been, at the centre of an almost successful farm, a white frame farmhouse surrounded by four barns, two hundred acres of only mildly rocky land, and a huge maple bush that backed down onto the lake. Since that time the estate had been eroded by successive waves of alcoholism and fire. The original house had burned and been replaced by an old pigbarn, converted by the Frank brothers into a dwelling of sorts. This new house was flanked by the two remaining barns which sat in front of it like twin warnings of disaster. Between them, leading from the house to the highway, was a hundred-yard driveway littered on either side with the dead vehicles and spare parts which Mark Frank somehow juggled and stuck together in a way that provided him with enough money for food to fuel him through the days and cheap red wine to help him survive the nights.

A stranger might have thought that this man, standing at his own front door with a cup of coffee boiled from last night's grounds, no wife or children, a twin brother going crazy, an eye lost to an accident, and hands scarred and made almost useless, would have been bitter in the recognition of his shrunken kingdom. But the truth was that Mark Frank liked his coffee muddied, and had long ago claimed his glass eye as his own, as much himself as the other. And as for the land his father had lost, though he sometimes dreamed of the rich and verdant farm that might have been, he was glad to have escaped the backbreaking and endless hours of tending and ploughing. Instead of being faced by animals and manure, looking out his own front door he was able to gaze on a cornucopia of ancient and rusting cars and trucks. They filled the barnyard better than pigs and cows ever had. Like crops they were planted from time to time and harvested when needed; but unlike crops they had no rhythm of their own, only the rhythms of his own days and whims. Looking out he could feel he had forged his own project in this life, that although his brother might read books and pin charts upon his wall, he was the true scientist and explorer. Because he alone had kept up with the times; its dead metal history filled his yard and in its few acres he had re-invented his father's farm without the labour.

He was standing on the grass in his bare feet, his plaid shirt tucked into his large and baggy pants, when he heard the beginnings of a mufflerless truck a mile down the road. Breakfast had carried him over the edge of the day; and his brother's shrinking brain and the killing of the pike had been dismissed from his mind. He listened and he blinked. Blinked once and blinked again. The truck, he now knew, belonged to Charlie Malone but was being driven by Randy Blair. Every day its noise had been getting worse, and now it was the worst it could get.

He went into the house and set down his empty cup. He was never conscious of looking out one eye rather than the other, but the world was always wider on one side, so as he brushed his hair in the mirror above the sink he tilted and craned his head, trying to see that he had gotten the part straight. It was wasted effort: his hair was so thin and so well trained he could have made the part by running his hand once over his scalp. By the time he went outside the truck had arrived, and Randy Blair and his young half-sister, Lynn Malone, were walking across the grass.

"Guh-day," Randy said. Tall and big-boned, he was still fleshy in an adolescent way. He had blond hair like Kitty's, which was already bleached white from the spring sun, and his fair skin had turned a deep pink. It was a year since he had finished high school. Until then, he had spent the winters in Salem, living at Charlie's and going to school until June when he helped Charlie bring in the first crop of hay. Then he would spend the summers in Toronto, with his father. In the divorce, that was the agreement: two months every summer and ten days at Christmas; but this past year Randy had spent the winter in the city and now it was only a month since he had returned to Charlie's. In that winter away it seemed everything had shifted. Though he had always been sullen and rebellious, he had always been a child too, seeing himself as helpless in face of the men. Now that had changed. Since coming back he seemed to have become more aggressive but also unsure of himself, as if his strength came from the city now and he was only waiting to be found out. Now he stood beside Charlie's current vehicular disaster, squinting at Mark and starting the ritual dissection of a new package of cigarettes.

"Smoke?"

"Just put one out," Mark said. He stepped back from Randy, watching the play of the sun on his face as he lit his cigarette. When he had first come back from the city he had smoked differently, holding the cigarette in his hand as if the weight of his fingers might break it apart. Now he was smoking again the way the locals did, gasping it down, quick and sharp.

"I come to get the truck fixed," Randy said.

"Okay." Mark looked away from Randy to Lynn Malone, who was so exhausted with staying still and waiting for the men to finish that she was standing on one foot and nervously rubbing it with the other. She was Randy's half-sister but might have been from a different planet. Although Randy had been out of high school a year, Lynn's first year of school was just ending. She was skinny, and her dark hair was parted in the middle, but it was her eyes that were exceptional: wide-set, deep brown, and almond shaped, they were an adult's eyes in a child's face, eyes exactly like the three real eyes of the Frank twins.

"Well," said Mark, "I guess we better get to work." Then, to Lynn, "Who you got here?"

Lynn nodded, her turn now. She loved the sound of Mark Frank's voice; it was like rusty iron being driven together. "Talk some more."

"Go on," Mark said, grabbing at her. She danced away.

"You know what?"

"No."

"I made fried eggs this morning for Mom and Pat. I broke open the shells and I landed the eggs in the pan." Telling this Lynn remembered the best part, the sound of egg hissing as it struck the hot metal, the thick transparent fluid turning white, setting and fixing itself just as fast as she could watch.

44

"Well," Mark said. "I hope they didn't die of it."

"They did," Lynn said, thinking he meant the eggs. "They died of frying."

"You're a killer," Mark said. "I should have had you fishing with me this morning."

"You should have." She saw Mark Frank's arms coming out for her and danced away again. She was wearing canvas shoes, her mother always made her wear shoes when she was coming here because she said the iron could cut your foot and make your blood go bad; but now, feeling good to be out of the truck, she kicked them off and stamped her bare feet into the grass. "Pat made me promise to feed the chickens."

"Then you better."

"I want to watch you fix the truck."

"You come back when you're done." This last pronounced by Randy, in a voice that told what she already knew, that she had been pigging for attention.

Kitty had told her that Randy had been born when she lived in Toronto and was married to a man also called Randy. The seasons he visited his father were always preceded by letters with real typewriting on the envelope and before she started going to school, when it was one of her chores to empty the postbox, she had sometimes been so hurt by Randy's snubs and mean jokes that she prayed for these omens of his departure. But it was never worth it, because when he came back he was always silent and morose, striking out at her randomly, talking about the city in such a confused way she never knew what he meant. Kitty had shown her old pictures of the other Randy, Randy Senior, and he looked in the pictures like his son looked now, fair-haired and full-faced; there was something about these Randys that reminded her of certain animals that never quite got their whole colour, so they always looked sick and precious at the same time.

She picked up her shoes and moved off through the yard to the back of the barn. The bits of chrome and mirrors shone through the air brighter than any flowers, and when she came to the place where the chickens lived, in the lee of a gigantic yellow junked grader, she climbed up into the driver's seat and let the sun and its reflections from the metal roast her warm.

The chickens, who were always being forgotten, came up to join her, scratching and gabbling until they were all around her, their wings fluttering and their necks jerking convulsively in the hope of food. "What do you want?" she asked, knowing. "Do you want to be fried, boiled, baked or eaten raw?" The chickens, six of them, began to hop about her, sometimes brushing her with their feathers. She reached out and grabbed one by its ankles, holding it out at arm's length and trying to look at its eyes. They were tiny, tiny black eyes circled with red, and they seemed to look out one to each side. In her palms the chicken's legs felt like wet skinny sticks. When the bird struggled in her grip she held it tighter, afraid and fascinated, the feeling of its movements jumping through her. "Settle down," she said, trying to imitate her grandmother's voice. "Come on now, settle down, settle down." The bird twisted, then opened its wings and tried to fly. Its legs bunched up in her hands and for a moment she felt dizzy, felt that the bird was going to have a surge of strength and tow her up into the air. She let go and the chicken fluttered a few inches up, then collapsed in her lap, scuttled across her bare legs, and fell off the grader to the ground where it lay on its side.

Lynn climbed down slowly. Its head was still moving in pecking motions but it didn't seem to be trying to get up. Although she had grabbed it before, now she was too frightened to go close. "Come on," she said. "You have to get up." The bird looked at her through one of its sideways eyes. For some reason Lynn became convinced it was trying to cry. She had never looked right into the eye of a chicken but now she did. It glittered, so tiny and shallow it seemed there could be no brain behind it. "Come on," Lynn said. "You have to stand up straight."

She went to the doorway of the barn and took out a tin of grain which she mostly scattered on the ground. The five healthy chickens began pecking so quickly at it they might have been having fits. But the sixth lay still, its head moving slowly, the rest of its body frozen.

"Come on," Lynn said. "Here's something to eat." She put a few grains in front of its beak. "Stand up now. Stand up and have something to eat." The bird didn't seem to notice. She decided she had to put out more, to overwhelm it with smell, and she dumped the rest of the tin on the ground so there was a mound of grain and seeds in front of it. But it didn't move.

"I'll help you," Lynn said. She stepped forward. She didn't want to touch it again, could already feel it turning on her as soon as she got close enough, trying to peck out her eyes. "Come on," she whispered. "You know I'm sorry. I'm very sorry. I didn't mean to hurt you."

Then she slowly reached out, putting one hand on top of the chicken's exposed wing, sliding the other under it, beneath the dirt and feathers. As she did her hand seemed to catch, pushing the feathers against themselves, and the chicken shuddered at her touch. "Come on," Lynn said. "I won't hurt you."

She lifted it up and set it on its feet. She held it out from her, as far away as she could, its beak twisted off to one side. "Stand up. Stay standing up so you can eat." She withdrew her hands. It tried to flutter its wings; one worked but the other just jerked spastically, and the imbalance made it fall over again. Immediately, this time less afraid, Lynn reached out for it: her fingers sluiced into the feathers and she could feel its heart battering as she set it on its feet again, right in front of its pile of grain. Hesitantly it bent down to eat. Lynn turned and started to run.

When she got out front Randy had driven his truck over the hole. Without asking she slid down under the bumper and joined Mark Frank in his welding pit. The sudden dark surprised her eyes. She had to close them and when she did her field of vision filled with the image of the chicken, a white cloud of feathers hobbling about its grain, then collapsing, dying, ready to be found lying in a small white circle, head invisibly tucked underneath, waiting to be turned over and inspected, to be confirmed dead in the sudden immobile neck and dusty eyes.

The sizzle of the welding torch was like the sound the eggs had made when they hit the hot metal pan. She looked up at Mark. In his welding goggles, standing on a wooden box to be close to the tailpipe and his teeth bared in concentration, he was a stout wide-necked fish reaching for the surface. From one end of his torch a long blue-white pencil of flame reached out to the rusted metal, making a circular shower of red sparks round

Mark Frank's head. From the other extended two rubber hoses that led out to the twin tanks, oxygen and nitrogen, strapped together on the dolly that Randy was holding still. Lying at the side of the pit was the old muffler, and the attachments for the new one, which Mark was trying to weld to the old tailpipe.

"I hurt one of the chickens," Lynn said. "It fell off the grader."

She saw Mark Frank stop and turn off the torch. Then push up his goggles. Welding always made his face sweat, so when he took the goggles away the skin around his eyes was white and coated with small drops of water.

"I couldn't help it," Lynn said.

"Help what?"

"The chicken. I hurt a chicken." Now she saw her brother crouched down at the edge of the pit, looking angrily at her while Mark Frank rubbed his face and tried to catch up with the conversation.

"Goddamned tailpipe," Mark Frank finally said. "It's so rusty it can't be joined again." This pit where Mark Frank worked, welding the various undersides that were brought to him, was completely dark—except for the perimeter of light that seeped under the edges of the truck, and the glow of a grease-covered lightbulb. The warm yellow light turned the welding pit into a comfortable cave. And it made the belly of Randy Blair's truck seem like the insides of a person. Long tubes and shadows implied a vast tangled network of iron arteries and nerves. Looking up at it Lynn felt vaguely afraid, as if it might be sick.

"I think it broke its wing," she said. "The chicken that fell off the grader."

Mark Frank came closer to her. In this light his eyes seemed both the same, only the one that was real needed to be rubbed and blinked every few seconds. "Hey," he said. He reached out for her and this time she let his big hands fall on her shoulders. "We better go back and see."

"All right."

Randy started the truck and moved it so they could climb the wooden ladder up to the ground. She watched Mark go first; his flannel shirt had come untucked and when he leaned forward the shirt hiked up to show his back, fat and hairy as a bear's. She had seen Pat's back too; it wasn't hairy at all, though her mother said they were twins. Then she followed him up the ladder, her feet testing each rung carefully, bare feet brushing off the dirt left by Mark Frank's boots.

In the sun she saw that her arms had gotten so cold they were covered with goosebumps. She slapped at them with her hands, walking with Mark and Randy back through the heaps of iron to where the grader stood. That night she had woken up twice to hear Pat and her mother talking. Usually they sounded like they were trying to drive the bed right through the floor, but last night had been quiet, whispering, the sounds of secrets being passed back and forth. She didn't like secrets, secrets that were hidden from her or secrets that she had to keep to herself: like this chicken that she was sure they would find dead, keeled over where she had left it, and even as they came up to the rusting yellow grader she knew it was too late. She had wanted Mark Frank to find it while it was still alive, so it wouldn't be her fault when it died.

But when they rounded the machine there was no sign: a small pile of grain remained, what she had dumped out, but there was no body. Over near the barn door a group of chickens shoved and pecked in their convulsive way, but going near them Lynn couldn't tell if one of them was hers, the one that had been hurt. "It must be somewhere else," she said. "It must have hid in here." She looked under the grader, around the machines, in the shadowy door of the big barn. And as if this was what he did every day, Mark Frank looked with her, getting down on his knees to peer under rusted cars that had been parked for decades, slowly walking the circle around the grader, trying to search out any place the chicken might be.

It was Lynn who found it. "Here," she called. "Over here." She had in fact started to believe that it wasn't hurt after all, and that the worst that was going to happen was Randy's anger. And then, standing beside an old green Chevrolet, trying to warm herself in the sun reflected off the cracked windshield, she had just happened to look inside. And to see, huddled in the corner of the green velour seat, a white chicken, shrunken down into a perfect white ball, its feathers tucked closely around itself as if it intended to die by disappearing.

But its neck was stuck straight into the air and its eyes were wide open, staring one to each side. "It's okay," Randy said. He opened the back door and reached for it. As he did, it toppled out onto the ground, completely stiff, and lay with its legs sticking out one way and its head the other.

"Well," said Mark. "It's only a chicken."

"Are you going to eat it?"

"No."

She watched him as he went and got a spade from the barn. The goosebumps from her arms wouldn't go away and she had to keep slapping them warm as he dug the hole and put the chicken in it. Then he made her shovel the dirt back on top. With every motion she was afraid she was going to slip into the hole after it, though it was only a small one, and when she was done she was afraid the dirt would collapse if she stamped on it.

"It's okay," Mark said. He lifted the shovel high and pounded the surface flat. "It could have been any chicken. It might not have been the one you thought."

"It was."

"You don't know."

"Yes I do." She stared up at him. With his welding goggles pushed back on his head, his glass eye was almost transparent in the sun. She let him put his arms around her and lift her up in the air. Randy had moved away and was picking his way back to the truck. Mark smelled like grease and sweat and fishguts.

"Do you want to cry?"

"No. But you can carry me."

As they walked back to the truck he bounced her up and down, up and down; it seemed that he had been doing this forever, that she could always remember being in his arms and being jounced like a baby against his chest. And he carried her down into the pit again, let her stand beside him as the truck rolled back into place and he held up the torch again.

She stood beside him, her hand hanging on to his pocket. He smiled down at her and then pulled the goggles over his eyes.

"All right," Randy shouted, as if there were a great noise to be overcome.

"All right." The taps from the welding tank were opened. Mark took out a match and held it to the nozzle. There was a loud pop, a loud red pop, then the blue flame leapt out and Mark Frank held it up to the tailpipe, sending sparks in a perfect circle around the seam. Lynn closed her eyes. The sizzling metal carried her back to breakfast, to the eggs dying in the pan, then back to the night before, the sounds of secret whispers. Now she had her secret too; she could feel it folding up in her mind, finding a place to hide that would be covered in white feathers and dust.

A man finds out his brother is crazy and he begins to wonder about himself. Who knows what could happen to a person who is taking care of someone whose brain is getting smaller. He is lying in the room next to me and the same blood runs through us. I breathe his air. Maybe I dream his dreams.

As she dozed Mark Frank could feel Lynn's sleeping weight grow heavy against his leg. He shifted his foot to prop her up, then squinted closer to where the flame touched the metal. It was growing red, red and redder. He had a sudden image of the pike hanging up out of the water curved like a crescent moon. Then finally the metal gave way and ran together.

Four

Friday night had passed and Saturday morning begun.

Ellen Malone sat stone still in the kitchen of her own house. On the wall was a small grandfather clock. It was an antique miniature built from yellowish oak wood streaked with a bold flaming grain, and fronted by a glass etched in delicate flowering vines. Today, however, she did not notice this fragile beauty. Today she was afraid of the ornate metal arrows that pointed out the time. It was eleven in the morning and with her eyes closed Ellen Malone could see the Indians: dusky bodies tumbling shapelessly through the dark, their souls gleaming from their bellies like full moons.

She sat in her wicker chair. Beside her was the woodstove, an old-fashioned model that was more than six feet wide and four deep. Its two baking ovens were set in the centre, between the outside fireboxes. In a row above the greased surface of the stove, suspended like pregnant black marshmallows, were the warming ovens, their bellied doors trimmed with chrome and provided with chrome handles so they could be opened to receive everything from bread dough to wet woollen mittens. The stove was so old and so familiar she had forgotten when it came into the house, though it was when she had not yet borne her first child; and it had been in the same place for so long that she couldn't remember if it had ever been moved in all those decades, which it hadn't.

She sat beside the stove, and with its medley of pots and pans, its warming ovens above her, its long zig-zag of stovepipe disappearing into the ceiling, she was enclosed in a black iron forest. She liked to sit in its shadow; she was safe here. Behind her, on the wall, obscured from most angles by the stove, were two pictures, both in oval frames and covered, like the clock, in flower-edged glass. And this glass, like the glass of the clock, was kept religiously clean. In one frame was a young woman with a high forehead and a black dress that buttoned up to her throat. She had been leaning forward when the picture was taken, anxiously showing her neck and chin to advantage. With her the camera had succeeded in portraying the lie; but not so with her husband. In his picture he wore glasses, but with a peculiar squint suggesting the habit might have been invented that very day. His round face, ending in a double chin, was marked by a curious tiny smile that might have seemed either charming or mean. He too was wearing a high collar and though he wasn't leaning forward it strained; it was easy to think that here was a young man who had prospered with his wife's cooking and was starting to grow out of his wedding clothes.

Ellen Malone seldom looked at these pictures. They were of her parents. The pictures were almost a hundred years old. She had gone to their funerals long ago and now the photographs simply eluded her sight, because at some time they had started to remind her of something she no longer remembered.

But the people who came to visit would inspect the parents and then Ellen Malone and think that they were not so different, that this woman in her wicker chair and her black dress and her grey hair divided in the middle and then pulled back was the perfect daughter to these ancestors on the wall. She looked the part and most of the time she was as still and as dead, only bigger because she was more recent. The rest of the time she was considered to be remarkably crazy; with her metallic false teeth and her strange statements she seemed to be as crazy now at eighty-two as she had been twenty or thirty years ago. Her craziness was undiminished by age.

She sat in the wicker chair and looked down at her hands. Arthritis had knotted them up so badly that every joint was swollen and the skin was veined in thick blue threads. They were so useless that there were days she had to depend on others to light and rescue cigarettes for her; to avoid her fingers she had to drink her coffee out of bowls the way Frenchmen do; to make her mouth fresh she had to let her daughter-in-law take out, clean and replace her false teeth. Those bad days were laid end to end now but the old woman didn't mind, she wasn't fussy about time; it turned itself into other things, the way she had sometimes seen people changing into each other, pretending they didn't know.

The oak-cased clock had been placed so she could easily see it. That clock now said eleven, in the morning it was, and now she remembered it had said eight exactly when Randy had come downstairs to make coffee.

"Up early," Ellen had said.

"I got to get the truck fixed."

"You like to keep it fixed."

"Sure," Randy said. Ellen never knew where he came from. He was her own grandson and she couldn't see anything of any Malone in him. His skin was too fair, his hair was too red, even his eyes were wrong: brown and liquid they were like a cow's eyes. She didn't know how Kitty could take seriously a son who had eyes like a cow. And yet he was mean sometimes; the Malone meanness but much worse because he never meant anything funny by it. Other people changed around but this boy never seemed to change.

"It needs a new muffler," Randy said. "Charlie broke it last night and they're driving Kitty into the city today."

"That's nice."

"It's not nice. They're taking her to the hospital." *It's not nice.* For a moment Ellen focussed on his fair sunburned skin, the eyes that were still his child's eyes, and remembered the first time he had said that, crying when he discovered that Charlie had drowned six kittens from an orange barn cat he didn't want repeated. And remembered how Randy had gotten his revenge, nine years old he'd tied a rope around the cat's neck, lowered it down the well and then brought it back and left it on the porch for Charlie to find.

"She must be having a baby," Ellen said. Remembering. "She's always having babies."

"All right," Randy said. "Christ." He found some cigarettes on the table, lit one and gave it to Ellen. Then put the coffee on the electric stove to boil.

"Don't swear," Ellen said. "When I was your age I didn't know the meaning of bad words." She put some of her weight into her arms and tried experimentally to shift in her wicker chair. When the centre of her spine was dead, she had to be helped with every step, didn't even dare drink for fear she'd have to go to the bathroom when Charlie or Sadie weren't around. Today the base of her spine was alive and sensing. She stood up and tried to push her shoulders back.

"Careful," said Randy. He was right beside her, his hand under her elbow.

"I'm all right. For Christ's sake let an old woman take her walk in peace." She put one foot forward. Her legs didn't lift too well these days but she had developed a special step, a flat-footed glide that was almost like skating and kept her firm to the ground. She slid the sole of one slipper forward, then the other: good, this was a rare good day, she slid and skated out of the kitchen, through the front hall and past the downstairs bathroom they had installed specially for her, and to the parlour. In there the temperature was cool and the colours of the morning came like petals through the window. She stood, not daring to risk sitting down, breathing in the old smells of winter-dried bittersweet, horsehair-stuffed furniture, leatherbound sets of books unopened since the day her husband died. In that room too was his picture: forty years old, it lived yellowing in its frame. It had been taken just before the accident, so it was almost exactly as old as he wasn't; and in the picture he was standing beside his new car, wearing a wool toque with a knotted top that fell to his shoulder, and a coat so padded it swelled him out like a cow on summer pasture. He, and the car, and his friend Stanley Kincaid had all ended their timespan together, going out in a brief chorus of two tons of metal, odd bits of upholstery and rubber, plus their few hundred pounds of flesh, bones and detritus coming to an abrupt halt in the face of a rockcut that sustained no injuries.

The clock said twenty minutes to eleven. She was in the wicker chair again – her morning excursion over, and now she put her hands on her hips and pressed her thumbs into her dead-feeling spine. She had looked at the clock so often, seen it at so many different times, it was useless to attempt to sort them out. The hands of the clock were ornate black arrows. She had learned a new trick with her eyes, the trick of making things come close and grow large so she could see the black wrought metal arrows in every detail, right down to the black lacy barbs at their very tips. She had known Indians when she was young and they still had the reserve, and her father had said he killed one once and threw the body down the well behind the big barn. "Don't look down that well," he had told her, "or them red bones might reach up and grab you down." Other people's fathers had gone to war, but her father had killed a real Indian. Now only their poison was left. It was in the barbed arrows and one of these days those arrows were going to jump right out of the clock, through the glass, and jab themselves into someone's eyes.

Her arms were pressed into the arms of the chair. She pushed her thumbs in deep, trying to make her spine straighten up. The feeling of aliveness returned, and the morning came back into focus: she had stood in the parlour so long Randy had brought her a mug of coffee.

"You ever kill an Indian?" she had asked.

"No," Randy had said. "You seeing Indians today?"

"I killed an Indian once. I threw him down the well and his bones turned the water red." She looked at Randy's face; it was pink. Not pink like an Indian's, but pink like a pink marshmallow. God knew where he came from. "I used to bounce you on my knee," Ellen said. "And you used to bite my arm like it was a sucker."

"Do you want me to help you back to the kitchen?"

"I'm all right. For Christ's sake, can't you let a person alone?" Her anger had made her stand up straighter; and then the unexpected motion surprised her knees and made them go blank. She was suddenly falling, the coffee spilling forward in a great black spurt, her head rushing up to the old brown and red braided rug. And then not even letting her alone to fall on her face, Randy had grabbed her up into the air, his hands like metal hooking the insides of her elbows, hurting—the little bastard knew it hurt—and dragged her back to the chocolate brown wicker chair where they stored her these days.

Eleven twenty. The clock on the wall said eleven twenty. One day those poison arrows would take Randy's eyes out. "To hell with you," Ellen said. She stared defiantly at the clock, her eyes fixed on the constant flaming grain. Its face and barbed arrows were masked with glass; the hours were marked on the face with Roman numerals. You had to admit those Romans had known a thing or two: clocks and roads and numbers. She had been standing in the parlour all alone and that bastard Randy had brought her coffee, made her spill it, then had his excuse to put her back in the kitchen, stuffed in the wicker chair like some old cushion. "Oh no you don't," Ellen said. "I figure things out in my own time." She took her thumbs from her spine, which now felt supple and alive, and pushed herself up to her feet. Then, with her careful skating step, she returned to the parlour.

The soft morning colours had dissolved in the rising day. Growing out from the windows were yellow blocks of light: they stood like buildings in the room, their straight lines cutting across the horsehair furniture, the bookshelves, the braided rug. She had helped her mother make that rug, twisting it together out of old wool skirts and dresses. She walked into one of the buildings, letting the sharp edge of the light peel her clean. Sometimes it seemed it was she who lived at the bottom of the well; her bones felt so cold and numb they could have been surrounded by icy water for a whole hundred years. In the old days she had kept this parlour as its own kind of forest, a green forest of hanging plants; hydrangeas, ivy, wandering Jews, spider plants, parsley, begonias, African violets—all had dangled in their pots from copper hooks screwed into the wooden ceiling. And when Kitty was born Ellen had not gone to any hospital. She had lain on a cot in the middle of this room while the cramps tore through her muscles and the doctor stood in the corner, too polite to look.

On the horsehair sofa, woven into its covering, were a young couple sitting at the bank of a lake, a picnic spread out in front of them, a willow tree hanging over. When Kitty was born the sofa was so new the picture looked almost real. Between cramps Ellen remembered she had stared at the woven lake, trying to imagine herself on the water, the young woman being courted by the handsome young man.

She had been forty-one years old when Kitty was born, exactly half her age now, and at the time, she thought, about exactly twice the age she should be. Because her body had been too old for this baby; her gut and breasts already slack, her kidneys sore before the first month was out, her bones starting to freeze even then so there were whole days she had spent on the sofa in the parlour, watching her belly rise with Kitty.

"How are you doing?" Charlie's voice.

"I'm okay." Somehow she had come to be sitting on the sofa, her hands folded in her lap, leaning back against the faded willow tree. Behind Charlie's head her husband's picture peeked out; she didn't notice this, didn't care. The time had long gone when it was a loss, even a ghost for her. When she noticed it she was only surprised at how indistinct his face was; behind the hat and scarf it could have been anyone, blurred by the movement of the camera that had been seeking something else.

"By God," Charlie said. "I never know where I'm going to find you these days."

"You're getting old," Ellen said. "You don't know where to look." Now Charlie was someone who knew how to change. Right now he was fat and bald, jolly as a baby, covered in smells from the barn.

"You want something to eat?"

"You know me," Ellen said.

"I was going to make some bacon and eggs."

"I don't know," Ellen said. "I don't eat much these days."

"You could keep me company." Charlie reached out his hand for her and she took it. He was her firstborn and faithful; when she touched him she felt her own warm blood and knew it had never turned against her, not with Charlie, he was more faithful to her than herself, more her flesh than her own.

"Okay," Ellen said. "I might have a bite."

"That's right," said Charlie. "We get to live in the house, we might as well eat."

Ellen felt her belly go loose, she was starting to laugh and her muscles were giving way. "Don't make me laugh." But it was too late, catalepsy the doctor had called it, but she was no goddamned cat, only laughing made her feel like one, loose and woozy she could piss her pants laughing and now she felt it coming in waves, breaking up from her stomach and bursting out her throat.

And then she was in the forest, the real forest: no trees, no iron pipes, no plants, only the true black forest that was all darkness and absolutely still. *This is how it was.* Before there were people, before anything, there was only this forest of darkness. She could feel God's breath hissing through it; too lazy yet to make the world it rolled through the forest like a train rolling down a gentle grade. *This is how it was.* God's lazy breath breathed through her and she could feel the forest growing in her: every muscle, every particle of flesh, every cell breathed through by darkness. There was a long time when nothing happened. And then she could see the dusky bodies tumbling shapelessly through the dark, they crissed and crossed like finger shadows on a dark wall. Back and forth they went; there were hundreds of them, even thousands, she could see them pouring through the forest in vast numberless legions, their souls gleaming like full moons.

Gradually the forest started to break apart: trees, sinewy green leaves, vines flashing up out of the ground. And through it all thick ropes of light; they burned away the Indians and the dark, sent white shoots of pain through her muscles, making them feel like the frozen ground being forced to thaw again.

"Ma?"

She opened her eyes a slit. Charlie's face was close, very close, his washed-blue eyes like tiny waterpaint discs. Then she felt the tension in her back, he was lifting her: not yet, she wanted to be back in the forest, not yet. But he had her in his arms and then she was drifting through the air; he was carrying her as she had carried him – Charlie, the truly faithful.

"You scared me, " Charlie said.

Before her open eyes scenes from the forest still flickered; and the ropes of light that broke them apart swung back and forth as if they would smash right into her brain.

"You want some tea?"

She forced her eyes to the clock on the wall. The black arrows had shifted their position; today they had missed her and now the time was twenty minutes after one and she was safe for the afternoon.

"Tea makes you pee," Ellen said. "My father told me that and now I am telling you." Catalepsy the doctor called it, but she was sure she was no goddamned cat because a person could turn into a cat but a cat couldn't turn into anyone at all. The first time it happened was when she was having Kitty. Lying on a cot in the middle of the floor, contractions hammering her bones soft, looking at the picnic on the sofa while the doctor looked out the window. Old Doctor Laverty he was called now, but he wasn't old, he was younger than her then and afraid to see a naked woman's parts when she was pushing out a baby; and the sight of him blushing as he looked up her had finally made her laugh. That was when it happened the first time, when his head disappeared down over the horizon of her belly, and his red blushing neck and the feel of his breath on her thigh had been so funny she had laughed until she fell right into the forest. And then they had given her a needle to bring Kitty on. Kitty, she had called her; and though she never said why it was after the disease that was started by the doctor's blush.

"Now," said Charlie. He leaned towards her with a glass of water and two white pills.

Ellen inspected the pills, then Charlie's eyes. "You sure got cat's eyes," she said. But now she was distracted by his smooth scalp, patched by summer sunburn. "You are like the Thousand Islands," she said. "You could ride a boat across your head."

"If I was a boat," said Charlie, "I'd ride me to a tavern."

He took out a frying pan, set it with a clatter on the electric stove, then broke four eggs into it; four Ellen counted knowing two were for her, knowing that with Charlie here it was all right to eat, he would help her from her chair to the bathroom. "Did you take those pills?"

"They're gone."

"Gone where?" He came to her and took her hand in his. She looked down, willing her hand to stay closed but he had his fingers under hers, prying open her palm until they could be seen, two white dots sitting side by side on her thick skin. "For Christ's sake," Charlie said. "You're worse than a kid."

He lifted her up again. Her back was still alive but she didn't mind making him do this, now that he was forcing pills on her, tearing her away from her own parlour and making her sit like a goddamned captive in the kitchen. With his hands under her elbows, him standing behind her, she stiffened her arms for support and skated slowly forward. She could feel Charlie's breath on her neck; everyone was breathing today. Her husband had breathed too. Before he died she would wake up in the night and hear him breathing, sometimes light and gossamer like lace cloth being waved through the air, other times deep and heavy, every breath reaching down to his gut and straining for more. Even after the accident she would wake up alone and hear his breath, and then finally realized that all those nights of her marriage it had been only herself she had been hearing, only herself changed into him, and after that she didn't miss him anymore. She looked down at the floor and watched her feet traverse the polished maple of the kitchen, then the wider pine boards of the hall. He pushed open the door of the bathroom and sat her down on the toilet. Even as her body lowered, she could feel her insides starting to give way. "All right, Charlie. Leave a person alone." She crossed her arms in front of her belly and leaned forward into them.

"All right," Charlie said.

Back in the kitchen he put another pan on the stove and started the bacon. These days when Ellen got bad he went numb inside; he wanted to cry, to slap her face, to get into the truck and drive without ever coming back. "Hey Charlie-boy," everyone would call, "how's your mother?" and grin and slap his arm because it was better known than the weather that she was crazy, crazy yes, crazy and sharp like a handful of razors spat out into the air, and even funny to those who only had to come and visit and see her false teeth shining out of her mouth like a cheap wedding ring. One day she would swallow those false teeth and she would be gone.

When the bacon was done he stuck it in the oven with two plates, then started the eggs. From the bathroom he could hear Ellen, she sounded like a truck blowing all eight cylinders. *Don't kill the Indians. I got to pee.* Jesus Christ. At this rate she'd soon be telling dirty stories, like the women at the Old Folks in Belleville. He grinned. The Charlie Malone grin they called it, quick and like a fish: whenever he grinned he could feel the corners of his mouth biting into his cheeks. Sometimes it felt good to smile; other times he felt as if it was being forced on him, people would say things and he would find himself grinning—it felt as if his face was being slapped. Like the other day when Kitty had come back from the doctor in Salem and told him she had a cyst on her insides.

"He says it's bigger than a grapefruit. They want to take it out at the hospital."

"Where is it?"

"Right here." She had taken his hand and pressed it into her side; it was thirty years since he had felt his own sister like this. Her flesh had changed from being tight and elastic, drawn taut like deerflesh over her bones, to a soft and muddy field. Through this new terrain she had drawn his palm until he felt it, a round tough edge, the shell of an unknown planet.

"Not so bad," he said.

"Charlie."

"You scared?"

"I thought I was pregnant. Can you imagine?"

"Well," Charlie said. And that was when the smile was slapped onto his face, a hardening of the muscles he couldn't help, he could feel it plastered there, the stupidest grin in the world. "Well," Charlie said again, to cover, "I guess *that* wouldn't have been so bad." He stepped back and pretended to assess his sister's wide shifting eyes, high forehead, and wispy Malone hair. "I guess *you're* not so bad."

They had been standing out in front of the house. Him with his bald head, his pot belly, and his hands starting to crinkle up on the back like roasted turkey skin. But Kitty, though she had this lump eating up her insides, with her wispy yellow hair and the sun shining through it, she almost looked like a girl, like Kitty Malone.

"You going to tell?" And they had both looked guiltily through the kitchen window, as if Ellen in her wicker chair could have heard their whispers through the two-foot walls and glass, as if her goddamn teeth had a passport into their minds.

"Tell her after I go," Kitty said. "Tell her it's nothing to worry about."

"Is it?"

Her wide eyes swung and stuck to his.

"All right," he said. "Don't you worry." And grinned at her again, a quick fish-smile of reassurance, drew her close to him, into the narrow circle of his arm.

And now, standing at the stove, he found himself leaning back and with his arm in that same tight circle he took the spatula and ran it under the outside edge of the eggs. He was a patient man, Charlie Malone, he didn't mind doing his cooking at a low slow heat, and he knew when he was done the whites would rise up smooth and full of the butter below, ready to hiss out steam as they parted. He had cut open enough pigs and cattle to know how flesh fled from itself when it was cut; and now remembered too, in the animals he had butchered, cysts he had discovered: buried between the muscles and bone, black ovoids covered with glistening grey tissue: nothing to get excited about.

Ellen, finished, leaned forward until she had both hands round the door knob. She rocked herself on the seat, pulling at the same time, trying to snap her legs straight so they wouldn't go blank. Then, securely standing, took one skating step to the sink where she washed her hands. Above the sink was a mirror and she was reassured: her wide-boned face had never given anything away; it seemed as it always had, square and forward. She took up a plastic bottle and squeezed cream onto her hands, managed to rub some between her palms, and then applied it to her gullied cheeks and her high white forehead. Her hands hardly felt the

cream but her face and scalp drank it in. She twitched her skin
with pleasure, watched herself doing this and almost laughed
again. *Oh no. No goddamn cat again.* She showed herself her false
teeth and then, leaning with one hand on the doorknob, skated
out into the front hall.

"Charlie."

He came and took her arm. He was a gentleman, this son; a
prince, he came and escorted her to her wicker throne. Where
she let him help her down. Emptied now, her back felt clear and
light. And she already had the taste of bacon on her tongue. For
the first time in months she twisted around to look at the pictures
of her parents: her father, with his tiny mean eyes that Charlie
had gotten, trying to blow them up with glasses; and her mother
looking younger and more foolish than anyone. "Would you believe it?" she said.

"What?"

She turned to Charlie and saw the black hands of the clock. It
was two in the afternoon. In the morning Randy had come
downstairs and tried to tell her something about Kitty.

"What did you say?" Charlie asked.

"Them Romans sure knew their numbers."

"That's right," Charlie said. "You could never fool a Roman
about a number." She watched him open the oven door, take out
the plates, and add the eggs to the bacon. "You know," said
Charlie, "there was something I wanted to tell you."

"Not now," Ellen said. "I'm tired." She closed her eyes. She was
hovering at the edge of the forest and God's breath was skitter-
ing through her veins.

Five

Saturday afternoon: in the middle.

Pat Frank lay on his back with his eyes closed wishing it was night, wishing what was ahead was already past. It was one of those days when there was something inside him that needed to be filled.

"I don't know what we're doing here," said Kitty Malone.

"I don't know," agreed Pat. Her voice had sounded as if conducted by metal; they were lying side by side, connected from shoulder to wrist. Against his bare chest lay the weight of heavy blankets. Their feel was strange to him. Absolutely even and firm, they were flat and cool on his chest and tight against his upturned toes, tight and almost uncomfortable, the closeness of blankets that have been ironed and tucked in properly, with the corners reinforced. But more foreign than the neat and uniform lie of the blankets was the sheet itself, a starched white sheet that was so bleached he had showered twice, trying to rub his skin clean enough for this fancy linen that made him feel as if he had spent his whole life immersed in grease and manure.

These days when he slept he dreamed he was his own self as a boy sleeping. He would lie in his bed, sensing his own brain floating restlessly in his skull, the big veins growing up from his neck and pumping blood into the magic places. Sometimes it seemed the boy he had been was being born in him again; and somtimes it seemed this resurrection was lighting up not only his brain, but his heart too, making it swell and open with bursts of irrational sentimental love.

On this Saturday afternoon that love lay in him, but curiously brittle; he had not only dreamed himself as a boy, but dreamed his waking up, his discovering himself ten years old again with skin white and elastic, eyes that opened wide and took in everything without caring, lungs so innocent he could feel the air when he breathed it. He had dreamed that memory, the memory of how air felt when he breathed, and now as he lay awake he was trying to remember if it had really seemed cleaner then, if he had been truly aware of every breath, or if that pure boy-feeling existed only in retrospect, invented by age and too much cheap brandy and tobacco.

Now, lying in this rented room of the No-Tell Motel, Pat Frank wasn't sure if it mattered whether he was asleep or awake. Neither the brittle feeling of love nor the dream of himself as a boy seemed to be what he needed. With three pillows, each covered in a javex-smelling slip, piled between his head and the fake walnut headboard, and with his legs stretched out their full long length so his heels were pressed against the base of the bed and his toes jabbed up into the tightly fitted blankets, he looked at the red curtains with their synthetic gold stripes. Like everything else in the No-Tell Motel they were stiff with artificial cleanliness; in fact these curtains were so starched they hung askew, giving a narrow triangular view of the parking lot.

"Your brother Charlie told me," Pat said, "that in the lounge they have a new singer with green tits."

"Green tits," Kitty said. "I'll be sorry to miss that, you can believe."

"I can." In these years they had come drinking to the No-Tell Motel maybe a hundred times, and on at least a half of these hundred occasions they had almost stayed there, not wanting to bother with the drunk drive home from the lounge. The green-titted singer was new, but it seemed they had seen everything else here—from gold bellied Go-Go dancers to a man who played the accordion with his nose to the one-legged stripper who took it all off ten times between supper and midnight. In their visits to the lounge, the essential moment of indecision always happened coming on two in the morning, in the very parking lot indistinctly visible through the curtains. Then, standing beside the truck, Pat would fold Kitty into his arms and say, "You drive." And Kitty would say, "You know I can't"; and finally, resigning himself to the forty miles of twisting highway that he knew so well it wasn't a case of being bored by it, but of travelling through a section of his own brain that had been actually and literally worn away by the repetition, Pat would climb into the driver's side, roll a cigarette, and start the motor going.

"Well," Pat said. "Here we are." His tongue had already made the long traverse: dug into the backs of her knees, her spine, investigated every contour of her body, sought its way into the bittersweet and sour places. He had tongued her, touched her, made loved to her, and through it all she had been curiously inert, as if this idea of stopping at the No-Tell Motel on the way to the hospital had lost its appeal, as if the one long last mutual exploration and climax before the operation was impossible for her, it was already too late, and like last night she was committed to turning her body in on itself—her nerves, her whole focus inward so that like her mother she was preparing to float to her grave in a cocoon.

"Jesus Christ," Pat said. "To tell the truth, this is depressing." He swung out of the iron sheets and switched on the television. Coloured static broke out from the screen; he had read somewhere that colour television was radioactive and he could almost feel the mysterious particles buzzing in his genitals. "Goddamn, I'm sterile." He looked at Kitty, she looked at him, they both looked down at his body which now appeared so gaunt, so bony, so tentatively held together by ropy lengths of sinew and muscle, that the whole idea of such a mechanism reproducing seemed almost too absurd.

"Sterile," Kitty said mournfully. "Don't make me laugh." She held out her arms to him and like a boy he leapt onto the bed, forgetting, landing full on her so he saw her eyes roll as the pain registered.

"I'm sorry —"

"Don't." She had her arms around him. "Hold me Pat. Just hold me."

He slid his hands down her back, digging the heels of his palms into the muscles that crossed her spine and then further; into that triangle made by the small of her back and her buttocks. From there he could sometimes lift her whole body; it was the secret place that made her so weightless she rose with sheer motion.

"Like that," she said. He was lying above her and on top of her but the blankets were between them and the sensation of the wool on his skin was sharp and glassy, like the tough glassy sand on the lakes near Salem, each bit so glittering and sharp you thought it was going to cut you. And lying with her, at rest, he remembered a summer night years ago when he had been so furious with her, so furious with himself for persisting with her, that he had walked down to the lake where his brother fished, taken off his clothes and rolled in the sand, rolled and ground himself into the sand just for the sensation of the sharp bits cutting into his skin, wanting them to cut him open in a thousand places and release his blood.

"Like that," she said. And now he came under the covers and slowly placed himself against her, lowering himself down onto her, into the circle of her arms, watching the long length of both their bodies, her pale skin that was shining and silky for him, his own body which seemed simply knotty and brown, brown down to the waist where it turned dead white; and between their bodies was a golden shadow that closed as they closed together, sweet and easy, closed until it came to a point where their bellies met and he was up inside her, rooted in her as deep as in himself, rooted in her these twenty years as if he were a tree grown old in her juices.

"Don't be sick," he was pleading. "Don't let them take you apart for this"; but of course he knew better. The doctors would cut her open and up; they would take their knives to her and she would yield her body to their cheap wisdom without thought, without criticism, without anything at all except a night of fearful dreams followed by a morning begun by a long sweet needle bringing her to the table. That was how it would be. And then he would come to see her and she would be in her hospital bed with sheets as white and starched as these, and she would be smiling weakly, and the lump in her side would be gone, replaced by thirty stitches black as twin rows of teeth, a few layers of bandages, and half her insides gone. The doctors could do anything. They played doctor because everyone wanted to live. Even Ellen Malone, eighty-two years old and scarcely able to shit without being squeezed, wanted to live. Even he himself, Patrick Frank, forty-nine years old with a forty-nine-year-old glass-eyed twin brother, wanted to live, wanted to see his own bastard child survive one more day just in case she turned into someone, in case he learned how to love her; wanted to see himself survive one more day just in case the unfillable need was suddenly requited, in case he suddenly became his own true self. Yes, the truth was that lying rooted in Kitty Malone and the first rain of sweat coming slick to his skin he had turned into his own brain and, like a fox, was locked tight onto the tail of his own convoluted vision. Even he himself, Pat Frank, could believe that at any time, the very moment his whole body and soul yearned for was just around the next corner, and that at this perfect and totally desired moment he could finally, suddenly, undeniably, permanently, ecstatically come into true possession of himself, find himself alive and conscious in the absolute living centre of his own being, alive and finally full and bursting.

"Kitty."

"What?"

"This is good, eh?"

"This is good."

Alcohol made the brain shrink, television withered the knackers, but finally it wasn't going to make any difference; he could feel it clenching in him the way it always had, the force gathering from the soles of his feet and his neck, all through his back and belly and gut; and then waves of it started through him, the pain in the centre as great as the pleasure, and as it came to the crest it seemed the pain was so sharp it could last forever, he would be stopped on the edge with this tremendous growing pain opening up, and then the waves started again: *one more time*, he thought, *one more time for show*; and then it was started and he was spurting into her, not knowing if it would last seconds or forever, and she was coming with him. "Kitty, I don't know if I can make it."

"Baby Pat, be my baby now." Her hands holding and squeezing, helping him through, new layers of sweat washing out the old until finally he relaxed and his long legs curled around hers. "Lie still, Pat, just lie still."

Her hands were warm on his back, he could feel life seeping through her skin to his; gradually his muscles loosened, his neck stretched and grew calm, his head sank into the corner between Kitty's shoulder and the pillow. She was breathing slowly; he had twisted away from her bad side and one of her breasts was cushioned into the hollow of his chest. She breathed and he breathed with her, starting to doze again, returning to his dream of himself as a boy.

In his dream it was dawn and he was lying awake in his bed. He discovered himself there, staring through the blocky shadows to the window, a blue-grey rectangle on the wall. In the room were the sounds of his own breathing and, slower and deeper, the sounds of his sleeping twin brother, breathing with his own dreams. He swung out of bed—the noise made his brother whimper—then pulled on jeans and a jersey. His feet, white and supple on the pine floor, took him soundlessly out of the room and downstairs into the kitchen where he saw himself in the mirror: a boy, a smooth boy's face with brown wavy hair, wide eyes, cheeks smooth and hopeful. But then, looking at himself, saw the man he would become, the bony skull peeking out from the thick hair, the caverns waiting to be revealed from behind the temporary flesh of his face, even the nose waiting to grow and be broken, grow from a straight boy's nose to the nose of the man he would be, twisted near the top and veined around the sharp nostrils. *Will I remember me as I am?* He had looked at himself in the mirror and then gone outside. It was sunrise. His room when he had woken up had been grey, the stairway grey deepened with shadows, the kitchen a blue-grey turning with the light; but outside it was tinged with yellow, the yellow rim of the sky showing through the grey mist that lay across the fields and blurred the barns. But even at this hour his father had been awake, sitting on a wooden crate outside the house, dogs at his feet, a plaid jacket carelessly thrown over his shoulders, his hands firmly wrapped around one of the yellow bottles he favoured for the product of his still. Beside him, older and greyer, sat Simon Thomas, a neighbouring farmer who sometimes joined his father in these nightlong watches.

"Pat."

"Dad."

The dewy lawn like beaded ice on his feet, then his father's sudden movement, the arm circling out for him and drawing him up on his lap.

"You come to see the old men?"

"I woke up." His father's voice carrying the whisky breath to him, bristles digging into his neck. He tried to twist away but his father held him tight. Then he remembered grabbing onto his father's hand, it was pressed against his whole belly and the skin was tough as hairy bark; each of his father's fingers filled his whole boy's hand as he tried to pry free.

"Let him go," Simon said.

"You're like a little greased pig," said his father. Digging his fingers into his belly, trying to tickle but only hurting until in a panic Pat whirled and punched at him, finally slipping away when his father's head snapped back in surprise. Now the icy grass was welcome to his feet; he skipped away but his father only sat, grinning at him, looking to Simon for approval. "Tough," his father said. "I suppose you're getting pretty tough." He laughed and Simon laughed too; Pat's father, stout and heavy like his twin brother Mark, seemed to be laughing out of blank good nature, not caring that he had been outwitted this time; but Simon, skinny as vinegar, laughed with a question, as if he could hardly wait for Pat to be older, as if the knife he held in his hand, paring his nails, was one day to live between them.

And then as he watched, his father raised up the bottle to his lips, his eyes closed, the lines on his face smoothed out, and Pat could see his throat jump with each swallow, like a curse.

He woke up from his dream with the heat of Kitty's breath pulsing on his own throat, warming its whole length as if she lived inside him, breathed her love through his own lungs. Without thinking, automatically, he pushed himself up off her and went to the motel dresser. On it were two empty glasses, into which he poured dollops of rye from the half-empty mickey beside them. Then went into the bathroom to add water. His face in the mirror was stubbled, caverned, broken with drink and weather. As a boy he had been able to see his man's face, but now, as a man cresting his own prime, he could scarcely imagine how hair could have grown out of the tough skin of his scalp, how flesh could have ridden the sharp knobby bones of his face.

"I was asleep," Kitty said.

"I was too." He came and sat beside her on the bed. In the first years they knew each other any kind of proximity had made the blood turn sharp in him, wanting her, needing the feel of her skin against his. Then there had been, it seemed, a whole decade of fights and recriminations, they had turned on each other like animals penned too close; and it was only lately, only in the last few weeks that they had started to grow easy again, so as the mattress gave way to his weight and he stretched out his hand and set it on her belly, Pat felt himself opening up to her, feeling awkwardly sentimental yet wanting her again too, the two feelings that seemed so contrary to him now running together.

"You know," Kitty said. "I was dreaming about us." She sipped at the drink Pat had given her, making a sour mouth at the taste of the pale, coppery rye. She had a wide mouth: every expression it made always seemed doubly forceful to him, and when she kissed him, placed her lips against him, he always felt enveloped and warmed, sucked into the heat of her whole life. Her eyes too were wide: they looked at him, looked away. She had restless eyes, Kitty Malone, sometimes it seemed those eyes that couldn't stay still were her whole restless story, refusing ever to fix on one place and move towards it, refusing anything except whatever she could see in the centre of herself. "You remember the last time?"

"Sure," Pat said. "Is that what you were dreaming about?"

"I think so. We were driving to the hospital. I was so fat, sticking out to the dashboard, and you were smoking those damned cigars."

"A father has to celebrate," said Pat.

"What about the mother?"

After Lynn was born they tried to live together in Kitty's grandfather's house, a disaster that lasted only two months before Kitty attacked him in the kitchen with a fork and a broken bottle, so hopeless and furious she was laughing even as she tried to gouge out his face.

He got up from the bed and poured more rye into his drink. There had been only the one child, but there had been two pregnancies, and both times they went to the hospital that way, her swollen, him drunk; and both times it had been in the afternoon, and he had learned to co-ordinate his arrival at the hospital with the evening hours of the liquor store. That is: he would take her into the hospital to get registered and settled, and then he would say he was going out for dinner and would come back for visiting hours.

Now Kitty had barely started her drink but he, in one swallow, had finished his, even with the additional rye, and he felt its only effect was to open his throat that much wider; he felt he could finish this bottle and the one he had in the glove compartment just by pouring them straight down his throat; and maybe that would settle him or maybe it would just warm up his serious thirst.

"Ellen was with us in the truck," Kitty said. "We were all driving to the hospital and she was yapping away about the goddamn Indians and her goddamned teeth were biting through my cigarettes and she said, Why don't you get married?"

"We should."

"I was thinking that," Kitty said. "I was thinking we could have a secret marriage." Her eyes were stuck to his now, wide and blue; in the whole twenty-two years since the night they first became lovers, they had never talked like this and he felt himself opening wider, stupid sentimental love pouring out for her as if his whole self would be emptied. He watched her eyes, she was starting to cry, her hand had slipped away from his thigh to her own side which swelled with the cyst they were going to take out.

"All right," Pat said. "We'll get the licence now; and then we'll get married when you come out."

"Do you want to?"

"Yes."

"Do you really? Or are you just saying that because I'm sick?"

"You know," Pat said. The coloured static on the television set had resolved into a baseball game. Tiny white figures were rushing about a vast bright green synthetic turf. "These things take a long time." Now he looked at the rye in his glass, straight, muddy as the colour of his piss the night Charlie Malone chopped him in the kidneys from behind, the night Charlie Malone found out he'd gotten Kitty pregnant and jumped him right here in the lounge of the No-Tell Motel, beer bottles in each hand and screaming over the noise of the band, not waiting to hear Kitty say it was all right, she'd wanted it. Leaving him lying on his face on the floor, feeling every bone in his back had been crumbled into burnt gristle.

Now the television screen was filled by a huge tanned face, beneath a peaked baseball cap a city pitcher was chewing a wad of tobacco bigger than the lump in Kitty's side, bigger than his own face, it hung out over the side of his jaw like a sac of wet sand. Charlie Malone: he had played baseball with Charlie Malone often enough, without uniforms, but baretopped in their jeans in the field behind the Catholic church they used to play baseball on Sunday afternoons, against teams from all over the county. Charlie Malone, Kitty's brother; Charlie Malone, once his own best friend; Charlie Malone coming at him from behind because he had been fucking his sister and had never gotten married to her.

"Do you want me?"

"Sure," Pat said. Every day this summer it seemed his heart was bleeding love: crazy, sentimental, mawkish, indiscriminating love, and now Kitty had opened it that much wider, anything could, he could love anyone at all, even Charlie Malone. But now mixed with the love was something else, something altogether different: a deep-running current that caught at everything he felt towards Kitty Malone—the old resentments and disappointments that still lived in him, the irrational desire to smash into her, to smash apart anything they might make together—and suddenly he found himself on his feet, almost running across the room to the dresser where he took the bottle and swung it to his lips in a long careless arc, pushing back his head the way his own father used to, but he knew not even the rye would smooth out the lines on *his* face, no swallow or ten swallows was going to make any difference.

It was between innings and the television was showing commercials of people drinking beer, city people sitting beside a waterfall drinking beer. They had drunk beer between innings at the Catholic church too, sometimes one every inning so by the end of the game the only way to get on base was if the pitcher hit you. That was when he was young, when Kitty was in school, and his own sex still fluttered around like a weather vane.

"What's wrong?"

"Nothing," Pat said. The brandy and the hate in a swirling confusion.

"I was only joking about getting married." She had lit a cigarette and, though she was still in bed, had put on her shirt, wrapping it close around her belly and breasts.

"Sure," Pat said. "I bet you were."

"We couldn't get married now. It would be too crazy."

"Too crazy," Pat Frank said, finishing the bottle. "What we should do is keep seeing each other the way we do, sneaking around at night and fucking in the fields until we're seventy-five years old and we've still never known one goddamned week of peace together."

"If that's how you feel."

"That's right," Pat said. "If that's how I feel." There was a line inside his throat that scraped raw whenever he raised his voice; it was already raw now and starting to hurt, and it felt not like a physical sore but like a wire connected to his brain, a wire smoking hot that destroyed vast resources every time he got angry, every time he let her suck him into hoping that finally their lifetime battle of wills would be over and they could spend one second in actual harmony that wasn't just one of them appeasing the other. "Look at me for Christ's sake," he shouted. "Can't you ever look at someone? Who the fuck do you think you are, Kitty Malone?"

They had been driving down the road at Saturday noon, Pat

Frank taking Kitty Malone to the hospital to have a cyst removed from her ovary on the right side. On impulse they had stopped at the No-Tell Motel, taken a room and gone inside: one last time, just in case.

Now they were out in the parking lot again. From their truck, the only vehicle in the parking lot, they could see the yellow electric light lying in a thin band between the red curtains of their room. All day Pat Frank had felt there was something in him that needed to be filled, something that neither his own brittle love nor the feeling of himself as a boy could meet. But now, still furious with Kitty, it seemed that he had come to himself, that what had been missing was only anger, and the line inside his throat had been scraped dry and raw, and the rye bounced carelessly through his blood, and he felt quiet and exhausted.

He eased the old truck onto the highway and, holding the steering wheel steady with his knees, rolled himself a cigarette. It was an old truck, this, it belonged to Randy Blair, Kitty's eldest son, and right now it ran quiet and smooth, its insides greased and lubricated by his own hands, its muffler replaced and welded together this morning by his own twin brother.

"Well," Kitty said. "Is that better?"

"Sure. That's better." The motel was located a few miles north of Kingston, flanked on one side by a drive-in movie, and on the other by a cemetery. Here the farms were gradually giving way to subdivisions, and the early summer fields were equally stubbled with the bright green beginnings of new hay and the even brighter colours of real estate signs.

As Pat finished one cigarette and started to roll the next, he looked over to Kitty. She was slumped against the door, her hand reflexively on her side, her eyes closed and her wide mouth slack. He stuffed the tobacco and paper back in the pack, then reached over to her thigh. He had always liked her legs, long and muscled, her thigh fit in his palm; but where the flesh was usually taut and alive, now it seemed to have given up.

"I'm sorry, Kitty."

"Don't apologize."

"Sometimes I don't know what to do with you."

"Don't do anything with me. Just drive me to the hospital."

"*Just drive me to the hospital,*" Pat mimicked. "And while you're having your operation I'll make you a nice little coffin so you can just give up and die with a good conscience."

"Fuck off."

"*Fuck off.*"

She pushed his hand away and now he could feel the life jolting back into her, her head swung round and her eyes opened, flashing for at least this moment the same fire they had when they fought for the first time, the night she decided to leave him and go to the city, the night he had goaded her to it and she had finally broken down and lost her temper.

"You're a heartless bastard, Pat."

"Am I?"

"Yes." He reached again for her; she grabbed his hand and twisted it away; the truck swerved and for a moment the sound of gravel on the metal body ran through them both. And then they were back on the road again, past all the fields now and into the outskirts of the town.

"You know," Pat said.

"What?"

"Maybe we should get married."

"Sure," Kitty said. "What a great time to get married. What we should do is have a few more drinks, get married and then we can fry in hell full-time for the rest of our lives." She was pushed over into the corner of the truck again, but her eyes were open now and her mouth tense, small lines like wire fingers growing out of the corners. It was times like this that he walked away from her and didn't see her again for weeks or months. It was times like this he drank until his body could do nothing but throw up, and then went through the same cycle again and again until he was too sick or too broke to continue. Now the need was already in him, every cell was opening up, every nerve twitching and crying for it; and his hands were shaking on the wheel, even his bones were unable to keep themselves under control.

"Jesus Christ," Kitty said bitterly.

And then he was pushing himself back from the wheel, straightening out his arms and back, the anger opening up in him, sparking right out of his bones he was so angry he was laughing. "Jesus Christ," he repeated. "If only Jesus Christ could see us now. What a circus." He pushed down hard on the gas and accelerated through a yellow light. "Here we are exhausted, fucked out of our pants, you're going to the hospital and we're sitting in this goddamned truck and shouting at each other. We've been doing it for twenty years and we'll do it for twenty more if we get the chance, goddamn, I never would have believed it, *goddamn*, I never would have believed I was born for this." And finally Kitty was laughing with him, she pulled over to him in the seat and clung to his arm as he drove wildly through the city—past the graveyard, past the university, past the hospital—laughed and then began to cry as he finally slowed down for the downtown intersections, turned, and manoeuvred himself into a parking spot outside Kingston City Hall.

Pat opened his door, reached in, and pulled Kitty out on his side.

"Let's do it," he said. "Let's go in and do it right now."

"All right," said Kitty. "Why not?"

Six

Kitty Malone was standing in an open Johnny-coat, her arms stretched akimbo, her feet freezing through paper slippers on the tile floor, when the intern stuck his hands under her armpits.

"Just checking," he said. "Once they get started, anything can happen."

His knuckles dug around sharply, pushing against her bones, and she felt herself starting to sweat. When he took his hands away he rubbed them on his white linen coat; he was so small and skinny she couldn't help thinking how easy it would be to slap such a runt right down to the floor. That would be something to tease Ellen about. An Indian from India. There were no yellow bones in the well behind the barn.

He was writing something down, his back to her to protect the page. Then he turned to face her. Her own doctor, the man at Salem who had sent her here, had a round gentle whale's face; this intern's features were dark and compressed, and he looked so unhappy she couldn't help feeling he would want to rub it off on everyone else.

"Just taking notes," he said. He pronounced his words in a precise and peculiar way. Even in his high-heeled black shoes he was not quite as tall as Kitty; but he had stepped so close his face was pushing into hers and Kitty could smell the mint and tobacco that were laced into his breath.

"Here."

His cold fingers followed hers, probing, pushing in until she had to turn away.

"Lie down." Then up from the inside with a rubber glove.

"They grow big there," he said. No hint of a smile. "It's just a cyst."

"Just a cyst."

"Just a cyst," the intern repeated, tapping a shiny black toe on the floor: polite, casually skeptical. Kitty wrapped the coat around her and swung down from the bed. She was standing above him, wearing a gauzy white hospital gown that was so thin and skimpy she felt like an explosion of age and fat. Protected only by the cigarette which she now took from her bedside table, Kitty found the tone of his voice rankling her worse than bad wine.

"Don't try to scare me."

"It is forbidden for doctors to frighten the patients." He had a peculiar yellowish cast to his skin, as if it had once been darker but was now being bleached out by successive months and years indoors. For a moment she began to feel sorry for him. "You'll be all right," he said. His features cramped, as if the very sight of her was painful, and he walked out of the room, his quick exit marred by the ragged staccato of his cleated shoes.

Late at night, she woke up. She had been dreaming of a trial, her own trial, that she had been caught in a network of carelessly invented minds, like a spider trapped in its own revenging web.

She knew about trials. She had seen them on television, because Ellen admired an intrepid wheelchair lawyer named Ironside. She had also seen one live. Her son, Randy Junior, had been on trial for setting fire to a car in downtown Salem. During the trial it had been established that he had indeed set fire to the car, which belonged to a man from Ohio, and that he had told someone this was to help celebrate the fourth of July, which was the day of the crime.

The man from Ohio had called the town policeman, who had been forced to arrest Randy.

At the trial there was no doubt that Randy had committed this deed. Twelve years old, his hair freshly cut under the whipping-cream bowl, dressed up in a too-tight suit, he had stood in front of the judge and Kitty had listened while the judge mumbled something about a broken home, a father who had neglected his duty, extenuating circumstances, and let him off with six months probation.

She had changed from her Johnny-coat into her flannel night-gown, and now she smoothed it down over her thighs and knees, making it into a soft cotton lake.

Her own trial, she felt, had not gone so well. In her dream the intern had been both judge and jury. One face had stared down at her, pinched and yellow under its white judge's curls, while twelve identical doll's heads had nodded hostilely from the jury box. He had looked at her, felt her, prodded her armpits and belly like a man prodding a cow's belly to see if it was pregnant, but he hadn't really *seen* her. Somewhere he would be sleeping easily enough, entirely forgetful of her, while she was dreaming of him, couldn't shake the close frightened face pushed together like a rat's, the clean fingernails bitten past the quick, the brown blood-veined eyes.

Her hand was always at her side now, holding and exploring. In the next beds were two old women. When the intern jerked open the curtain and strode out of the room, they had stared at her curiously. Now they were in a shallow rattling sleep. They reminded her of Ellen; like Ellen they had to be helped to the bathroom, but unlike Ellen there were two of them, so they could unravel with each other like two senile turkeys, gabbling and pecking every moment into the ground. Ellen, alone, never gave up anything: she had scrambled up the whole world and then had squeezed it into her mind; and there was not one inch she would surrender. When Kitty had dared to ask her about going into a nursing home, Ellen had snapped, "When I die, the whole goddamn world dies with me," and then pulled back her lips to display her shining teeth: thirty-two lies.

Her hand was damp on her side. When she pulled it away cool

air hissed through the wet spot on her gown. To keep the hand busy she reached for a cigarette; lighting it and listening to the gravelly breathing of the old women, she tried to smooth out her own.

Forty years old. The years were just so many numbers now; more important was the iron judgement they implied – the time that was already past. The intern, she now realized, hadn't really meant to dismiss her, to sentence her nor even to be hostile. He was only passing on a message: that as of this moment she could forget about youth and future; that although her body was still strong its automatic right to life had expired; that what remained was only the question of whether or not to close the small gap that existed between herself and the two old turkeys across the room.

She had told Pat to leave her alone tonight, had insisted that no one visit her until the next day, after the operation. "I'm too tired," she had claimed. "I need to sleep." But that wasn't the whole truth. She needed one night alone, one more long chance to sense her own self.

The room door opened out to the hall and from the nursing station she could hear strains of radio country music and voices talking. Saturday night. Now she realized it was Saturday night and the rest of the world was going its usual crazy weekend way, shaking and jiggling itself in search of the last twitching nerve – while she was sitting on a bed, holding still, trying to talk herself out of a bad dream and trying to convince herself she wasn't going to die.

When her father was killed it had seemed as if a veil had been torn away, and Kitty Malone had found a space in herself that was only dark, only wanted to cry, only wanted to hide.

By the time of her first summer with Pat Frank, when she was eighteen, the place torn open by her father's death had begun to heal. Following Pat Frank around, teasing him and her brother Charlie, was almost a joke to begin with, barely an infatuation. Even when she first seduced Pat in the field she felt only a crazy flirtation with herself, the possibility of being trapped. There were echoes of panic and danger, but they only made the game more interesting; they sparked through her veins every time she moved towards him, with his every touching of her. Without ever really making the decision she had stopped resisting; then she was drawn in deeper—by her need to feel further whatever was being teased, by the long lazy summer filled with breezy bug-free nights that favoured outside lovemaking and long romantic walks across the hills, and finally by Pat Frank, whom she at first admired, then discovered to be even weaker than herself, so insistently needing that there was nothing in himself he had the strength to deny.

"This is easy," she thought, the night she came home from seducing Pat Frank. And every step of the way it was easy until the night he turned on her, called his feelings love, and then said, "I'm too old. You have to make your own life."

The veil was ripped away again. The first time, when her father died, she had passively cried. This time she turned her back on Pat Frank, ran through the fields to her house, and sat on the porch the whole night, clutching her stomach, every few minutes leaning over the rail to retch. The next morning she was on the train, one suitcase only, headed for Toronto—the biggest, most confusing, most exciting city she had ever heard of. That she could catch a train to. And the whole way she imagined Pat Frank changing his mind, Pat Frank grieving, Pat Frank looking for her, Pat Frank searching disconsolately through the whole township, the whole country, the world.

She was still so angry when she arrived in Toronto that within the day she had a job in a restaurant near the station, and a room in a boarding house on Jarvis Street. Then the current of her anger ran out. She would find herself lying on her bed, curled up tight, her knees pushed in against her belly, trying to still it. And now it wasn't the same as when her father had been killed; what she felt was not empty, but bitter—not so much betrayed by Pat as by herself. And promised herself not to care again—not that much—not care so much that her caring made the person leave.

Every night for a week she lay in her room and listened through the walls to the sounds of other people watching television, other people making love, other people fighting, laughing, begging, even sitting contentedly in their rooms alone.

During the day she somehow got through her work as a waitress. Then, after eating her supper in the restaurant, she would come back to her room and her bed. Until one night she sat up, looked at herself crouched over on this strange bed, her arm pressed into her belly to stop its cramping, and realized that since the night she had fled Pat Frank and sat retching on her own front porch she had gone nowhere at all, that if she was going to be like this she might as well be at home again. With each breath her chest and stomach opened and she felt terror welling up in her. She made herself walk around her room. "I won't be afraid," she said. "I won't be afraid."

"I won't be afraid," she heard herself saying, "I won't be afraid." The whisper of her words sounded ridiculous. "I won't be afraid." She tried to make herself shout it but her voice merely croaked. She forced herself to stand upright. In the corner of her room was a small sink with a mirror and, pacing back and forth, she stopped in front of it. Her face was unrecognizable. Around her eyes the skin shimmered and twitched. Her hair stuck out from her head in random straw-like clumps, like the hair of a crazy woman. "Look at me." Her voice died away. The terror swam up in her now, it was rising through her body like water in a pipe, she could feel it coming up from her feet, through her legs and belly and chest, and soon it was going to stream from her eyes, stream from her throat in a long banshee shriek. She put her hands over her ears but she could hear her own wailing already, a shrill piccolo scream splitting apart her head.

"No. No, I won't." She tore her eyes away from herself, turned her back on the mirror. Her purse was on the bed, where she had dropped it after coming in from supper, and now she rummaged through it until she found her brush. Furiously she pulled it through her hair, yanking and tugging at the knots, forcing it through again and again until her hair crackled and her scalp pulsed and burned.

She started to sit down again but caught herself and forced herself to stay on her feet, pacing, but this time refusing to look in the mirror, averting her eyes every time she came near that corner of the room. Until finally she found herself at the door, her eyes fixed on the yellow peeling paint. She paced away and came back. Beneath the yellow paint was green, and in places where wide strips of green were revealed it too was cracking apart to show its predecessor, a violent purple. She scraped with her nails at the purple. The high brittle sound went through her bones, but she couldn't stop. Underneath the purple was yellow, the same yellow that was on top, the colour of boiled eggyolk, and when she had scraped through all the purple that showed she started back on the green. Finally she had a circle of yellow scraped free. Both her thumbnails had broken; to smooth the edges she was using her other fingers, all at once like claws, still muttering, "I won't be afraid." And then suddenly she pushed the door open, forced herself to walk downstairs and out onto the street.

Once walking it seemed all the pain and fear were miraculously left behind in her room. Even her thoughts of Pat were gradually hyphenated by the spectacular rush of cars and people, buildings and neon signs, forests of telephone poles and wires. It was a carnival. She was so happy she wanted to cry. It was a huge spectacular fantastic side-slapping beautiful carnival and she was absolutely right in the middle. No one in the world knew where she was. She walked through the city, every step a wonderful rubber bouncing on the pavement, energy pouring through her legs so they felt like electric wires, so happy her face was pulled back in a huge smile, smiling at everyone she passed, tears still moist in the corners of her eyes.

Then, as quickly as the good feelings had started, they threatened to fade. Suddenly her legs were heavy and tired. She stopped, looked up and down the bright street, then found she was standing in front of a bar.

At first it seemed to be all leather: a leather-padded counter with leather-topped stools, all black, and red leather booths. She was instantly cheered again. Even in this absurd carnival of a city, this bar seemed out of place. It reminded her not of her dreams but of places she had already been, towns near Salem, Kingston and Gananoque and Belleville where the bars on the edges of the suburbs were opulent and lit with coloured lights and where the managers always wore toupees. She sat down in one of the red leather booths. Spotted over the ceiling were dim yellow globes. The light they gave out was soft and friendly, streaked with red and black so it was thick enough to hold the music, the smoke, the need of her own body to find somewhere to relax.

It became her place. Two weeks after that first night she was sitting there, in the red booth, watching television and sipping slowly at a gin, waiting, waiting for nothing, waiting as it turned out for the moment when Randy Blair, strawberry blond with a crazy bomber jacket in the middle of summer, walked in, zippers everywhere, and sat down beside her.

"Hiya. Mind if I stop?"

"Oh no. I don't mind."

"I guess you haven't been here long." His teeth were white and even, his lips full: he was like a teddy bear, a city panda. His eyebrows and lashes were thick and blond. Even his eyes, which from that first moment she found round and brown and dumb, attracted her because they were so deep, so well fed – he was padded and healthy and content, like a calf that had spent its whole life sucking its mother's milk.

"Not too long," Kitty said.

"I didn't think so." He reached into a zippered pocket and drew out a package of cigarettes. When Pat Frank smoked he rolled his own: hastily he put them together, tapped the ends, then sucked the smoke in deep quick drags. Not this man. He rubbed the tailor-made between his fingers, put it gently in his mouth as if it were flesh, smoked it so slowly and tenderly she wanted to take him home right away, not even knowing his name, just take him back to her room and be surrounded by his warm padded arms, feel his warm contented breath on her skin: sleep.

"What are you doing here?"

"I was having a drink," Kitty said. "I was just sitting here on my ass having a drink."

"Girls don't talk like that."

"Oh don't they. How do they talk?"

"They say, Please Mr. Taxi Driver, I've just come to the big city and I don't know what to do. Help!"

"Help," Kitty said. She stood up and walked down the narrow

alleyway between the red leather booths, out the door and onto the street. Then waited. Waited a minute and then ten. Then went back into the bar where Randy Blair was sitting where she had left him, two new drinks on the black-topped table, a new cigarette slowly dying in his mouth.

Saturday night: in the middle.

Kitty Malone sat on her hospital bed, her nightgown spread over her crossed knees. She had not turned on her light, but had been sitting on her bed for what seemed like hours, smoking cigarettes, listening to the hoarse rattling breath of the two old women across from her, letting her mind race in long circles. With one hand she reached down to smooth the cotton flannel of her nightgown, stretching it taut, making it into a red flannel desert. The other hand was pressed into her side.

She sat on her hospital bed and realized, sitting in the dark, that she had been sleeping, sleeping sitting up and dreaming about Randy Blair. The lump in her side seemed to have receded. She moved her hand up, to her heart, which was tripping and stammering in her chest. Only a few hours had passed since the intern had probed her, and already she had had nightmares about him, forgiven the nightmares, and dreamt again: of Randy Blair, of coming into the city and finding some small speculative part of her soul blown wide open and expanded into a hundred thousand streets and houses, lights day and night, a million people living their lives uninterrupted by anything except their need for each other.

From the hallway, through the open door, she could hear the strains of country music. Swinging her feet down to the floor, she searched out the paper slippers, then walked out into the yellow hall. The music grew louder; it was coming from the nursing station and she went towards it, her arms folded across her gown, her slippers scraping along the tile floor.

"Well, how are you?" A birdlike girl in white opened the door and stood in front of her, her head cocked to one side, smiling as if she had been waiting for Kitty all night. Her hair was gold, a blonde gold that reminded Kitty of how her own hair once was.

"I'm all right," Kitty said. She followed the girl into the nursing

station and let herself be seated in a wide leather chair with
chrome arms. The girl, looking socially towards Kitty, fidgeted
with the radio.

"Isn't it nice that you got up? I've been sitting here waiting for
some company. My name is Sandra." In front of her, set out on
the desk, was her jewellery. It was, like her hair, absolutely gold:
earrings, a necklace, two gold bracelets.

"That's nice," Kitty said. "That's a nice name." First the intern
and then Sandra. Two new people in one day. It was so long
since she had met anyone new she felt like she was going to the
city again. Suddenly she grew self-conscious in front of Sandra's
stare, and for a moment it was as if Sandra was assessing her,
measuring her the same way the intern had, like the social
worker who sometimes came to visit Ellen. Then the stare was
gone, replaced by a smile. "For Christ's sake," Kitty whispered
to herself. The girl was at most twenty years old. But she looked
so confident in her seat she could have been sitting in the centre
of the nursing station of the whole world, taking it through the
night with the aid of her gold totems, her white hands so perfectly formed and delicate Kitty suddenly thought that the men
must be crazy for her; and then Kitty saw as Sandra sat down
opposite her that one leg was shorter than the other. Thin and
twisted, it ended in a white shoe grotesquely large.

"I'm Kitty Malone," Kitty finally said, remembering to intro-
duce herself.

"I know, I saw you sleeping. I always like to come see anyone
new, even if they're asleep. You know." Then her smile widened.
"But I would have come to see you anyway." She turned and
reached to the counter, picking up something Kitty had already
been eyeing: a potted plant. The pot had been wrapped in shiny
green paper and glowed like a Christmas tree. Inside was a
sinewy plant, green-leaved with deep-red flowers. The entire
thing was wrapped in plastic and then Kitty finally knew why
her eyes had been both attracted and repelled; it reminded her of
the plants they put in the cemetery on new graves, wrapped in
plastic so the flowers might last against the weather.

"Isn't that beautiful?"

"It's really nice," Kitty said, forcing herself to receive it from

Sandra's outstretched hands. She set it on her lap and stripped off the plastic; exposed it wasn't quite so bad.

"A man brought it."

"Oh he did."

"He was so drunk I had to spray the hall."

Kitty looked up at Sandra and for a moment, seeing the array of gold, the helpless twisted foot, saw not Sandra at all but a smiling angel. Her eyes were grey and cold, and though the surface of her skin was smooth and tanned there were somehow intimations of lines, a fine-drawn quality like a mesh beneath the soft surface of this angel who, Kitty saw, was staring back at her frankly: a beautiful golden angel of death. Then the image was broken and Sandra, concerned, was talking again, offering Kitty a cup of coffee and a sleeping pill.

The first few months Kitty had loved the city, needed it, turned herself open to it as if only her whole life could soak it up. Through the days she floated to the nights, and there she was anchored by the pink comforting body of Randy Blair.

Sleeping with him was perfect. Lying beside him at night, half-drunk and half-euphoric, she would happily sink into his warmth. But if he turned to her, touched her and came inside, she couldn't respond. Somehow that place in her that had been exposed by Pat Frank was covered over now so thick she could hardly sense herself with Randy.

"Is it good for you?" Randy asked one morning.

"Oh yes." She felt wary, that some unspoken agreement had been breached.

"Sometimes I wonder."

"Don't you worry about that."

That was in the morning, a weekend morning when she was making coffee for him on the hotplate. There was a metal table in her room and they sat on either side of it, him playing with his eggs and toast, dutifully eating while she served him, suddenly the housewife in slacks and a shirt, kerchief over her hair that needed washing.

"We could go out to the country today."

"The country?"

"You know," said Randy, irritated, "I could take the day off and we could go for a drive."

"That would be nice."

"Don't you ever miss the country?"

"Oh sure," Kitty said. "I do." It was strange to hear someone call it *the country*.

"I thought you would," Randy said. "Being a farmgirl and all." He seemed different today, campaigning, planning attacks and diversions, looking for something inside her to grasp and possess. And though they were silent in the taxi, driving north out of the city and away from the lake, she was uneasy.

"You like this?"

"Sure."

"This is where they grow all the fruit and vegetables for the city." Long fields absolutely flat: it was a warm October day and there were no more crops, only the dense black soil, thick and moist, waiting for spring. "That's good land," said Randy. He stopped the car and they got out to see it close. She stepped into a field and picked a handful of the loam; it was creamy and smooth, the glossy particles crushed into mud in her hands; it was soil so rich you wanted to plough it with your fingers.

Then they were in the car again, driving north past the flats into hillier, rockier country. Randy Blair: he wasn't like Pat Frank at all. Randy Blair: his hair was slicked straight back into a duck's tail, one careful strand curled over his forehead, arcing over one round brown eye.

In the city she had hardly noticed that the season was changing, but here the trees crowded the hills in yellow rolling waves and the colour of the sky was deep blue, that dense deep blue fall skies have when the sun sinks a little lower and the earth starts to draw its heat out of the air.

"I was thinking," Randy said. The edge in his voice that had started at breakfast had now grown sharper. She saw his hands were clenched on the wheel; he was staring straight ahead and there was a curious set to his mouth.

"I was thinking," said Randy, "about whether we should get married soon. What do you think about that?"

He twisted his head to look at her. The set lines about his

mouth were matched by ditto marks between his eyebrows where they were pushed together with worry. He looked unhappy. Kitty was going to tell him that this was the first time she had ever seen him unhappy, that he didn't have to marry her just because they had spent these few months sleeping away the nights together. But didn't. Instead she let her eyes skim by his, settle on a distant hill.

"What are you looking at?"

"A place," Kitty said. "A place we could get out and walk to."

When they had stopped earlier, to inspect the gardening land, the sun had been strong in the clear sky. Now it was clouding over and a wind had picked up, so as they climbed the pagewire fence and set off across the pasture to the hill, Kitty had her arms wrapped round herself, shivering, and for a moment she was reminded of her own home, of the fall there and the way the blood whipped itself up to combat the winter months of cold nights and overheated wood fires.

After they had finally reached the height of the land they could see valleys running on either side of the ridge, like twin hollows pressed by giant fingers. She had in fact almost succeeded in pushing his question right out of her mind when he grabbed her arm and pulled her around to him, so he was looking into her eyes and she couldn't avoid him any longer.

"Well?"

"I don't know, Randy. I have to think."

"I love you." This was the first time he had spoken these words; they sounded forced and hollow. The wind in her face seemed to batter her; she was trying to keep her eyes on the trees on the opposite hill, but her eyes were filling with tears, and suddenly she could hardly tell if she was outside Toronto or back at her own farm again, standing on the hills and letting the autumn wind tease her, blow winter into her face. She remembered Randy but it was as if he was hardly there, she couldn't focus on him, it was as if her feelings for him had been blown away by the wind, by her own sudden need for Pat Frank and her own home. Randy was tugging at her arm now and telling her again that he loved her. And though the words still sounded recited, they only reminded her of how she'd used him, and made her feel worse.

"I'm sorry."

"Don't be sorry, for Christ's sake, don't be sorry that I love you." And his close face and brown eyes were so demanding that she threw herself against his chest, her arms desperately around his neck, pulling him to her, on top of her, down onto the ground into the bed of yellow leaves where without answering him she drew him into her: naked, unprotected, unsafe—for once feeling his skin against hers, wanting the feel of him and wanting to give him for once the true feeling of her. And when it was over she thought, *All right, it was all right*, because the wind dried his leavings on the insides of her thighs.

Close, they were almost close as they walked back to the car. His arm around her, she let him lead her down the hill and across the field again, and at the pagewire fence she let him cup his hands so his fingers laced a stirrup for her shoe. Then he came over too, stood in front of her, his hands printed red with her weight.

"Kitty, will you answer me?"

"No. I can't." The wind had come up; there was roaring in her ears, drowning out the sound of her own voice, of his response. She stood in front of him with her eyes shifting off over his shoulder, sticking again to the yellow waves of leaves, to a hawk circling over the ridge.

"Look at the hawk." It drifted in ever-wider circles, its wings slanting and edging through the air, a living humming knife slicing out cylinders as it climbed.

"Birds," Randy said. Close, his face was close again as he leaned to her, took her shoulders in his hands. "You have to answer, Kitty. You have to."

"No." She felt vaguely tired and contented, their lovemaking still crisp on her skin.

"I won't take you home until you tell me."

"Don't be silly."

This was the first time she saw it, the first time after all these months: his face went brick red, so sudden a light might have been switched on, and his hand swung back as if to hit her. She wasn't afraid, only waited, his face and neck had gone so red now that tiny white stripes showed through. "Don't push me."

"Don't threaten me." He turned around on her. The back of his neck was red enough to singe the blond brush of his hair.

"Randy, I have to think."

"Fuck off."

"Don't say that."

"Cunt."

They stood, Kitty Malone and Randy Blair, each to their own side of Randy Blair's black Ford taxi. "You have to tell me," Randy Blair said. "I won't start driving until you tell me."

"Tonight. I promise."

Each opened their own door and slid in to sit on the yellow leopard-patterned covers. Randy looked so solemn that Kitty wanted to laugh; but she didn't, she only watched as he slowly slicked back his hair, guiding himself in the rearview mirror, then reached into his bomber jacket for his cigarettes.

"Let's talk about something else," said Kitty. She was cold and she could feel bits of leaves clinging to the backs of her legs.

Randy switched on the motor. It caught with a high whining sound, like thousands of blades meshing together. Then he skidded the tires in the gravel and turned the taxi round so they were heading south again, back towards the white fan of light that marked the city. A whole afternoon was necessary to get them out, but only an hour passed before they were back at Kitty's place, climbing the narrow stairs to her room. At every step she could feel Randy tugging at her.

"Will you marry me?"

"Please. Wait."

"Why won't you tell me?"

The stairway was dark and smelled of boiled meat and cabbage: foreign food. She felt close and panicky; a fast pulse had started up at the base of her throat, choking her.

"Randy. For God's sake let me think." His hand dug deeper into her elbow and for a moment she thought she would turn and bring her knee up into his face.

"All right," Randy said. "I'm sorry."

She left him in her room and got into the bath. First she slapped water on her face, and dug the dirt out from her eyes and ears. Then she rubbed shampoo into her hair, foamed and coiled it around the crown until she had made a gigantic white helmet of bubbles. Finally, with the soles of her feet pressed together and her knees wide open, she gently sponged the dried sperm from her thighs.

The morning after her wedding Kitty had woken up and started making breakfast in the new apartment Randy had rented for their marriage. With the bedroom door open she could see him sleeping while she washed cups and ashtrays from the night before. In those days it seemed she smelled everything, everything from the furry warmth of Randy's skin to the manure on her brother's shoes, and so while she washed away the traces of cigarettes and Charlie's two bottles of rye she opened the window and let the wet spring air blow in across the sink.

They were in an apartment above a store, with an extra room for the baby that was coming. When the coffee was finished cooking in the shiny tin percolator Ellen had brought, Kitty stepped out on the narrow balcony with its yellow Italian-curled iron railing and looked down at the street. There were cars passing by, long ranks of black cars all covered in ribbons and flowers, and ceremoniously honking at each other. For a moment she thought it was a funeral but then saw, in the centre of the parade, a car containing the bride and the groom. The bride was dressed in white. With olive skin and a too-wide lipsticked mouth she looked grotesquely sensual, like a whore, and the groom, with his oily black hair and black eyes, like a greedy gourmand ecstatic with the knowledge that for every night of his life he would have the privilege of devouring her. Their diamond rings flashed in the pure spring air. They were sitting in the back seat, the top down, and as they passed beneath Kitty's window they looked up at her and smiled, their faces wide and open, their teeth white and shining like silver bands, like Ellen's teeth, like the whole false life she would never lead and standing there in her own wedding nightgown she smiled back at them, showed them her ring; and then suddenly crying waved once more, throwing them her coffee.

She remembered turning away from the window, starting back into the apartment and seeing Randy struggling up out of sleep. The memory was so strong it locked; she was frozen in the moment when Randy was trying to focus his eyes on her and the outraged bride and groom were shouting from the street. And then, struggling, she was awake. Somehow the sheets had gotten wrapped around her neck and, with the panic still in her, she finally got them untangled.

She was back in her hospital room. Across from her the two old women still rattled the night away, but through the window the spring sky was just beginning to show signs of light. And now she remembered that with her coffee, Sandra had given her a sleeping pill, and had finally led her, dazed and stumbling, down the hall to her bed.

Her neck hurt, felt sore and strained as if someone had been choking her the whole night through. She stretched slowly, exhausted from the pill but knowing that she wouldn't be able to sleep again. When she had finally told Randy she was pregnant and agreed to marry him, it had seemed so simple she hadn't known how she ever could have resisted. That night, the night after their day in the country, she had been so ashamed of herself for fighting with him, for washing him off herself, she had let him come in unprotected again. That was when Randy Junior happened.

Astride Randy Blair in the narrow darkness of her boarding-house room, guilty and afraid, the sounds of television coming through the thin walls, riding him full of hate and despair and pity until, for once, her body found itself with him, gathered together and bouncing to the rhythm of her Jarvis-Street bed, released.

"Did it hurt?" he had asked.

"No."

"Do you feel good?"

"Yes. Really, I do."

The sound of a door being shut. Then slow irregular steps in the hall. That would be Sandra, she thought, that would be Sandra limping her way past the rooms. Not wanting to talk, but too lazy to put out her cigarette, she sat and waited as the step got closer. And then Sandra was in the doorway.

"I must have been tired," Kitty said. "I didn't know I was so tired." She wondered how Sandra, with her twisted foot, had managed to get her from the nursing station to her bed.

"That's all right. You should try to get back to sleep now."

"I will."

Sandra stood still for a moment, framed in the door. Then came into the room. As she walked, Kitty noticed, she turned with each step, her full weight twisting down onto the special shoe, until she got to the bed where she reached out one hand for support before lowering herself down onto the chair beside it.

In the early morning light Sandra was pale gold. Her fine white hands were folded together, the fingers intertwined, ready to wait this way forever.

"You've got company now," Sandra said.

"I know."

"You'll be able to see your brother Charlie tomorrow."

"Charlie doesn't drive to town too often."

"He's downstairs," Sandra said, "in the Veterans' Wing." Her hands, cool and white, unlaced now and moved to Kitty's arm. "He came in last night with a broken leg. They've got a cast on it already and they say he's going to be fine."

Seven

Although it had been an hour since the sun's shadow swung from one side of the yellow junked grader to the other, it was only starting to be Sunday morning for Mark Frank. Because when the sun had risen, Mark Frank had not. And even after he had climbed out of his sagging bed, limped slowly downstairs and stood on his front lawn, taken out and cleaned his glass eye, pissed out the remains of the night's beer and replaced it with two cups of coffee, washed his hands and sat down at the kitchen table in front of his orange scribblers, the sun had not risen for him.

He was, in brief, depressed. Depressed, melancholic, blue, cheerless, disconsolate. Unsmiling and even atrabilious.

His condition was a large grey cloud inside of him that could not be discharged. For hours he had lain in bed, afflicted by this unusual and uncomfortable cloud, so weighed down by it that the thought of going fishing, which always cheered him, was soured, so weighed down that after lying in bed and smoking cigarettes for the whole morning it had finally come to him that maybe he could get rid of the grey cloud by writing down the events that caused it.

So now, with his eyes shut, his ballpoint pen pressed against the page, his mind rebelling, Mark Frank was trying to remember, to recreate, to compose his own particular Saturday night.

Saturday night

he wrote on top of a fresh page. Somehow this reminded him of composition class in school, an instance almost as depressing as the present, and of the only instruction which had stuck, which was to start at the beginning.

I drove down with Randy and Charlie to the lounge of the motel to meet Pat between visits to the hospital. We were watching the new singer when Pat comes in drunk.

He wrote this and then remembered again his composition class, which had been taught by a crazy townie called Henry McCaffrey, and McCaffrey's second piece of advice, which was to visualize the scene. Though he had never been able to do it in class, he now closed his eyes and effortlessly conjured up the four men sitting at an arborite table at the No-Tell Motel watching the green-titted singer. And felt again in his blood the feeling that had started there, the tense combative feeling that always sprang up whenever Pat and Randy were in the same place. He wanted to find a way to write that down, to explain that it wasn't the ordinary sort of feeling, but then for background information he began to concentrate on something else that had come up, when Pat told them about Billy Maclennan, who had gone to the hospital a year ago because, he said, his mother's soup was giving him such a bellyache he didn't know what else to do.

He says Billy has a touch of gangrene now and they have a plastic tube sticking into his side where the gall bladder used to be. Stuff comes out the tube into a bucket and it's thick and black as molasses. Pat said it smelled so bad he had to leave. I had Billy's mother's soup once. It wasn't so bad though it might get worse after it sits awhile.

At this thought Mark Frank pushed the orange scribbler away, set down his pen and moved to the stove, where he poured himself another cup of coffee. He was thinking of Billy's poor stomach and now, Pat said, it was turning green inside with gangrene so they had to pipe the shit out of him through a tube.

He had decided he would write by simply putting down what was in his mind, but now his mind was as full of disparate thoughts as the lake of different kinds of fish swimming in their own directions, and even as he tried to imagine how they would fix up Billy Maclennan so he could walk around without leaking molasses he found himself going back to the look that had passed from Randy Blair as Pat came into the lounge of the No-Tell Motel. Because Randy hadn't just looked at him, he had measured him like a young bull measuring the old: a pure curious appraisal.

And Pat, seeing this, said to Randy Blair, "How're you liking being home again? You having a good summer in the country?" Because Randy spent last winter living in Toronto with his father when Pat thought he should have stayed home to help Charlie.

Mark sipped at his coffee and tried to remember exactly how it had started. From the beginning, from the day Kitty brought Randy back on the train, it had been bad between him and Pat. Like the time Pat had bought Kitty a radio when she moved into her grandfather's house, and the very first morning Randy, only three years old then, picked it up and smashed it into the kitchen floor so on top of the linoleum there was a new carpet of broken glass and plastic.

> Then Pat grins at Randy and pulls out a piece of paper. It was a wedding licence. "Look at this," he says. Randy of course is ready to piss his pants. But Charlie picks up the licence and smiles across at Pat as if he's been waiting for this his whole life.
> "Pat," he says. "You should of done this twenty years ago."
> "She wouldn't let me," Pat says.

Now his fingers were already getting cramps and Mark had to put down his pen and crack his hands. The truth was it sometimes seemed that everyone around here was getting older, even the chickens were starting to die right in the middle of spring. He went to the counter and took a piece of white bread from its plastic bag, then covered it with a thick layer of butter, followed by some of Kitty's strawberry jam. It was the first morning in three weeks that he had missed fishing and, still being in the house this late in the day, with the taste of jam in his mouth, it felt like winter again. Like the whole cloud of winter was blocked up inside him.

Then, crossing back from counter to table, he remembered exactly what he was trying to avoid: Charlie Malone's face as he lay on the pavement in the rain, his leg twisted under him, his eyes blood red in the receding light of Randy Blair's truck as he drove away from his own uncle, the man who had fed and housed him for fifteen years while his father sat on his ass in Toronto and wrote cards every Christmas. Charlie Malone's eyes clenched tight and his mouth wide open, crying like a baby.

Yesterday it was cloudy all day but the rain didn't start until night-time. When Pat came in the shoulders of his jacket were wet and he wiped his face off with his sleeve when he sat down. I've seen him drunk more often than I've seen my own face but last night he was looking for a fight.

"We all thought she should have stayed home and married you," Charlie said. Then he tries to make it harmless by slapping the table. Knocking Randy's glass over by mistake and Randy's up and standing over him.

"Fuck off, Charlie."

"Take it easy," Charlie says. "We're all old men here except you. Don't give us a heart attack."

Randy fills his glass from the pitcher and the truth is that since he went to visit his father he is a stranger here. He drives his truck around and he doesn't know what to do with himself. He helps Charlie a bit but he is worse than he used to be, worse than a hired man, and although he does what he's told he never offers anything himself. The truth is that no one here owes him anything. The moment he came back to visit we knew he had lost himself.

"Not too old to get married," Randy says.

"That's right," Pat says. "A man wouldn't want to die fucking out of wedlock."

Again Mark Frank got up. He and Charlie often joked about getting old, but what he felt was punched around. His back and kidneys would get sore, his shoulders would hurt in the morning from being slept on wrong, or from doing less work in a day than he used to do in an hour. On this particular Sunday the base of his back was a sharp mass of pain. He pushed his hands into his spine and tried to stretch around, but it seemed his whole body was stiff, that every night's drinking now took days to run out of him.

This morning his glass eye felt gritty in its socket. He took it out and washed it again, splashed water in the socket too, then patted it dry with a soft towel he kept for that purpose. Although he was a man who ordered and remembered details, a man who knew, for example, every usable and nearly usable part scattered through his barnyard, there were certain things he could not remember at all. He could not, for example, remember what it felt like after he lost the eye. There had been a brief moment of horrible intensity that started on the edge of his pupil, fading to the almost absent sensation of being cut by something very sharp, and then that benevolent sharpness had suddenly exploded in the very centre of his brain, making him scream. That is what he remembered: not the continued pain but the sound of his own high-pitched boy's scream.

He went to pick up his pen but the nerves in his arm jumped, his fingers couldn't grasp it, so he reached for the coffee and watched his arm jump again, this time veering away from the pot towards the emergency bottle of cheap sherry he kept on the top shelf of the cupboard. A place even Pat wouldn't look because the top shelf was where Mark put pots too burnt to be worth washing.

Looking back at Saturday night it seemed that Pat had been seeking out trouble, nosing for it as he always did when things with Kitty got too strained, and when he had goaded Randy the boy had jerked up to his feet like a puppet. And Pat, instead of placating him, as Charlie had done, had pushed his long red nose in further. "What the fuck is bugging you tonight?" Pat had said.

The sherry was sour and bitter, but it steadied him. He took a second swallow, a third, then brought the bottle to the table.

And then him and Randy are standing with their faces close enough to kiss or spit. "What the fuck is bugging you?"

"Don't push me," Randy says.

"Don't make me laugh."

"I'll let you go this time. I wouldn't want my own mother marrying someone with a squashed nose."

"Go ahead. She ain't marrying me for my nose."

Then that Goddamn fool Randy takes a swing at Pat. His ring cuts him. He swings again but this time Pat grabs his arm, turns him around, and delivers him such a boot in the ass it sends him half-way cross the room. Throws the truck keys at him and walks out of the lounge.

Their last dog had been killed by a snowmobile that winter and so it was that Violet Kincaid, the widow, could sneak up on the Frank household, such as it was, and be standing in the doorway before Mark looked up and saw her, him caught with his head down carefully writing in the scribbler.

"Well," said Violet Kincaid. "What are *you* doing?"

"Nothing." And flustered stood up and put the scribbler on the counter, leaving the bottle of sherry alone, with no glasses, on the table.

"That's okay," said Violet. "I'll drink it like this. Now that you invite me."

But Mark, his mind now returned to itself, grabbed the bottle from her. "That's kerosene for the lanterns. You could die of it."

"If a person could die of *that*, you wouldn't be here to be visited. What happened to your eye?"

"I forgot it." Jesus Christ, the way a person could be walked in on during his day of rest. He put the kettle on to boil and started searching for his eye. This quest ended in the sink, at the bottom of his coffee cup, where the eye was located, plucked out for examination, rinsed clean again, and popped into place. Binocular once more Mark turned to survey the widow. For a time he had spent most of his nights with her, then those nights had dwindled away to weekends, now even the weekends had started to scatter themselves through the months.

"I've been hearing things over the phone."

"You have."

"I heard that Kitty and Charlie Malone are both in the hospital and your brother is in jail."

"What happened?"

"Randy ran them over, all of them. Imagine. Ran them over in his truck and almost killed them."

"You better sit down," Mark said. "Before he runs you over too."

"They say he ran them over just like frogs and you could hear them squishing on the road.

"Here," Mark said. "Take a drink of this kerosene before you die of fright."

He handed her the bottle and she had three swallows down before she choked and spat it across the room. When she had recovered from coughing, she took a package of cigarettes from her purse and started one. Then leaned forward. "Now tell me the truth."

"The truth is, I should have gone fishing this morning."

The widow Violet Kincaid was plump and grey, but no one thought her harmless, least of all Mark Frank who had spent hundreds of dark hours in the lee of her shadow and breath. Her eyes were the colour of her name, and in the dark, in the light of lamps and candles, they were bruised glowing pools. She used to say she was a witch. In the morning he would take himself away, his bones buzzing, renewed, his mind blank as if he had dreamed dreams too powerful for his habit, and all the following day he would have glimpses of his dreams, her dreams he knew, dreams of foreign places and planets, dreams that belonged in the graveyard.

The kettle was boiling and Mark Frank began to make himself more coffee. It was a long time since he had stayed up all night; his body had lost the rhythm of it, and though the first light had given him a new burst of energy he now felt simply exhausted, both his eyes gritty and sore, the muscles in his shoulders so heavy and aching he might have spent the whole night lifting Charlie Malone up off the road and carrying him back to the motel. Charlie's head cradled in his elbow, his eyes open and his leg hanging down as if the bones had been boiled right out of it.

"The truth. For once in your life, Mark Frank."

He contemplated reaching for the bottle but saw that she held it so firmly her knuckles were turning white, a virtual virtuoso death grip, and seeing him eye the bottle she lifted it up and tippled it like a man. That was the thing about the widow Kincaid: she was tough and greedy. You couldn't take her anywhere without her drinking you out of your pocket; you couldn't take her to bed without her sucking the marrow right out of your bones; you couldn't even have a car accident without her surviving and leaving you dead to pay the insurance. Which is what happened to her husband, Stanley Kincaid, whose accordioned car still lived in Mark's barnyard (minus the horn, the upper steering assembly, the left windshield visor, and the left rear wheel, all of which had been contributed to other, more ambulant vehicles), whose shadow Mark saw from the very first night he bedded down with the widow, whose ghost still swam and drowned in the bruised pools of her eyes.

Sometimes as Mark slid in and out of her he could feel old Stanley's ghost sliding with him, urging and spurring and whooping him on, coming along for the ride and showering sweat through his leathery old skin as if he were one of his own goddamn high-stepping horses, laughing at him behind every deep breath, pushing him so far into the widow there were times Mark thought he would never come out, times he came so deep into her that when the cloud burst out of him he felt he would spin dizzily forever, conscious of nothing but his own old sweat and Stanley's exultant graveyard laugh. And sometimes it was so bad he even wanted to ask her if she too heard Stanley's laugh as she writhed under him. But didn't dare.

When the coffee was finally made he set the pot along with two clean cups on the table.

"The truth," said the widow Kincaid.

"We were all there," Mark began. "Me and Randy and Charlie, when Pat came in from the hospital."

"Drunk?"

"Not too drunk to walk." He looked across at her, found himself forgetting about his story and wondering whether she might loosen her death grip on the emergency sherry. Then suddenly remembered how it had been when Pat walked out of the bar leaving Randy on his belly; when Randy got up his nose and mouth looked like a big spoon of strawberry jam. "Well," Mark said, "it seems Pat and Kitty had been hanging round City Hall, because when Pat came into the motel he was waving a wedding licence around like you'd have thought he'd got a brand new pecker. Before ten minutes are gone, so is Pat, after he and Randy have a go at each other. But Randy's so stirred up he starts at Charlie and finally sneaks up on him and pulls his chair out from under his arse."

He paused and looked across at the widow. "A man gets dry."

"Drink your coffee."

"A man gets dry for his own liquor."

Her knuckles whitened; Christ, she was strangling the sherry. "Not until you're finished."

He could almost taste the sherry. It would be sweet and it would burn in his gut. Maybe he didn't want it. Maybe it would taste better later. He sniffed at his coffee but even the fragrance made his exhausted nerves jitter and he pulled away. He began rolling a cigarette, watched his stubby thumbs carefully crease the paper.

"You know Charlie," Mark said. "In two seconds he's up and has Randy stretched over the table, his hands around his throat. But then Randy comes back at him." The widow was watching him and Mark knew his story held her; yet somehow, in the telling, it lacked everything that had been so real in the bar. Because what he wanted to relate was not just who-hit-who-when, just to satisfy her gossip's curiosity, what he was worried about was how out-of-season they all were, him and Pat and Charlie, to be still drinking and fighting and fucking like teenagers. Because the truth was they were all too old for it; the truth was that the beginnings of the impulse were still there, but they lacked what it took to carry it out; so while in the old days Charlie or Pat could have laid Randy down so he would never have caused another scene for ten years, in these days the truth was they could only try. First Pat had booted him half-way across the room and then he had left, but Randy had just gotten up from it, wiped the blood from his nose, and gone on drinking. The fight had driven Pat away but Randy was just warming up, getting ready for the main event with Charlie. And Charlie, though he had tried to strangle him, hadn't even hurt him. His bald head shone like a goddamn lawn in the green lights, green as a tit on the green-titted singer, but he couldn't hurt Randy, couldn't do anything but surprise him and slow him down, because the moment he went easy Randy was on his feet, swinging, his thick arm driving his knuckles into Charlie's gut.

"Well?" demanded the widow.

"Well," Mark said, "he takes Charlie's hands and pries them off his throat, and suddenly he has his feet again and he is putting his fist into Charlie's big belly so hard you hear a big *whoompf* of Charlie's air being let out. And then Charlie is on the floor and Randy turns to ask me if I want to be next. But before I can help on this, even the manager of the motel was bored with the show; he and that big bouncer of his grab Randy and throw him out into the parking lot."

At which point, Mark now remembered, he had been relieved to know the evening's nonsense was finished without anyone being killed, and a person could go back to having a few drinks and trying to listen to the green-titted singer over the brassy sound of the No-Tell Symphony Horn Band. And then he recalled what his teacher had told him, to start at the beginning, which now seemed the night Pat had told him his brain was shrinking. Because if Pat had not put so much worry into watching his own brain disappear he would never have started chasing after Kitty Malone again and she never would have gotten a lump in her side. And if she had not gotten a lump in her side she and Pat never would have got close enough to City Hall to even think of marrying.

"Then Charlie gets up from the floor to follow Randy out to the parking lot. Damn idiot, he is too old for that, so I went too, to make sure he didn't hurt himself. Randy was in the truck, so drunk and angry he couldn't unpark except by crashing all the other cars out of the way. He was making the place look like my barnyard. By then it was starting to rain pretty good, you could hardly see anything but his headlights smashing around, and Charlie running across them, trying to fight his way into the door. But Randy threw him out again and Charlie must have slipped in the wet. He was just lying there when Randy drove over him."

"Well," said the widow Kincaid. "He was never right."

The widow balanced the bottle of emergency sherry in her strong hands, and while Mark watched she set its mouth to her lips. He was so tired now that everything seemed to be registering on his senses at once. Not only did he see what she did, but he felt it too, felt the cold green glass against his own lips, the nauseating sweetness of the sherry down his own throat, trying to settle in his stomach which was not settled. She licked her lips and he could feel her tongue on his own mouth. That was the way it was. You would meet a woman and soon you would live your whole life beside her, so mixed up you couldn't tell your mouth from hers.

When the widow Violet Kincaid had finally gone, Mark Frank finished the rest of the emergency sherry in one small swallow, poured himself a final cup of coffee, and then prepared to go outside. Sunday. It was Sunday and in the old days when a trip to the No-Tell Motel was an excursion into the wilderness of city music and beer in clean glasses, when Stanley Kincaid lived a mile down the road and he could walk that distance without being passed by a car, in those days when his world felt full and Sunday was a long full breath that stretched from the drunkenness of Saturday night to the chores of Monday morning, then Mark Frank liked to pass his Sunday afternoons walking back through the maple bush to the lake and sitting by the shore.

It was raining again. It had stopped for the morning but it was starting all over, and with the rain from last night it had soaked the ground spongy and green, turned the grass green as new oats, and was forcing the leaves out of the trees, forcing them open like a hand unclenching, like Charlie Malone's hand being pried off Randy Blair's throat. So now Mark Frank put on his old felt hat that kept the wet off his eyes, glass and real, a quilted nylon ski jacket Kitty had given him one Christmas, and set out for the lake.

It was that borderline time between spring and summer when there are still piles of dead leaves from the previous fall, a time of grace before the insects get thick, a time when you can still see spaces in the sparsely covered trees, when you can still see bare patches in fields unevenly ploughed and planted.

Through pasture and cornfield that had once been his own but now were farmed by a cousin of the widow Kincaid, Mark walked to the edges of the maple bush. The sky was grey, with lakes of yellow where the light seemed to be gradually thinning the clouds. But once in the bush, the light deepened. It was strange to be without a dog, their last dog had been killed so messily that neither Mark nor Pat had yet the heart to get another, so when walking, instead of a succession of flushed birds, treed squirrels and raccoons, gophers, porcupines waddling slowly out of the way, there was now only the sound of his feet slapping through the wet piles of leaves, the sound of rain falling on the crowns of trees a hundred feet above.

It was cold but there was no wind. He had his hands jammed into his pants pockets and only his wrists were exposed, the rain making raw bands around them. It was almost a week since he had spent an evening drinking alone with his brother.

"You know," Pat had said, "I think I am going back to being a boy again."

"You don't say."

"I do." There was something about this brother of his that defied his eye. There were times when their joint presence seemed too much for the house, times when the sounds of Pat moving about the place were not familiar or welcome, but an intrusion right into his nerves.

"Yes," said Pat. "When I lie down to sleep at night I dream I am a boy. Do you ever dream like that?"

"No."

"I never used to dream."

"You don't say," said Mark.

"You know," said Pat, "sometimes I think I'm going to die. If I am dreaming myself as a boy it means my brain can't go forward any more so now it is going backwards. When it has no further back to go I'll be dead."

"You act your age and you'll be all right."

"Act my age," Pat had said. And he looked at Mark so curiously that Mark wondered who or what had been growing under this familiar twin's skin; Mark wondered so much that when he wrote it down, he tried to used Pat's words exactly.

"Act my age," Pat said. "When our mother was our age she was dead and our father was close enough. Charlie Malone is going senile, Sadie is a walking broom, Stanley Kincaid is hardly remembered by his widow who is a witch, you are wearing the same glass eye you wore out twenty-five years ago, and I am only alive in my sleep."

The trouble with Pat is that he has never found out the order of things. A man grows old and dies and if he resists it only makes things worse. Pat can look for his brain on the wall all he wants but it won't make him any smarter. He says he is trying to improve his mind but I say if he put more of it into eating potatoes and less into searching for itself, he would feel a lot better. If a man doesn't act his age things fall on his head.

He had walked through the upper part of the bush, the place where the trees were past their maturity and limbs were beginning to rot from within and split off with their own weight, to the lower part that had been planted by his father and should now be tapped but wasn't being, was now sixty years old and coming into its first full bloom but there was no one to draw off the sap. Here the trunks grew straight and smooth, and the limbs arched up easily to the crown. For years this bush had been kept trimmed and thinned, the one place on this farm that was being readied for the future, but now it too was going; there were thousands of saplings growing up between the trees, the surrounding fences had been let go and cows had trampled around the roots, the odd tree dead from lightning or disease was let lie where it fell, its place in the sun taken not by another maple but by fast-growing softwood and prickly juniper bushes. In a few years the man who owned this land would take this same walk, survey the bush with his calculator, and decide to sell it off for timber before its whole value was lost.

By the time he got down to the lake Mark Frank was exhausted. The sleepless night seemed to have settled in his bones: no matter how often he stopped and stretched he couldn't seem to get his body lined up right, no matter how quickly he walked his blood didn't seem to warm his body, so even though the rain now was spitting hard into the water he was glad enough to sit down in the shelter where three pine trees grew close together at the shore.

There, on a rock whose base had been edged with snow only a few weeks ago, he rolled himself a cigarette, pulled his hat down further over his eyes, and watched the lake fight the rain.

This afternoon, before she left, the widow Kincaid had walked round the table, the sweet powdery smell of her suffocating as she placed herself beside him, her hands folded across her belly.

"Well?"

"Not today." Not because he didn't desire her, vaguely he did, but because somehow it seemed to require too much effort to climb the stairs, take off his clothes, get warm with her in the cold bedclothes.

And now he felt as he sat and let his back stiffen in the rain that he was turning away from himself in some way Pat hadn't, that his life seemed to be narrowing down; and for just a moment as he sucked in the smoke he could hear a faint rushing noise, as if he were in a tunnel and time was hissing past. Opened his eyes wider to bring himself to the lake but saw instead Charlie Malone, Charlie Malone in his arms with his face turned towards him, his leg drooping, Charlie Malone's eyes wide open too: hearing the same sound.

He sat at the lake and listened to the sound of his own life hissing by. And then he went back home, to his kitchen, where he finally made his judgement.

What Randy did was bad but people have done worse to each other. Charlie will be all right. He will lay on his couch until his leg is better and then he will get up and work again. I would have been as dumb as him. I would have tried to take Randy if they had not thrown him out. I'd try it still if I got the chance. In my mind is a picture of Randy. He looks like a potato no one could eat. I could. I can do things others won't. Pat used to say I was too stupid to know better. He can think that.

Eight

It was Monday morning.

The sun was already high in the sky, out of sight, but from the tin-roofed barn that housed the chickens it shot its dazzling reflection through the kitchen window. This light Pat Frank tried to avoid by squinting his eyes as he scooped sections of the pink-fleshed grapefruit he had found in the refrigerator.

Over the cut Randy Blair had given him with his ring on Saturday night, Pat wore a bandage that extended from below his left eye to the long bone of his jaw. The bandage irritated him as he chewed, stuck into place not only by adhesive and dried blood, but also by the beard hairs that were growing into it; and aside from contemplating the painful collision of citrus juice with the raw spots inside his mouth, and the new and resolved direction of his life, he was trying to decide whether to go around the bandage when he shaved, to take it off first, or to defer the whole exercise until another day.

In his eyes was the over-bright glare of the sun, and in his stomach were the remains of Saturday night's drinking softened by the terrible food they had served him Sunday in the Kingston lock-up. As he worked his way around the grapefruit he absorbed its sharpness with pieces of thickly buttered bread, sliced raggedly off one of the loaves which he recognized as being from the generous hands of the Pillow Kincaid.

Pat pushed aside the grapefruit and set coffee to boil on the stove. Then he tore the bandage off his face and washed his cheek with hot water and disinfectant. In only a day and a half the skin beneath the bandage had turned white, Randy's temper like a stripe on him now. That white he covered first with soap, and then with foam, until his whole face was bearded; and then, pausing to allow the soap time to soak into his skin, he leaned forward and inspected himself in the mirror. It was at times like this, when his face was half-covered or he saw himself in the almost dark and only his eyes showed, that he lost track of himself, of what he looked like, and could imagine those same eyes coming out of faces more fully fleshed than his, less marked, not caving way where teeth were missing or arching up like an old mountain to his bare skull.

He was just picking up the razor when Mark slammed the screen door, walked in and put down on the table a brown bag of groceries and a carton of beer.

"You're looking at yourself again."

"Just catching up."

Mark took a bottle of beer out of the carton and held it towards Pat. "You thirsty?"

"Not yet."

"I'll put it in to get cold."

"Sure," Pat said. He looked at Mark, and then past him out the kitchen window to the front yard where Mark's old Ford coupe was sitting, black and dusty with chrome around its top, waiting for Pat to drive it to Toronto. He heard Mark shutting the refrigerator door on the beer. Mark had offered it to him, and he had waved it aside as if everything were the same; but in fact it was different. He was not going to drink the beer now, or fifteen minutes from now, or any time at all. Because from the moment he had stood in the parking lot of the No-Tell Motel, sheltered by the flashing sign from the rain, and watched first Randy Blair and then Charlie Malone run outside, ending in Randy Blair driving over Charlie while he lay in the slippery wet, Pat had known that everything had changed, that he had stopped drinking and was now focussed on the hunting down of Randy Blair. Even when the ambulance had come for Charlie and the police had taken Pat away, drunk and protesting, Pat had not lost sight of this new purpose. All night in the lock-up he had nursed it, and the whole next day he had let the knowledge simmer and ripen inside of him.

He began to peel away the soap, each stroke of the razor preceded by his fingers to feel out old pockmarks and scars. When he was a boy he had looked into the mirror and wondered if he would ever shave, and now, as he did, he recalled that his father had told him that when men get old their hair falls away not only from their scalp, but also, finally, from their face and even their chest and pubic bones, so finally they end up as pink and bald as they started, like Kitty Malone's grandfather who was at that time eighty-seven and whom they sometimes met, in town at the store, or on their very occasional visits to the church, powdered up like a baby with handkerchief twists sticking out of his pockets as though beneath his pants he was wearing diapers; and after his father had told him this he couldn't help looking at old Hank Malone and thinking that under all those clothes he was smooth and shiny as a pink rubber doll.

"Everyone in town wants to know what happened."

"Everyone here does too."

"They say Randy's run away to Toronto and Kitty wants to call the police on him."

"Fuck the police," Pat said.

"I bet."

When Pat was finished shaving he took his wallet and dumped it out on the table: the wedding licence came with it, its bulky white paper already creased into place. He counted out seventy-four dollars in bills, then rummaged around in his pocket until he found two more, fives, which he flattened and added to the others.

"You better take more than that," Mark said.

"I ain't going to the moon."

But Mark had already dug into his hip pocket for his own wallet, a bulging black leather billfold that he opened to reveal a thick wad of twenties, which he halved.

It was always Mark who had the money: where it came from Pat had never exactly figured out, he only knew that Mark perceived a secret landscape hidden behind the everyday, a terrain of opportunities for turning metal into cash, so somewhere in the midst of what appeared to a random and chaotic stream of visitors, wrecked cars and trucks, junked transmissions and engines, was a logical and systematic outpouring of twenty dollar bills. Some ended up in Mark's wallet, some in his own, and most in a bank account in Salem which had long been big enough to buy back the farm their father had drunk away. All this had started, perhaps not coincidentally, shortly after Mark had lost his eye, and sometimes it seemed to Pat that it was through his beige glass eye that Mark saw what most men, him particularly, missed, and that though his dark, more human eye might be twin to his, it was the glass one which was Mark's special gift.

"So," Mark finally said, as he uncapped the bottle that Pat had refused, "this could be it."

"It could." Pat's wallet was now swollen with Mark's money and his face felt raw and renewed. He was going to Toronto to get Randy Blair and he felt edgy and nervous. He didn't need the coffee he was trying to drink, even less did he need the knife Mark had put on the table between them. He found himself pacing about the kitchen, stretching his legs and grinning nervously. His cut was now a purple slash down his cheek, hedged narrowly by whiskers where he hadn't wanted to risk the razor. He was aware only of a feeling of excitement, a curiosity about Toronto – Kitty's one-time mecca that he had never seen – and a patina of fear and anticipation.

Mark's old Ford coupe ran like a fat belly, sighing and swaying, threatening to lose its balance at every corner, complaining when the speed was stepped up. But its sound was deep and smooth, and the tires, though bald, were made of that old thick rubber that would never quite wear out. While driving Pat thought about Randy Blair and what he was going to do to him. *What he was going to do to Randy Blair*; it was at this juncture that his plan faltered. He knew that he was on his way to Toronto, that everyone, himself most of all, required that he be the one to search out, confront, and revenge on Randy what he had done to Charlie, but the exact method of revenge, what exact thing he might actually *do*, still eluded him. So he was prepared for the hunt, resolved and ready for it, but there was a place in the future where his imagination went blank. And just thinking about his mind going blank made it slip around to thinking about the fact that he *was* thinking; and then trying to get his mind to sneak round the corner to catch a look at itself working. Because it had struck him that the mind and the brain might not be in exactly the same place.

"What I mean by this," he had explained to his brother Mark, "is that either my brain made me think I have a mind, or on the other hand my mind might have existed first and out of its smartness might have invented my brain. Like a person inventing his clothes."

In Kingston Pat stopped at the hospital and went first to see Charlie, who was lying on his back with his leg coated in white plaster and wired to the ceiling. By this time Pat had reinforced his pocket with a mickey of his favourite Barclay Five Star Brandy; immediately on coming in he pulled out the brandy and handed it over to Charlie, who was waiting with his hand extended. Like Kitty, Charlie was in a room meant for four, but in his room he was the sole patient.

But although he was in the biggest and fanciest room of his life, and although his leg was swaddled in decorator white adhesive and plaster, and was strung up to a shiny chrome hook in the ceiling, Charlie did not look well. Prosperous, there was no doubt that in this elaborate room, wearing his Christmas housecoat, his face cleanly shaved by the nurse, his hair combed back over the temples, Charlie Malone looked absolutely and untypically prosperous. But he looked grey too; his skin was soft and grey as if it hadn't seen the sun for a lifetime, and there was suddenly silver laced through his sideburns. It seemed that in this one weekend Charlie had passed from being one of those perpetually middle-aged men whose bodies stay constant and sinewy even while their faces take on wrinkles and age, who have worked the ground right into their bones and run their farm forever, to one of those indefinably old grandfathers who haunt the hotel and liquor store like ghosts in search of their former selves.

"You son of a bitch," Charlie said as he twisted off the top, "you must be crazy." He took a small swallow, coughed, and set the bottle on the night table. "Can't drink lying like this. They said they were going to take my leg down today and let me walk with a cane."

He was even starting to complain like an old man. His cane was hung over the end of the bed, stout brown-varnished wood with a rubber tip that grew out of the end like a fat black mushroom.

Pat picked it up. "Heavy." He leaned into it, practised hobbling about the room. His stomach felt clear and sharp; it was in fact now two days since he had drunk anything, since he had walked out of the lounge of the No-Tell Motel, but it was still easy enough to look away from the brandy to the window, where the afternoon sun now lit up the park across from the hospital, turned the grass a bright moronic green while the lake glittered with thousands of tiny wavelets. Then his mind slipped into the million scattered reflections on the lake: if he could throw himself out there and say Goodbye Charlie, if he could just disappear into the light.

"You're not drinking."

"Not this morning," Pat said. "You know how it is." Goodbye Charlie. It would be easy enough, everyone did it in their way, even when they masked it as his father had—the all-time, all-world, Goodbye-Charlie champion—so days he didn't want to work he didn't even have to think of avoiding his labours, only started drinking in the morning so by the time he was supposed to be meeting whatever emergency was being denied, he would be so far gone he could only sit on his bench outside the house, waving away the flies and grinning foolishly while the cows wandered into the corn, while the milk leaked out of their swollen teats, while the machines sat idle in the only week dry enough for haying.

"I drink to escape," his father liked to say, and then he would give everyone that big charming smile that broke his face into a good-humoured mask. Pat always remembered him in the same pose—sitting, leaning forward, one arm flung out in vacant good fellowship. Good old Terry Frank always had a place for someone to come and drink the day or night away. And when Pat thought of his father he thought not of a brain that had the usual minor problems of shrinkage but of one that had passed the critical point, so impaired that neighbouring farmers and townspeople used his sieved mind as a hotel from their problems.

"You know," said Charlie, "if that little bastard hadn't run over me, I swear I would have killed him. He knew I was after him."

"He couldn't help himself."

"Christ Pat, don't give me that bullshit. I saw his face when he was driving at me."

"It was raining."

"He wasn't looking for the brakes."

"No, I guess he wasn't."

"He lived in my house," Charlie said. "I fed his little bastard face for sixteen years." He sat up so angry that his weight shifted too suddenly and the chained cast ripped its hook out of the ceiling and came thunking down on the bed. "Jesus Christ." In that one second Charlie's whole face grew slippery with sweat, and his hand snapped out to the brandy. "That's okay."

"I could get the nurse."

"Christ no. Let me have another drink."

"Sure," Pat said. Goodbye Charlie. Sometimes it seemed Charlie had Goodbye Charlie'd himself, because if he didn't know the child Randy Blair would resent first being pulled away from his own father and then being given away by his mother to a house run by crazy Ellen Malone, then where had he been?

"You all right?"

"Sure," Charlie said. He had the strangest face, Charlie Malone did. It was round and the eyebrows were burned blond and his small fish's mouth almost spat out the words, but altogether he looked almost like the boy he had always been, chippy, and now that the pain and the brandy had given him back his colour Pat thought Charlie hadn't suffered too much after all, that he would be home soon enough, the whole incident written off as another night at the bar. And then Pat saw Charlie leaning towards him, the boy's face screwed up and anxious, caving away at the edges so the boy and the old man in Charlie Malone were joined: "Pat. We're not going to let him get away with this." On the line between a question and a statement.

"No, Charlie."

Pat drove slowly, Mark's black Ford coupe going smooth and steady in the slow lane, riding like an old balloon-tired bicycle. Despite offers from Charlie and then Kitty, he had kept his resolve and remained dry, and now the pain of needing a drink was forming a fine and interesting edge in his nervous system, sending signals of need and deprivation to territories he had long ago surrendered. Periodically he would ball his long hands into fists and dig them deep into his kidneys, trying to force out the poisons which, now that they weren't accumulating, were starting to hurt. At every service station he stopped and both drank and urinated copious amounts.

Although he had spent the whole day looking forward to his mission with Randy Blair, by the time he had finished with all of his preparations, procrastinations and detours, and had actually gotten onto the multi-laned highway connecting Montreal to Toronto, the sky was turning pink, beginning to soak into the clouds that layered the western horizon. It was the elongated twilight time of day: it split the sky into long pastel stripes and deepened the colour of the whole country around, making the fields greener, more fertile, making clumps of trees into magic fragments of forest.

In this gentle melting time between day and night Pat Frank felt his new sober hunter self finding breath and blooming. In the glove compartment he had Mark's knife, on the leopard-patterned brushed cotton seatcover he had a map, and in his back pocket, folded carefully, the wedding licence still resided, with only twenty-four more hours needed until it would be good for one marriage.

"A person could rush around all day," Terry Frank used to say. "He might better have a plan."

Pat at least knew that he was driving in a broken-down car to Toronto, a city he had never seen. The image of Kingston, and its surrounding terrain, was reduced by dark and distance to a few shadows in the rear-view mirror; and his new hopes for his own self were being reduced too, dissolving into the blank wall of what he was going to do when he finally got to Randy.

Every time he stopped, Pat sat at the counter drinking his cup of coffee and three glasses of water, trying to put his plan into focus. Kitty had given him just one piece of advice for the city: "Don't forget to lock the car." With Kitty, for example, he had tried to have a plan. Jesus Christ, a hundred plans, a hundred different strategies to get her to yield her unknowable enterprise and collapse with him into domesticity. But she never had, even when in desperation he pulled a Terry Frank on her and went so vacant he refused to fight or make love for months; and though right now he could feel the lump of the licence in his back pocket he was sure she had only consented in a moment of weakness, in the sudden fear that her body would collapse without companionship. The sly, fearful bitch: the moment she was out of the hospital it would be back to total war again, her sitting complacent in her grandfather's house while he mouldered about the township, planning, plotting, drinking.

Total war, yes, they had states of peace and war. Peace was, like now, times when they admitted their need for each other. Before Kitty had gone to Toronto, there had been peace, at least she had chased him constantly. He had gotten so used to her pursuit that he expected to see her every time he looked up from a bottle of beer, or a lady tourist needing a hand with her car. But after she came back, though she had sought him out that first night, the balance had slipped the other way. "I need to learn to be alone," she said. Her declaration of war – as if every person wasn't alone every second of their lives. Sometimes, to fight back at her, he would retreat for months at a time. Into drinking. Into someone who needed the consolation he expertly provided. Then, one night, he'd wake up to the sound of her in the house, padding up the stairs to sneak into his bed, as if whole months and years hadn't passed; or he'd wake up needing her, her image so strong in his mind he'd set out across the fields looking for her, walking the whole twelve miles in the hope that she would have been having the same dream. Sometimes this would lead to a quick and perfect reunion; others it would bring on a fight where he would finally find himself drunk and screaming so much his throat hurt, screaming she was a drunken asshole slut that deserved to be knocked up by anyone crazy enough to climb into her bed; and he would be standing there screaming, his throat raw and the words drowned out in the noise of his own voice roaring in his throat, and suddenly he would be able to smell it, his brain burning itself out with the sour electric smell of an overheated battery.

The more he thought about this, the more the coffee started to race through him, and the closer to the floor he pushed the accelerator of Mark's old Ford coupe till finally he was going almost seventy miles an hour, swaying from lane to lane, his teeth clenched and his eyes half on the sun, which now rolled gigantically red on the horizon, and half on the shimmering white line of highway. "Goddamn," he was muttering to himself, "goddamn. First she twists me around like a goddamn pretzel and then she gets me sent to get her own stupid bastard son. And when I get back she'll be gone." Not physically removed of course, but in her heart; and just as he sometimes cried with gratitude because at every moment he truly needed her she was right there for him, he equally felt she had deserted him a thousand times, that she was as callous and organized as a little windup toy, a galling wind-up robot machine that had no more need of him than he had for the dogs he had carelessly buried and missed only vaguely.

He had left her in the hospital bed, her map in his hand, but though she was sending him after her son he hadn't really been close to him, it hadn't really *felt* close; and when he had leaned over to kiss her, her eyes had shifted in the old way, past his head out the window, as if she was afraid someone might be taking their picture for kissing in the hospital. But then her hands tightened around his neck and though she was withdrawn he couldn't help wanting her. Furious, he had backed out of the room.

Kitty Malone and Terry Frank: it had occurred to Pat more than once that his reaction to these two had something in common; and though the exact details and words were impossible for him to find, the feeling was not: the tension of a wire stretched tight between him and them; the need to have that tension recognized, soothed, to have the need he felt returned.

"I'll admit this much for you," Mark had said when Kitty came back and Pat started seeing and agonizing over her again. "You might be getting old and droopy, but at least you still know how to make a fool of yourself." And now it was nearly twenty years later. If he had been old then he was absolutely ancient in foolishness now, and from time to time Mark still slapped him on the back and congratulated him. As if his own digression with the Pillow Kincaid was supposed to be more dignified.

The thought of Mark, his own twin and another of the self-contained robots he had somehow surrounded himself with, made Pat that much angrier. With his foot flat to the floor, the needle in the old Ford crept up to seventy-five, and alongside the deep smooth sound of the engine Mark had so carefully rebuilt came a grating, protesting noise, like someone beginning to puff as they approached the limit of their endurance. Kitty tranced out in the womb of her grandfather's house, Terry Frank drunk on his wooden bench every summer morning of his life, Mark complacently grown into his big belly and viewing the world through his glass eye all rolled around in Pat's blood, all mixed in with his two-day-old need for a drink that was growing sharper every moment.

The harsh whine of the engine began to break apart into coughs, and Pat eased up on the accelerator. Now the sun had fully set and the double lines of cars had their headlights on, white and yellow rows winding like armies through the hills whose shadows he could still see.

"Come on," Pat said aloud, "for Christ's sake." He tapped his foot impatiently and the old coupe surged forward, cleaning everything out save the image of Terry Frank sitting on his summer bench, leaning forward with his welcoming vacant smile. And when the explosion came and the sudden skid began he could barely push it out of his mind, only glimpsed the cars and highways through it.

He was still pushing at it when he began to fishtail and was suddenly stuck to the side of a transport that was trying to pass him.

His father's face: wide, open, smiling; hair grey-black and combed straight back from his forehead, which was broad and deeply wrinkled.

Eyes a bright and idiotic blue, the colour of ice fields in the sun.

"You have to have a plan," Terry Frank would say. For example, there was the day he and Mark came home from school to find their father with one of his plans. He was standing in the fields separating the house from the road, rifle in hand, beside a wagon loaded with drums of water and a pile of dead gophers. With a big smile for his twin sons he showed them how to dump water down one exit from the tunnel and blast the gophers' heads off as they scurried out the other, piling the wagon with what the dogs refused.

And then the Ford came loose and homed for the ditch: Pat saw only the onrushing gravel and cement. There was a bump, one corner of the car bit into the ground and everything snapped free. Wind whipped through the open window like a long last death-tunnel whistle. And in the air he heard a curious sound, the screeching alarm of thousands of birds, as if this crazy flip-flop dying was throwing him through heaven's walls and all the doves were going crazy.

"You have to have a plan," Terry Frank would say. In winter his favourite plan was to lay trap lines in the bush of his own and adjoining farms. Mornings Pat would be the first up, standing on the freezing oak floor of the kitchen in three pairs of wool socks. He would look out the frosty window into the glare of the morning sun, and beyond the littered front yard and the stained barnyard snow he would imagine purer and whiter pastures: the bush, the snowed-in fields, and best of all, the lake—an expanse of crystal ice and white snow that shone and glittered in the cold sun. Inhabiting these white places of his reckoning were the animals caught in his father's traps: squirrels, foxes, rabbits, out-of-season gophers were the usual prey, but it was beavers and even wolves that they hoped for—beavers for the value of their pelts and wolves for the bounty.

Most often the animals they came upon were still alive. If it was a wolf they would stand at a distance and shoot until the noise was unbearable. The others were detached from the traps to be gutted and thrown into the burlap bags they carried.

The freeing of shattered legs from iron traps, even the first plunge of the skinning knife were so much a part of his boyhood, activities learned in the unusually alert presence of his father, that an acceptance of these things was somehow in him before he knew it. But the killings were harder. When he was alone with Mark, anticipation and revulsion mixed together so completely that as he raised his rifle he would feel them darting through him in lacy electric flings, blending into a tension that sometimes paralysed him halfway through the shooting, leaving him shaking with his eyes closed, keyed to the wild echo of the rifle against the cedar and maple.

Then one day his father was too drunk, and Mark was sick, so Pat went out alone, the old burlap coal bag tied to his belt and the repeating rifle under his arm. In that winter, which was his thirteenth, they had two rust-coloured bitch dogs that loped over vast territories while the Franks walked their lines. It was a day so bright and dazzling, so totally sharp with winter, when the sky was so blue and the cedars so crisp and green, that everything was more real than real: the cedars rose into the cold sky like dreams, dark and explosive; the snow was so slick and white, each crisp step making sounds so sharp and glassy, so complete and unto itself, that it seemed to him even then that he was walking not only the landscape of this snowbound farm, walking not only the path that he was walking on the way to somewhere else, but that he was walking in that place in his own mind that had invented this need for clarity, walking in his own dream of pure and perfect snow.

That winter the snow had fallen early. By late November there had been a foot on the ground, by Christmas three feet. Now, in February, the snow entirely covered both the shrubs that in summertime dotted the hills, and the fences that separated the bush and scrubby pasture from the few ploughed fields. Between the layers of snow were thin sheets of ice, from times when the temperature had jumped and then dipped. These thin sheets gave support for the smaller animals, even rabbits and foxes. But for the heavier animals, it was impossible. The wolves, desperate, travelled in packs, howling close to the houses at night, hiding by day. They fed on deer who struggled and starved in the deep snow; and on occasion they captured sheep and young calves right from the barnyard.

"Even in the winter," Terry Frank had explained, "the deer digs through the snow to eat old grass and leaves. When the snow's deep he can't get at his food, and it's so much work to move that he dies struggling." It had snowed that way one winter before, several years ago, and Pat could remember being towed by his father on a toboggan to see the frozen deer kneeling like ice statues near the back pond.

On this day the sun had a bright hot glare. Nothing alive would freeze in a sun like this. It was rising in the clear sky, promising spring, and its light broke apart on the glittering snow so the whole white rolling terrain was sparked with bits of red and blue. With tobacco stolen from the teacher's desk, Pat rolled himself a cigarette. As he lit it, he tried to squint the way he had seen the men do, narrowing his eyes against the light and the smoke, and it was at just that moment, out of the corner of his vision, that he saw his first wolf. As he turned full towards it, his hand snaking out for the rifle, it was gone. The dogs, who had collapsed near him when he started to smoke, hadn't even noticed; and for the time he thought that the wolf and the shadows that seamed it into the edge of the far bush were only in his imagination.

When he had finished his cigarette he began working his way on the snowshoes again. Though the temperature was low, the hot sun warmed the still air and soon he was sweating in his clothes, enough to open his jacket and the top button of his shirt, and then, finally, to leave his jacket on a tree branch and continue in shirt and heavy sweater. The dogs raced around, barking at whatever they could tree, anticipating his direction. He had never travelled so far from the house alone in winter, and the sensation of his increasing distance made him feel tense and independent; he found himself continually clenching the rifle for re-assurance, and running his hand against his pocket, where he kept his hunting knife.

He had agreed to limit himself to one of the lines, half a circuit. To save carrying he was first walking to the point furthest from the house; and by the time he got there, which involved a trip through the back bush and two miles along the curve of the lake, it was noon and he stopped to eat the bannock and cheese he had brought with him. Twice he had climbed up from the shore to the bush surrounding the lake, and both times had seen layers of dense wolf tracks. "They'll come round you from behind," his father had told him. "You don't have to worry about surprising them."

He threw the scraps of the bannock to the dogs, then rolled himself another cigarette. The heat of the burning tip made the air above it shimmer like liquid glass. Looking through it he could see the whole flat surface of the lake stretching out miles in front of him, so smooth and icy-serene it could have been a giant eye frozen and buried in earth and rock. And the trees around the lake were like dark green lashes, thick and tipped with snow, so still in the cold air that for a moment the boy forgot about his father, himself, the place he had come from and the place he was searching for, and saw only the lake and the surrounding trees, a sudden oasis that had lived its own life for thousands of years, freezing and thawing, breathing air fishes birds as easily as the passing seasons. And wondered if this was how it looked before there had ever been farmers, if Indians had seen the same lake, the same trees, the same liquid movement through smoke and fire.

"The trouble with Indians," Terry Frank liked to say, "was that they didn't understand the plough."

At the first trap he found a rabbit, caught by the leg and frozen. This was a good start, some days they caught nothing at all. He cut the rabbit free and threw it in his sack. But then he followed the line a whole mile back on the upper reaches of the shore before he found the next—a squirrel. Black, its huge tail was fanned out on the ground. It too was frozen dead, its lips drawn back so far it seemed its mouth had been pried open for its spirit to escape. Working the squirrel free his hands got cold and there was the sudden awkward sound of bone scraping metal. At one point he thought he heard movement in the bush. He jumped around, reaching for his rifle and scanning the trees for wolves. The dogs, unconcerned, lolled a few yards away, eyes incuriously closed and tongues laid out against the snow.

The traps had been set out in the hollows of the streams that fed into the lake. In places the drifts were so deep and powdery that the snowshoes sank in and left him floundering, buried to his thighs. Even the dogs grew tired, and where on the way out they had perambulated five miles to his one, now they were content to struggle in the ragged track he was breaking.

The sun shone only weakly through the dense bush, and Pat was alternately flushed and shivering as he worked. The trap line was clearly marked with blazes, but he had never travelled through such slow snow; and at each empty trap he grew more discouraged until finally he stopped to roll a cigarette and think about giving up.

He could already see the look of scorn on Terry Frank's face as he came in the door carrying only one small rabbit and one torn-up squirrel. Following the line it would take him three hours to get back to the field where he had left the jacket; by that time it would be dark but not, in the snow, impossible to see his way home. But if he gave up and cut back to the lake he could be back at the house before the sun set.

"Well dogs," Pat said, "you decide." The two bitch hounds, named by his father Rusty and Red after their colour, looked at him speculatively. Even more than most hounds their skulls seemed spectacularly pinched and narrow, and allowing for the thickness of bone, Pat had often calculated that the size of their brains must be about that of a baby's handful of peas.

"Well dogs, is it home or hunting? Does the early rabbit get the carrot? Will you guide me through the evil forest?"

At the sound of all this human voice the dogs rolled over in the snow to be patted on their bellies.

"Jesus." Pat was thirteen years old, and though Mark was wider and stronger, it was he who was the tall one, the first to be stretching up into the world of manhood. If he went home early he'd be saying he couldn't do it, that he was still too much of a baby to take the cold and the effort of walking the line. If *he* had been sick, Mark would have gone alone; Mark, he knew, would stay outside till his stocky boy's body froze before admitting defeat.

Pat stood up, clapped his gloves together until his fingers hurt, and took the census of his body: feet numb but without twinges of pain, the seat of his pants wet from sitting on the snowy log, cold circles where his wrists and neck were exposed. Nothing that wouldn't get warm or be easy to ignore once he was moving.

In the fall, when these traps had been positioned, it had taken only a few hours to walk the entire circuit. Not only did the snow make it harder to move, it also disguised the numerous deadfalls that had been scattered about by disease, lightning, and careless loggers. Sometimes Pat found their tops, gaining good support for his snowshoes; more often he stepped right in front of one, and when he went to lift his shoe found himself trapped and falling forward.

By the time an hour had passed, the afternoon sun was beginning to run out. During the second hour shadows began to block the spaces between the trees. He missed two traps entirely, and a third was empty. He was just about to reconsider going home when he came up to the crest of a hill and saw, in the small valley below, the dark form of a wolf lying motionless in the snow. At first he thought that the wolf was dead, that it had been caught in the metal trap, frozen and starved. He didn't even think about the dogs, who were labouring behind him, until they scented the wolf and began barking and running crazily down the hill. When at first the wolf moved Pat thought he must simply be seeing things with fatigue. And then the bush came alive with the weird howl of more wolves. Their sudden music twisted him out of himself, made him feel like glass suddenly shattered and thrown across the snow. The dark form whirled and turned on the charging hounds.

As quickly as Pat had his glove off and the rifle to his shoulder, three more wolves had come out of the bush and thrown themselves at the dogs. "Rusty," Pat shouted. "Rusty. Red." The four wolves were a circle around the two hounds, the black and grey fur blotting out the red. Pat's finger was on the trigger but everything was moving too fast, the shadows of dog and wolf intermingled. His mind, fixed on the confusion, suddenly froze.

And then the wolves were gone.

The dogs lay bleeding in the snow. He ran clumsily towards them, his snowshoes flailing and threatening to send him over on his face. He was sure the dogs were still alive, that at any moment they would leap up, dance around him with their muzzles poking wet into his neck, their paws pushing off his shoulders. But they didn't move; their bellies and throats were torn open and faintly steaming in the cold air. Frozen in the trap was a small fox, which might have made the whole trip worthwhile had not its hide too been ripped apart.

When he got home it was almost six o'clock. Pitch black. His father was sitting by the stove, bottle in one hand and watch in the other.

"Jesus Christ," he said. "I almost got to worrying about you."

"I'm okay," Pat said. There were lanterns on downstairs but no light from the upstairs bedrooms. "Is Mark asleep?"

"He's at the Kincaids. Gone to see if you were there."

"Sorry."

"You better feed the dogs before you get to taking off your boots."

Pat, without speaking, continued to pry off his rubbers. His feet were so cold he couldn't feel anything in them, not even the pressure of his hands massaging them.

"You heard me."

"They got killed by wolves," Pat said, and kept rubbing his feet. He could already feel the pain starting in his ears, needles edging up from the lobes.

"They did, did they. Them dogs wouldn't make a meal for a goddamned raccoon."

He was drunk, Pat could see, but not *that* drunk. He was still sipping from the bottle, not taking it in the big swallows that made his Adam's apple look like a fish being coughed up by the sea; or at the stage of being so drunk he didn't even bother with alcohol anymore, just boiled coffee and poured it into his belly in a useless effort to keep from getting sick.

Pat took a pair of dry socks hanging from the stove and pulled them gently over his toes.

"What kept you?"

"I don't know. It took a long time." He looked at his burlap bag with the one rabbit. "I didn't get much."

"That's all right," Terry Frank said unexpectedly. "It's a bad time of year. You did good to try."

This made Pat want to cry.

"I remember the first time I went out alone. I was lucky to get back." He smiled at Pat and leaned over to touch him on the shoulder. "You better feed those dogs now. They get tired too."

And Pat, his toes starting to hurt, his shins stiff from a whole day on snowshoes, his hands red and numb, finally started to cry and tell the story of what had happened. At first explaining it all unreservedly but then, seeing the look on his father's face changing from kindness to anger, cut himself short.

"I'm sorry," he finished.

"Sorry."

"I didn't know what to do."

"What did you think the rifle was for? Pissing?"

Pat was silent.

"Well?" His father's voice rising.

"I don't know."

"Didn't you have it loaded?"

"Yes."

"Well for Christ's sake, why didn't you shoot?" This shouted.

"I didn't want to hit the dogs." He was still sitting beside the stove, the snow melting through his clothes and into his skin.

"You didn't want to hit the dogs," roared Terry Frank.

His father's face: wide, open, screaming. Pat tipping back in his chair, the words rushing through him, feeling so small that when he reached for the rifle against the wall it was only to keep himself from falling into the stove.

"Jesus Christ," shouted Terry Frank. "Don't grab that thing at me." Which only frightened Pat more, startling him to his feet, holding the rifle across his chest now, his finger slid into the trigger, alive now where it had gone dead before.

"Put that down."

"Don't tell me what to do."

"Put that down or I'll beat the arse right off you."

"Fuck off, shitface."

The sound of the wet wood hissing and whistling in the stove; of his father's breathing, hoarse and protracted; of his own, high-pitched and gasping as if he had been running the whole day.

"Give it to me."

"Stay away."

"Give it to me."

Backing off from his father, who was edging towards him. Stepping back to the landing and then one by one up the stairs, Terry Frank following, his hand held out. And with each step he climbed, Pat was gradually swinging the rifle from across his belly to point first at the stairs and finally at the belly of Terry Frank—who followed just out of reach.

And then he was at the top landing and if he didn't stop he would be backed into one of the bedrooms, trapped.

"Give it to me."

"No."

His father's face: wide, open, generous. "I'll let you alone."

"Let me alone now."

These negotiations whispered, his father's mask beginning to slip and dissolve, Pat's eye caught by the empty burlap sack hung over the chair. His finger on the trigger, tense and jumping, his nerves needing the shots that should have been fired in the bush, already anticipating the echoing sound of this one shot fired in the narrow stairway, the sight of Terry Frank exploding backwards in one long last vacant fling.

"Come on."

"No."

Terry Frank's big hand, fast for once, whipping forward to the muzzle of the rifle, but Pat had caught it coming, had spied out the blue eyes surveying the gap, and he was ready, swung the rifle forward. "No," he shouted, everything contracting inside of him as he pushed forward with all his strength, springing as he jabbed Terry Frank in the chest with the muzzle, his weight behind it, sending his father cascading down the stairs.

The noise of his falling was so loud, and the blood racing through his hands so hot, he thought he must have shot him after all. And as the boom and clatter of the falling faded, and his father settled at the bottom of the stairs, the noise of his voice rose. At first Pat thought he was just shouting with pain, and then he thought that he was crying, but finally realized it was neither but only the never-heard sound of his father laughing unrestrained, truly laughing as he straightened himself out, unhurt. And finally he pointed up to Pat, his face scarlet with anger and pride. "You goddamned little bastard, Pat, you would have killed me."

Pat discovered himself lying on his back. Outside was the constant sound of cars on the highway. He pushed himself up in the bed, the clean motel sheets like warm glass against his skin. He was breathing deeply, each breath piercing through to the bottom of his lungs, as if old habits and layers of protection had been peeled away in the night.

He reached for his tobacco and rolled a cigarette. The smoke wanted to cling to his insides, caught lightly in his blood and circled lazily around, like smoke from a fire in dry still air.

According to his watch it was noon, which meant he had slept almost twelve hours. No No-Tell Motel this, it had advertised itself with a neon sign of a palm grove featuring a woman in a night-blue bathing suit. He had plunked a twenty dollar bill on the glass top of the registration desk and watched the vested man look unhappily at his greasy hands. Had to write his own name and address with a pencil stub so small his tired fingers could hardly tell one letter from another.

He sank down on the bed again to stretch his sore muscles. One bald tire on Mark's Ford coupe had not wanted to make the whole trip to Toronto; it was a right front tire and, when it exploded, it sent him first against that truck full of live chickens, and then into the ditch where he had flipped over. His whole body was so numb and disoriented it had taken him several seconds to register that he was alive. And then the driver from the chicken van had come and opened his door, started to pull him out; Pat had been in such shock that after the first step onto the grass he collapsed.

"What the fuck you think you're doing?"

"I don't know." The squawking of the chickens was like hail on a tin roof. They circled the car until they found the wheel in question, the tire blown right off it, absolutely nothing remaining but the metal hub.

"Jesus Christ," the driver said. "I ain't never seen nothing like that."

"Me neither," Pat said.

"You're lucky."

But not lucky enough to find much in Mark's trunk in the way of a spare. So after hitching a ride in the chicken van, the birds' noise finally drowned by the wind, Pat had waited for hours while the service station located a tire to fit his old-fashioned wheel.

Now he felt shaken and fragile. The long trip round in the air was still with him, the sudden freeing of the landscape to upside down, forming a sky made out of glass. The feeling of his head knocking into the old-style padded roof so hard he was bounced back down again, landing right in the seat just in time for the car to come to rest so his hands, still automatically gripped on the steering wheel, were the first thing he noticed. And second, that his feet too had kept their position; one on the brake and one braced against the floor. Without thinking he had done the first obvious thing, turned the key and started the stalled motor so when the driver came to pull him out it was running again, purring deep and smooth. Aside from the missing tire there were only two damaged points – the left front fender, which had taken exception to such antics and bailed out on the gravel shoulder, and the roof, which had a gently oval dint.

He was half-way through shaving before he remembered that he was now into his third day without a drink. The need sprang up in him suddenly, an edge, making his breathing shallow again, cutting apart his perfect day. For a moment he almost remembered dreaming. The dark torn shadows of the dogs raced across his mind and he closed his eyes, trying to search them out and make them live. But it was too late. The image was gone before he could catch it, and he found himself splashing cold water on his face, vigorously rubbing the sleep out of his eyes.

Beside the motel office was a restaurant. Slept and clean Pat Frank ate toast with butter and jam, and drank cup after cup of weak coffee.

It was now Tuesday afternoon, a whole day since he had set out, and as he ate he had an excellent view, through the grey-tinted plate glass window of the restaurant, of Mark's old black Ford. In this suburban parking lot it looked as bizarre and out-of-place as it had looked natural in the dirt driveway of his own home. In front of him Pat had the map Kitty had given him. Its purpose was to direct him from the outskirts of the city to the place where her ex-husband lived, and flattened out on the brown arborite table it looked simple enough.

Outside the day was grey but warm. He got into the car, spread the map on the leopard-patterned seat, and began driving in towards the centre of the city. Soon he had lost all the streets which Kitty had marked and found himself driving by instinct, homing in towards the densest section, what seemed to be the downtown.

Roads stretched out and collided with each other like a nervous system run amok. The low-rise buildings of the outskirts gradually gave way to scattered high-rises, and then the high-rises began crowding closer together so that even the dim grey sky that had hung over the motel would have been a brilliant relief. Not that light would have helped him see where he was going, he was so distracted by the unexpected; by the tracks in the middle of the street with red trains carrying people down their centre; by stores with writing in foreign languages on their windows; by armies of brassiereless women crossing the streets in blinding arrays of nipples pressed against sheer blouses.

He gave up trying to find his way and just let himself be carried along in the current of traffic, no longer resisting, just let the old Ford float down a never-ending maze of one-way streets, instinctively seeking the absolute centre of this mess, the tallest most jumbled-up concentration of buildings and smoke and masses of converging people.

He turned on the radio. Rock music pounded through Mark's

old speaker. He began seeing taverns out of the corners of his vision, happy oases with men leaning contentedly against the outside walls, full of what he wanted.

He was in a forest of gigantic skyscrapers. Traffic was crawling in a huge metal river. Heat and exhaust fumes swirled on its surface, smelling so foul he had to close the windows. When he saw a side street with an empty space he quickly turned in, parked his car, and climbed onto the pavement.

One of the hotel signs beckoned. Without further looking around he scrambled across the street and into the familiar cool and low-lit world. Like taverns everywhere it had a corner seat where he could rest his back against the wall and a television set in which he could lose himself. But not too deeply. Because when the waiter came he remembered what he had promised himself. "Tomato juice," he said. "A glass of tomato juice."

He rolled a cigarette and wiped his face with the back of his hand. Across from him was a mirror and in the dim light he could see himself looking amazingly respectable: shaven, hair slicked back, wearing over his checked cotton shirt a tweed jacket that he and Mark kept around for special occasions. In the pockets of the jacket were Kitty's map, his cigarette makings, and the knife Mark had given him. That he patted before taking the jacket off and hanging it on the back of his chair. When the tomato juice came he salted it and drank it back as if it were brandy.

"Again?" asked the waiter.

"Sure. I'm celebrating."

It was late afternoon by the time he managed to follow the map to Randy Blair's place. The apartment building was small, three storeys of red brick. On either side of it were tall narrow houses with sharply peaked roofs and windows so small and contracted with curtains that inside they must have been as dark as graves. He checked his pockets one last time, adjusted his shirt collar against the lapels of his jacket, then went up the cement walk to the glass door. That, to his amazement, just pushed open. He was in a vestibule with uncertain walls, as if this apartment had once been a house. And then he heard, coming down the corridor from one of the apartments, the sound of a radio playing, nice familiar sound of small-town music; and no longer nervous, nor even dazed by the huge size and complexity of the city, feeling only midly curious he walked slowly along the hall until he came to the stairway which took him to the second floor.

Randy Blair's apartment had his name in plastic letters on its door. Pat stood outside and listened. He heard nothing but the faint voice of a television set. He turned the handle, which yielded, and walked in.

To his left he saw the motion right away: Randy Junior sitting surprised on a brown sofa; with beer in one hand and cigarette in the other he levered himself up and came forward to meet him.

"Pat, for Christ's sake. Guh-day." As if nothing had happened. "How the hell did you get here?" Beckoning him in, the prince in his new castle, and so Pat advanced, suddenly feeling stiff and foolish in his clothes, following the honey-coloured broadloom through the short hall into the livingroom which was walled by shelves of books; every wall but the windowed one was covered and it was on one of the shelves that he saw the television, a small coloured glass square. "Quite a place," Randy said. "Did you ever see so many books?"

"No." Kitty had never said anything about this. There were as many books here as in the whole Salem library.

"He's got them in the bedroom too. Reads all the time."

"He does," Pat said. The sight of all these books was amazingly depressing.

"He does. But he don't make me. We just leave each other alone."

"Well," Pat said. "That's pretty polite."

"That's what my dad says. People should be polite. You want a beer?"

"Sure. Why not?" The books rose in dark-stained wood shelves from floor to ceiling. Each shelf was filled from end to end, and then on top of the vertical rows, more books and magazines were slid in on their side.

"He's got more in the bedroom too," Randy said, bringing in an uncapped bottle.

"You said that."

There were so many of them they were like insects; it was like picking up a rock and finding colonies of ants crawling over each other in swarming layers. "I was reading a book myself," Pat said. "It was about the brain."

"That so."

"I guess." He tried to remember the picture Kitty had shown him: a big soft man wearing a motorcycle jacket. She hadn't said anything about him being a professor. Taxis and racehorses, that's what she'd said he liked. Or maybe she had done it to him, maybe only two years spent looking for those goddamned shifting eyes and chasing after that hole in her centre had done him in, made him give up, resigned him to what could be bought and read and stuck up on his wall. Because there was nothing further from a book than Kitty. And now that he thought of it she was also driving him to books. He hadn't even been with another woman for three years now. If she didn't marry him he'd die lying in his own bed, reading Reader's Digest, waiting for his brain to shrink away to nothing and listening to Mark in the next room bumping and huffing like an antique steam engine sweating soot as he tried to bury himself in the Pillow Kincaid.

"This sure is a surprise," Randy said.

"It surely is." He lowered himself into an armchair, then set down the untasted beer to free his hands for tobacco and papers.

"I ain't allowed to roll them here. He says it gets tobacco on the rug."

"Ain't that something. You talk like your mother brought you up to shit in the barn." But when he was finished making the cigarette he neatly stuffed the end twists of tobacco into the paper, and lit it carefully, so the first burning embers wouldn't fall.

"Now," said Randy. "You don't have any business here."

The truth was that Randy had changed and though the process had probably been slow enough, Pat now started to see it all at once: he was wearing city clothes, jeans that hugged in close at the waist and flared like dumb-bells at his ankles, polished brown boots that wouldn't hold up for a day in the fields, a shirt that looked to belong on a banker. And his face had developed from a child's face to a man's. Where it had been round and almost pudgy, it was now growing heavier and getting square, the bones reasserting themselves through the flesh. And seeing him now, noticing the clothes, the set of his face, his delight with the money and surroundings of his father, Pat was reminded of him when he was first back with Kitty—in his little blue suit with shorts, pudgy complacent knees, looking all around as if afraid that if he took a deep breath he might die of the smell.

"How's Kitty?"

"Fine. They were hoping to give her the operation tomorrow."

"She shouldn't be in a hospital down there. You should've made her come to Toronto. They know what they're doing here." Randy looked at Pat. "My dad had the veins taken right out of his legs, you know. One day varicose veins and next day he was walking again."

"That's great," Pat said. He thought of the cold beer beside him. The feeling of need was like a nervous siren ghosting through him.

"Now Charlie," Pat said, "he isn't doing so well."

"Is that right?"

"Christ, Randy, what an asshole you are."

"My dad doesn't like people using bad words. You know what I mean? He says it messes the rug."

"Does he change your diapers too?"

A silence. Pat shifted in the armchair, moving his weight forward. Watching Randy, who still sat on the couch, half-empty bottle in his hand, one ankle crossed neatly over his knee as if he were the minister come for tea.

"I could throw you out," Randy said finally. "I was just being polite to let you visit."

His newly adult face now seemed to regress; and as Pat leaned further forward, his hands beginning to tighten, he sensed a further wavering in Randy's confidence. Randy was reminding him of a bull who has turned on you in the barn, ready to charge, then hesitates, looks up a second time, wondering. And a man knows he has that one long doubting moment to act.

"Don't get smart." Standing now. If he lets the moment pass without doing anything it will be like the time Charlie Malone got absent-minded with his best Hereford bull and ended up pinned to the nursing stall, two ribs broken and the rest turned neon purple with bruises.

"Don't tell me." Randy standing too, moving closer in his city clothes. His face was showing traces of his mother: the wide eyes that wouldn't make contact; the weird big-boned strength that blunted the air in front of it.

"You're going to be careful," Kitty had said. Asked.

"Sure."

"You won't hurt him?" Asking again, asking not only what would happen but what it was exactly that hung in the balance, what was being proven. As if he knew. As if with Charlie in the hospital and Kitty like this he could do anything else. As if it were possible to let Randy Blair run over his own best friend and just let it go. As if there were nothing that was owed.

"What do you want me to do?"

Watched her eyes stick to his briefly, then shift away, her hand moving up nervously to brush at her wispy hair. They had been not in her room but in the lounge, and from there they could see the lake. He started to feel sorry for her, her impossible situation, the shadow of her old marriage that still followed her. He had moved to touch her, which made her turn towards him, step to him and put her head to his neck, breath on his skin.

"Pat, you decide." Forgiving everything. A licence.

He had wrapped his arms around her and held her close, right in front of the others, right in front of the doctor he could see standing unconcerned in the doorway, in front of the window, the park that stretched down from the hospital to the lake—and had a sudden understanding of the lake itself: water filled with fish, abstracted empty brains swimming in cold water.

Randy was standing closer now, close but out of reach, slowly swaying back and forth, one hand still filled with the bottle, the other lightly curled.

"So," Pat said. "I was going to ask about your plans."

"Plans?"

"I was wondering where you were going to live."

"Well, I thought I might look around."

"Charlie could probably use some help up at the farm. Can't do much with a broken leg."

"What else?"

"What?"

"What else is wrong with him?"

"Nothing's wrong with Charlie. What's wrong with you?" And finally let himself take the tiniest first preliminary sip, just a few drops to take the dryness out of his tongue.

Randy standing right above him.

"Move back. You're making me nervous."

"Get out of here," Randy said. "Before I make you more than nervous."

"You're getting pretty tough."

"Charlie asked for it. He's been beating shit out of me for ten years. Now I'm as big as him and he can't lord it over me. So what? Didn't you ever stand up to someone?"

"Not in a truck."

"He chased after me. I didn't see him."

"Now Randy."

"I didn't," Randy repeated. They were standing face to face in the middle of the living room; standing, swaying, each with a beer bottle in his hand, and behind Randy's insistence Pat heard other, earlier echoes: Randy's own voice whining that he hadn't meant to lock Lynn in the chicken coop, Randy's own voice saying that he had to spend the summer with his dad in Toronto, Randy's own voice and Randy's own blue round eyes whining and insisting since the day he arrived in Salem. Pat could look right at him and remember picking him up with one hand and swinging him into the air, wanting to swat him; but because he was Kitty's by her city husband leaving him alone, feeling sorry for him.

"You saw him," Pat said. "And what did he look like going down?" And caught himself in the midst of his own familiar motion, the arm swinging bottle to his mouth: stopped: tasting it before he drank it: stopped: pushed the bottle away from his face, feeling the sweats break out on him as he did, sharp pains from his back and kidneys leaching out his strength, the bottle heavier to push away than an armful of cinder blocks.

And suddenly the pressure of the bottle in his palm released the dream: the memory of himself standing at the top of the stairs, rifle gripped in his palms, pushing forward with all his strength. Needing to be free. And the memory of himself facing the swirling mass of wolves and dogs. Unable to shoot.

"Get out."

"Now Randy."

"Get out of here before I have to throw you out." Face thrust belligerently forward, baby blue eyes bulging.

"You try to throw me out," Pat said. "You try." His head thrust forward, his neck stretched and corded. And he felt a surge of his own blood, confidence, and stepping back found the balance in his own body, his weight swinging through his legs and arms, ready for whatever happened.

"Right now."

"*Right now*," Pat mimicked. And saw before him not only Randy, whose face now swam in waves of red flushes, threat and counterthreat, but Charlie Malone: Charlie Malone who had been his friend all his life and now lay in a hospital bed because this stupid city nephew had run him over in a truck; Charlie, who had never backed away, now broken and resigned, asking his best friend to make the revenge that should have been his own. Pat now remembered the knife in his pocket, the knife Mark had given him. The money too. Old men's weapons to fight the young. Even as Randy reached out for him Pat had caught his movement and danced away, avoiding him around the corner of the chair, one hand still clenched tight to the bottle, his other brushing by his coat pocket for the knife.

"Come on, Pat. Fuck off."

"Now Randy. You don't want to talk to me like that. I tried to be a father to you once."

"I have a father." This hissed out. "You stupid fucking welfare drunk, where do you think I've been going every summer? Who do you think has been putting clothes on my back while I've been freezing my ass off in Charlie's stupid chicken-coop house? Christ, if I had an asshole like you or Charlie for a father I'd be sitting out in the middle of some field drooling with the rest of you."

"Now Randy."

"Don't tell me. Father, goddamn, I like that. Father. Sure Pat, you were just a great cuddly Dad, screaming and ranting around the kitchen, breaking bottles and plates like you were picking your nose. Jesus Christ Pat you're such a goddamn mean stupid joke I'm going to wipe the fucking floor with you."

They were stopped, absolutely still. The chair that had once separated them was now manoeuvered away and they were posed in the centre of Randy Blair Senior's tobacco-free carpet. On one side rose the unexpected wall of books; dark wood shelves packed with words by the million. And opposite, through the waist-high picture window, Pat could see the last of the afternoon light glinting on the metal of the city.

It broke up the edges of his vision, distracted him, pulling him away from himself so that when Randy finally came at him he was caught almost unaware. Randy Blair in his city clothes, moving through the room like taut pampered silk. And when Randy's thick young arm snapped out for his shirt Pat only barely managed to jump away, felt Randy's fingers graze the front of his jacket.

"Now, Randy, this doesn't have to happen."

But it was too late. Randy was already in motion again, his two hands diving out for Pat's neck while Pat sunk his right hand into his jacket pocket, his palm filling up with Mark's knife, his eyes now holding Mark's vision: Randy Blair, the stranger; Randy Blair, the alien spirit moving through the communal nerve; Randy Blair, the demon to be exorcised. And now the steel was flashing in the air, Randy stumbling back, warded off by Pat's left arm and his own eyes fixed on the knife.

"Pat, you bastard."

"Randy." Randy sprawled against the chair, his face round and desperate, his child's face ready to break open and cry.

"Randy, why did you try to run Charlie over?"

"I didn't see him."

Sullen and lying.

"Randy. You have to come clean."

"Don't you tell me, you stupid fucking drunk."

Pat felt his breath coming back. He closed the knife on itself, like fingers seeking their own palm. And folded it away.

And then Randy was up again.

Pat felt his balance suddenly go, he was bowled over by Randy's charge; and as he went to raise his arm to fend off Randy's fist his reflexes betrayed him. He could measure the too-long moment between the impulse and the act, the long silence while his arm stayed fixed, in position, unable to get started or deflect the power of Randy's fist slamming into the side of his face and sending his skull cracking against the door. Then finally at least his legs remembered how to fight; he got his knees bent and his feet braced against Randy's chest, kicked him away so he could roll over. But as he stood he was aware of new motion at his back, and even while he was raising himself from his knees he could feel the new presence in the room. At once Randy was on him again, pushing him into the shelves, helped now by Randy Blair Senior who stood above him, giving Pat a brief glimpse of his grey impassive face before his whole heavy body lashed out in a kick, burying his shoe in Pat's side.

Once. Twice. Pat felt his ribs being driven into his lungs. Blacked out. Then found himself under the window, where he started to his feet—was in fact standing and staggering forward when Randy pounced again, tearing him down to the floor where he stayed, consciousness slipping back and forth as they beat him, sometimes seeing shoes, fists, elbows coming at him. Then nothing at all.

When he woke his swollen tongue filled up his whole mouth. He tasted blood, swallowed, tasted it still, felt it drawing from the roots of his teeth. Then he became aware of his arms. He had them wrapped around his knees, pulled up into his chest. He tried to straighten his legs, went dizzy, tried again, brought up.

From the street he could hear the noises of passing cars. Looking up he could see the apartment building, and then remembered being carried down the stairs, dumped out the back door like so much garbage.

He looked for the moon but there were only wires crossing the sky, streetlights that burned in his eyes.

He had gotten to his knees but every time he tried to stand his ribs felt as if they were grinding together. With one hand he pressed against his side until all sensation blurred and went numb. Then with the other pushed himself up until he was standing.

He was forty-nine years old and it seemed, for at least this moment, that nothing worse could happen.

Nine

On a certain Tuesday night in June, Pat Frank lay at his lowly post in Randy Blair's alleyway. As he felt his life sliding into itself, and his ribs sliding into each other, he wondered what time it was and looked, by habit, up at the sky. His view was obscured by a tangle of wires, and the overhanging roof of a nearby garage. Holding his breath and cursing, he worked his way to his feet and began to move towards the street.

On that same night Kitty Malone's view was better. She spent the night in bed, dozing and sleeping under the influence of two shots of morphine administered by Sandra, and during her brief intervals of alertness she looked lazily out at the silvery moon that was crossing the sky in front of her window. And she dreamed: dozed and dreamed nervously of her operation to come.

For Ellen, fear and pain had never been further.

She was sitting in her wicker chair, and though her section of sky was dominated by nothing more than the tin roof of her son's barn, that tin roof, with its dazzle of moon rippling over the metal, had held her vision, fixed it on itself for one hour after another as she smoked her cigarettes and let the surface of her mind join with the tin, go as clear and unmolested as that moon-glinting metal.

She was thinking.

Not exactly in any active way was she thinking, not pushing her mind against any specific this or that, but she was having a good old-fashioned think, a whole night-long turning over of the entire situation, the whole universal situation dumped out like a fifty-thousand year purse spilled out onto the floor.

By the time the night was almost gone, four hours into Wednesday, with the moon's splash on the tin roof moved down to the lower left-hand corner like a scoop of ice cream ready to slither out of the cone, she was thinking about her father. Not about her feelings for him, or any of the trials and tribulations they had gone through: these she had long ago laughed off and forgotten.

She was thinking about her father in a different way, with a pure and perfect awareness.

Her father, she realized, had come. And then he had gone.

Just like that white inevitable moon he had started at the top with a whole life in front of him but, in the end, he had rolled right off the old barn roof.

But unlike that dumb roof-rolling moon, and especially unlike a scoop of ice cream, her father had had something to say about this wonderful phenomenon, a cryptic remark to encompass the fact that, when you come right down to it, when all grievances are remembered and gone, all you eventually do in this life is roll right off the edge.

Right off the edge, like ice cream falling out of a cone, like her father rolling off the old barn roof; and it came to Ellen Malone that the time had arrived for her too, that this long silvery night was the last she would be spending in this kitchen where she had mewled, cooked, then mewled again, her last night in this house. It was time, she thought, to be like that old ice cream scoop of a moon, time for her to be moving on.

On Wednesday morning, the morning of the operation, it was Sandra who woke Kitty Malone.

"Kitty," she whispered, "wake up Kitty." Kitty opened her

eyes and saw Sandra's face leaning close, her angel skin and angel hair glowing in the morning light, so young and perfect she couldn't help reaching up her arms for her, touching Sandra's shoulders with her hands as if she would draw her down onto the bed. Not to embrace her, nor even to love her; but to swallow and become her, to get out of her own cranky swollen body and into something new, something sweet and happy.

"There's a man here to see you," Sandra whispered. "Just for a moment."

Sandra moved back and to one side. And just as Kitty was registering the full brightness of the room, the fact that the sun was high and she had overslept, she saw the bulky figure by the door.

"Randy."

She would have expected him to look like he used to, to be his old strawberry-blond self with his waist thickened, perhaps even his hair faded and greying, but at least still slouching and wearing pants with cuffs that piled up on the toes of his black Wellington boots, a thick belt studded with tin stars, and most important of all, his bomber jacket, his crinkly black-leather bomber jacket with its miraculous topography of ridged and valleyed glossy leather, folds and canyons divided by shining silver zippers.

But save for the cleft in his nose and the slow shuffle of his walk, she wouldn't have recognized him. The round brown eyes were hidden by bifocals now, each lens with a tiny line across it, framed in tortoise-shell plastic. His hair was red-grey but receding, wetted down and combed straight back. He looked tired; everything about him from his high-domed forehead to his baggy checked suit looked tired out.

"Are you doing okay?"

"Of course I'm okay. I don't know what they've been telling you. And sit down for Christ's sake." Saw him flinch as she said that, too late. He had always been heavy but he was heavier now; the bed sagged and almost collapsed with his weight. She reached for him and took one of his hands in hers. Where the skin had once been smooth it was now rough and covered with tiny red hairs; and looking up at him she wondered if the rest of him was hairy now too, if his chest and back had sprouted new red forests sown by the falling hair from his head.

"You look okay."

"I am." His face, once gentle, was now like grey stone. But quiet, as was the touch of his hand on hers: so quiet it seemed he must have been away from women the whole long time since the day she had left him standing in Union Station.

"I'm okay too," Randy said.

Kitty suddenly realized she didn't remember his exact age and found herself doing additions and subtractions in her head. He had been twenty-seven in 1958, and so now, in 1976, he was forty-five. But he could have passed for ten years older because when he tried to smile his papery grey face wrinkled sad and resigned, and the corners of his mouth, which were passive in repose, drooped in defeat.

"I was curious to see you," he said. "Randy told me you were here."

"So you've seen him?"

"That's right."

"You think he's okay?"

"No. I'm worried about him."

"That's good," said Kitty. "It's time you were worried. I mean now that he is nineteen years old and big enough to run people over in his truck."

"It was an accident."

"An accident? What kind of an accident is it when you run someone over in a fucking parking lot for Christ's sake?" And now he actually flinched with the obscenities and she could feel him bouncing on the bed with discomfort.

"He was drunk. And he said the man tried to provoke him."

"Provoke him. What is he, a lawyer?"

"I don't know," Randy said. He twisted his large white hands together and for a moment Kitty saw them as she had two decades ago, soft and quilted, gentle baker's hands you wanted to settle in the vulnerable spots of your skin, gentling, protecting, closing off the raw nerves; and now she remembered that with him she had at least slept deep and well and protected.

"Anyway," Kitty said, "where is he now?"

"He might be in Toronto at my place."

"He might."

"He is."

"Jesus Christ."

"I didn't come to hear you mouth off, Kitty."

The bed sagged, bouncing almost to the floor as he stood up and found a chair. It was true, God it was fantastic that after only two minutes all the old feelings had opened up. Times she had hardly remembered for years were now clearer than movies in her mind; all the old anger was still alive and boiling in her; it would take just one word and she would be up on her feet ready to hit him. She reached for a cigarette, her hand trembling. Then it seemed she had passed through a cloud and saw him plain again, defeated, but violent and bitter.

"He looks like you."

"Like I used to."

"You look like you used to," she lied. She felt like crying for him, because now she suddenly remembered the force of his youth, saw laid over his balding skull the glowing hair that once streamed thick through her fingers, saw in his eyes the dark radiant colour that had gleamed at her the first day in the bar, saw his own casual violent way of destroying the space around him as he slouched through it, confident and aggressive, approaching her at the bar in his zipper-crazy way and with his foolish grin as if he owned this particular stretch of the world and could claim any part of it for the asking. And now he sat so stiff and scared, his big belly and chest thrust out for comfort, his arms miserably folded across each other: he looked tired, exhausted, out of life; he looked so run over and ashamed it seemed he must have fallen into some peculiar male winter that couldn't find a spring.

"You too," Randy said. "You look just like you used to."

She couldn't help smiling: he too was lying, his voice whining with the same old tell-tale giveaway.

And how could he help but lie, seeing her in a housecoat and nightgown, two days of hospital food in her belly, the colour fast fleeing her skin and her lungs starving on hospital air. So he was here to see her one last time, to check her out before she died; or, the bastard, he was probably as angry at her as she had been at him. And for a moment Kitty had a glimpse of how it must have been for him, running up to her in the station with panic beating through him, his one son at her hand and the other in her belly. Randy Blair: she had pulled the plug on him and he had never recovered.

She pushed back a wisp of hair and shifted her blue eyes to his. "What do you do these days?"

"I sell books. Technical manuals and things like that."

"I never knew you read much."

"The job's okay. And I don't mind the driving, that's the big thing the driving. There's no money in it but sometimes they send me down to the States."

"You still go to the track?"

"No. I gave that up."

"Too bad," Kitty said. "You shouldn't give things up."

He smiled at her, a different calmer smile, and reached into his shapeless beige raincoat. "They let you smoke in here?" And without waiting for her reply took out a cigarette and lit it. She was again remembering him as he had always been, the Randy Blair she had met that first night in Toronto and taken home to her room to keep herself warm; but no matter how hard she concentrated on the youth she had once known, she couldn't avoid the man who had walked in the door: the large balding man in a tent-like coat and a brown suit who couldn't possibly be anyone she knew, the kind of man who sometimes stopped at the No-Tell Motel, sample case in his trunk, sat in the lounge alone, and put back double rye-and-gingers while looking for someone like himself, another checked suit to drink with. Or, even better, a woman alone to stare at and fantasize about. Because although he had once been the man to cross the empty space and make contact, now it was beyond him. The edge had gone, worn away, disappeared. Age had transformed him into someone else.

Kitty sat up and wrapped her robe closely about her shoulders. She swung her feet down to the floor, searching out her shoes.

"You want a hand?"

"Christ no, I'm all right, they don't get me for another few hours."

She stumbled with the first step and had to accept his arm as they went out the door. Down the wide tiled hall they walked, until they got to the lounge and stood in front of the window that looked down over the lake.

"Nice view," Randy said. "I like coming to Kingston. In fact I've been coming here for years on this job and always meant to look you up."

She looked at him.

"I mean, I always felt stupid just calling you and making you send Randy down on the train. You know what I mean."

"Sure."

"One time I drove up to Salem. I went into the hotel and had a few drinks, then I walked around the town. It was pretty strange."

"Randy."

"What?"

"Go now. Please."

"What's wrong?"

"Just go now. You can come to see me again if you have to. But go now." Turned her back to him and closed her eyes. Wrapped her arms around herself until her housecoat stretched tight across her shoulders, holding her in, holding in the tremendous waves of resentment that battered through her. She felt a thousand doors and rooms had opened up in her, all filled with black moths trying to escape. Randy Blair: she had pulled the plug on Randy Blair. Randy Blair: he had lifted her up in the air and screwed her down on the ground, filled her up with himself and his kids and then he had left her. His mind and heart had walked out of hers. Nothing had touched him, nothing hurt, nothing changed.

"Christ Kitty, what's the matter?" He had his hand on her elbow, was turning her around. And as he did she felt her fists clenching, her right arm drawing back and she was ten years old again practising the famous Malone uppercut against a bale of hay. Taught and egged on by Charlie her fist was swinging, and she already knew how the dry hay would bite into the skin across her knuckles. And then she saw his face, bland and doughy, his familiar-strange face opening wide and surprised. His teeth cut across her knuckles as she gave it one last push, following through as Charlie always told her.

Randy Blair: lying on the floor of the sunroom, blood coming out one corner of his mouth, surprised. For once she had really surprised him. Kitty's hand bleeding too, his blood or hers she couldn't tell. And in a circle around them, their mouths open as if they had just seen the resurrection, other patients in their Johnny-coats, the foreign doctor with his fairy high-heeled black shiny shoes, and, in the doorway, limping towards her, Sandra.

"You were supposed to stay in bed."

It was only when she was back in her room, pulling the covers over her head and closing her eyes, that she remembered it was almost two days since Pat had set out for Toronto.

"Kitty, they're going to shave you now."

The whole night Ellen Malone sat in her wicker chair. From the upstairs she could sometimes hear sounds drifting down to her, sounds of breathing deepened by bad dreams, of Sadie's and Lynn's light bodies turning in the blankets like birds flailing in straw.

She had decided she was going to leave this house once and for all, and as she sat she let this new knowledge swell up in her like a baby getting ready to be born. She watched the moon traverse the roof and finally slip off the edge and leave it like a pale lucent sheet suspended across the sky.

She sat.

The more she thought about leaving, the happier she was, until finally the tingly sexy sensation of this secret started sweeping up under her skin, making her light and strong. And by the time the sky was beginning to glow with the first warnings of the sun, she was on her feet, skate-dancing herself around the kitchen and making herself a cup of coffee as if it were the easiest thing in the world.

While the sun came up she sat and drank her coffee. When necessary she pushed herself to her feet again and skated across the wide pine boards to the bathroom at the bottom of the stairs, and was so confident that as she skated back she made a detour to the stove where she poured herself a second cup.

But although she felt blithe and serene, even happy, laughing to herself that she was like a girl waiting for her first big dance—and hoping this wonderful anticipation wouldn't turn out to be as ridiculous as had the dance where she ended up sitting along a wall while the men she coveted simply did the usual, that is drank and fought themselves to oblivion outside—she had not worked out the details. In fact she was so confident she didn't even think about how to execute this wonderful and final extravaganza, only basked in its invention as the sun came full into the sky, and as Sadie and Lynn came down for their breakfast.

It was only at the very moment that Mark Frank stepped in the door that her plan arrived, borne into her mind as mature and fully formed as Mark Frank's belly.

As he shuffled in she saw in him a sudden image of herself: slow and removed, everything deliberate but without any real purpose, the world stuck out so far in front of him that nothing touched him any more.

Mark Frank whose diapers she had changed, Mark Frank whom she had powdered, bounced and babied, was getting old in front of her eyes and she was getting older. Mark Frank, who cried when he found Henry and Stanley run off the road and accordioned into the big stone cliff near the Catholic Church, was getting so old he was older now than they were then. Older now than anyone could be because there was nothing he cared for any more, nothing that dug into his gut so much he had to have it.

"Take me to the hospital," she had said.

"It's a long ride."

"I want to see Kitty and Charlie."

"It would be too much, Ellen. Aren't you going to offer a person a cup of tea?" And then looking at her, smiling as she had known he would. "Oh, all right."

It was Sadie who moved towards the kettle, so skinny her shanks boned out like a starving cow; even Sadie was getting old and now that Ellen had her own plan she felt sorry for her for all those years Charlie should have given her a home of her own, a place that grew into Sadie's body the way this house had grown into hers.

This house was what had kept her alive the whole time; it was living in this house built by her father and kept first by her husband then by her son that had propped her up, the every detail of wood and nail entering into her, feeding her soul and keeping her sustained, even while her body palsied and collapsed around her; Mark walking across the kitchen floor to the bathroom, goddamn, Ellen could hardly keep from laughing with the knowledge that it wasn't the kitchen floor he was walking, it wasn't the path from the stove to the toilet, it was practically her own goddamn body, her own blood and bladder and kidneys; the path from the kitchen to the bathroom was the path from her mouth to her what-for; because somehow the parts of the house and parts of her body had gotten confused. She had been there so long there was no telling them apart any more. Goodbye. That was all there was left.

Near the end of the barnyard she turned and waved once, quickly, not regretting anything. But kept her eyes open the whole drive down the trail, Mark silent and smoking his cigarettes, driving slower than an old horse to save his car from the bumps. Silent, that was what she liked about him. He hadn't bought any glass eye, hadn't had any accident, it had just turned that way, ossified after he spent a whole year looking out without opening his mouth. After that he practised a little more communication, afraid the other one would go too.

The last time, she kept saying to herself, rustling around like a little girl trying to find some spooky spark of fear to scare herself with: the last time I'll see that old maple, that clump of lilac, that mailbox. But the truth was, she knew, that the trees, the bushes, the roads, they weren't really important anymore. They were like the rooms where she had spent too much time; old places that could no longer promise her anything.

At three o'clock Tuesday afternoon, the leading edge of the sun had attained Kitty Malone's bedspread. She had been watching it since she returned from the operation: had seen it first on the wall, then sliding down to encompass Golda Gutteridge, the new woman who had moved in, then slipping to the floor.

"Look at that sun," Golda had said. "Bright. The sun used to be bright like that when I was a kid. Now I have to come into the hospital." Golda was not golden but grey: skin, hair, eyes all participated in different shades of the same porridge grey. Her cheeks hung from her face in strange mealy lumps, lumps resembling her chin and her Adam's apple; yet this was not her disease or a symptom, her disease was something Golda didn't mention except to say it was "kind of mental."

"You know," Golda said, "I lived in this town all my life. You know what I mean?"

"I guess so."

"This place," Golda said. "I left it lots of times but I always came back."

"Me too," Kitty said.

"I wouldn't have known that. Personally I would have taken you for a big-city type. Snappy, you know? I bet you liked the city."

"Well—"

"Of course some people like country life. Fresh air. Cows. Personally I always found the cabbages got worms. I never knew anyone to grow a decent cabbage of their own, yet you go into a supermarket and the place is littered with them. Cabbages."

Kitty let her eyes swim open and shut. She was not exactly awake yet from the anaesthetic, though she was not asleep either. Golda's voice was like a saw articulating the air, cutting it up into little chunks of words and ideas, flinging them around the room like sharp-edged blocks. Cabbages. A low-key shuffling noise from the corridor was so familiar that she opened her eyes and focussed on the doorway where Ellen appeared, escorted by Mark. Who pulled up a chair for her, sat her in the middle of the room and, grinning with embarrassment, started to back out of the door.

The sun had Ellen completely surrounded. She was sitting in the exact middle, turning the peaceful yellow patch into a frame for herself. It was so bright that she blinked her eyes and rubbed them vaguely with her knuckles, like an ancient giant bird bewildered by an early spring.

"I was coming to visit you," Ellen said. "Isn't it nice here?"

"Nice."

"I didn't know when you'd be coming home. Charlie said you were going to be all right. I wanted them to let me watch but they wouldn't let me in."

"You been to see Charlie?"

"Mark took me there first. Because the floor was lower. I ain't never been this many floors up."

The sun had now deposited a small window of light at the foot of the covers. This warmth she received, wishing it towards her centre, towards that mythical confirmation of her own ridiculous existence, towards that place Randy and Pat fought so hard to get themselves into. Beneath her hands she could feel the bandages, and at some distant reserve she could feel the pain too, the memory of the intrusion of forceps and knife. But it wasn't like after a birth, which hurt much more but left her feeling almost peaceful, not fulfilled but at least exhausted and knowing that she had gone through something to some purpose. This was different. It was less painful but sharper, like having offered up one's insides to a dentist. She felt she had done something not only painful but wrong, had crossed the law of her own body by letting it be numbed for the operation; and even by having the operation had tried to deny the necessity for her own death.

Through the remains of the anaesthetic she felt a weird primitive guilt that told her the pain had not been avoided, only deferred, that what she hadn't felt on the operating table had registered in her brain and nervous system, outraging them; and although the pain hadn't been experienced on the operating table it was still potent, alive, ready to spend whole years leaking into her from where it had been stored away.

"That Randy Blair," Ellen said. "You should never have had him."

"What?"

"You know. Randy. That little sucker was always bad."

Randy. Randy the child: his baby fingers had twined into hers, the child had shoved against her belly for warmth when he crawled into bed at night, that first year in her grandfather's retirement house. She closed her eyes. She opened them. Ellen's face was forward, concerned, she had somehow dragged her chair close to the bed and was leaning over her. Kitty could feel her breath on her face, her neutral false-teeth breath that used to taste like metal on her lips.

The sun had lifted itself half-way across the bed. Her sense of time, of the length of Ellen's visit, had slipped away and she felt herself covered by a thin layer of sweat. It was slippery, a grease-like sweat that lay on every pore, separate layers on her arms and sides so when she shifted she could feel her skin sliding against itself.

"I was feeling kind of sick," Ellen said.

Kitty had to close her eyes again. The whole day was spinning, a hazy drugged carousel. She remembered Sandra's face bending over her, her angel hair in the morning; again at noon when she drew the curtain around the bed and shaved her from the knees to the belly button not talking the whole time, only sliding the razor ever so carefully, the tips of her fingers following the blade. They gave her the first needle behind the curtain too; and by the time she had been taken down the elevator and was lying in front of the operating room, she was going into long spinny dozes, memories of children being born; memories so strong that every time she opened her eyes she expected to see her own belly mounded up under the sheet, full of a new baby.

"I feel sick different these days." Ellen's voice.

While she was still in the hall, the small foreign intern had given her the second shot, his smile suddenly reassuring; and then Doctor Connors himself had leaned over her, his face ballooning into a giant whale's face, the face of a whale you floated in your bathtub and squeezed until it squeaked in whale-talk.

"My goddamn bones aren't what they used to be."

Halfway through she woke up, opened her eyes to the ceiling mirror. There, floating in a glass pond, she spied someone's belly. One side of it was like a partially opened mouth, with a forest of shiny instruments dangling from the lips. Busy hands reached in, drawing things out as if they were cleaning a freshly dead chicken. And then, just as she was beginning to enjoy this bizarre sight, she felt a deep muffled tug, a sensation at some centre that had never existed before.

"She's awake."

"Kitty?"

"Don't. I don't want you to do it." And felt now like the earth from which a tree was being torn, felt the complex system of roots and nerves being torn out of the centre of her body, undone; they were planning to leave her nothing more than a shell.

"Don't. I don't want you to." Found strength in chanting, a soft chanted whisper. "Don't. Please don't. I don't want you to. No. Please. No. Please. No. Please—"

And fell asleep again to the sound of her own voice, the sound of her own voice trying but unable to sound itself. So she heard only the echo of what she wanted to say; like a bird high up in a clear sky it hovered, circled, climbed and fell.

"Kitty?"

Doctor Connor's whale face breaking through, smooth and round above her, peering down, his eyes made large behind his silver-rimmed glasses, his mouth slow as a whale swimming lazily through the calm seas.

"Kitty?"

"Please. No."

"It's over Kitty. You're going to be fine now."

"No."

"You were very good. Very strong."

"No. Please. No. Don't take it."

"You were very strong, Kitty. Very good. We got it all out."

The whole day the sun worked its way across the room, finally attaining her bed where it slowly climbed onto the spread, edged its way from one patch to the next, working its way across the room and towards her centre. With her hands folded gently over her belly Kitty could feel the emptiness, remember odd scattered moments. They were like the patchwork spread, sewn together but not connected; they could have come in any order. In each tiny frame she found a different picture: pictures of Randy in his grey tent-coat, pictures of Golda's porridge face, pictures of herself on the operating table, pictures of Ellen leaning over her. And babies too. Even with her eyes open she could go unfocussed and concentrate on the memory, on the image of them being held out to her, presented for inspection, wrapped in hospital white. And see leaning over them, proud and expectant, their fathers—Randy and Pat—their two heads rising out of one body, RandyPat the brand new Dad.

"You were very strong, Kitty. Very good."

The morning after her wedding she had gone to stand on her balcony, the wet spring wind waking up her skin, had stood on the balcony and leaned over, throwing her coffee to the flower-covered convertible. Then ran inside to the bedroom where Randy was asleep, woke him up, crying, lying beside him hitting his back and neck, crying, her fists pounding into his back until he rolled over and tried to hold her.

"No. Please."

Tried to hold her and then wrapped his arms around her, pulling her into him, forcing himself into her. She didn't know if he was asleep or pretending; if he was trying to love or rape her.

"So good, Kitty. You're so good."

But later that same day, still wearing the housecoat, sitting at the kitchen table while Randy cooked eggs and coffee, she had felt gentle, so gentle, washed by the yellow spring sun and her own crying, washed inside and out and wanting nothing more than to feel this way forever, quiet and protected, Randy's soft steps moving comfortably around her, the sun warming her hands and throat.

And now, again, she could feel the sun lifting her spirits. Finally it had attained her belly, her folded hands, and through its warmth she could feel the echo of the operation, the echo of the feeling of something being taken from her.

Things could have been different.

She could remember being a girl, sidling about the kitchen floor in search of a warm spot, looking at her mother in the chair and wondering why she was sitting, not standing; why one day did it rain and others sun; why had her father died and been wrenched out of her life.

She had spent whole days outside inspecting things for the certainty of their existence: examining trees to see why their leaves grew out of one place, not another; staring at the hay stacked in the barn and trying to figure out why it had been piled up one way, not another; going to look at the cows and trying to guess which would be the first to give up its grazing and sink onto its belly in the warm grass.

Over the years she had watched the empty places left by her father's death fill up with herself, with her own uncertainty; and it seemed this uncertainty had always been there, just waiting to be tapped. It travelled from her heart and her mind to her body. As she changed from a girl into a woman her blond hair grew dry and crinkly, angling away from her head, and even her eyes became anxious and uncertain, never holding to anything or anyone for more than a few seconds before shifting away, making the rounds to check that nothing else essential was about to change.

The sun on her belly was edging up the covers sending small licks against her throat and chin. She opened her eyes and at the sight of Ellen Malone, sitting in the hospital chair and happily smoking one of Golda's cigarettes, she couldn't help smiling. Crazy old Ellen with her silver false teeth; she always knew what she wanted.

"Christ," Ellen said, "I come to visit you and all you do is sleep. They told me you were getting better."

"That's right," Kitty said. "I'm getting better."

"You don't look better to me," Ellen said. "You looked better at home. And where's the father? The baby don't deserve to have a father if he ain't here."

As the sun crawled up her throat she made tiny wriggling movements, trying to accommodate it. It was warm, it made her feel good, but somehow it seemed the better she felt the closer she was to starting to be sad again. When her father had died she had been this way, each promise of recovery followed by a plunge into further tears. She had cried so much she ruined his funeral and then for weeks and months she couldn't shake it off. She would have these deep sleeps that lowered her into fluid, unremembered dreams. She would wake up so exhausted that she needed to sleep in the daytime too, missing a whole year of school with this mourning that wasn't only grief, but somehow an attempt to reach under herself to a place where he existed too. And there were the times she would walk in the bush and feel herself growing up out of the ground and see the cedar trees growing up out of the ground and then she would think of her father, suspended in it, the earth eating through his coffin and yearning for his skin as she yearned for the remnants of whatever he had been. *It could have been different,* but not those times, not when her feet were nailed to the earth and she could feel its current passing through her.

The year she came back from Toronto it was the same. She would find herself in her grandfather's retirement house, alone, afraid even to have Randy with her, her arms wrapped around her own waist walking the house and crying for herself.

Poor Kitty.

Poor Kitty Malone.

Her father died and gone pie-eyed, poor Kitty Malone she has no bone: she would pace through the house and mutter these consolations to herself, crying and laughing at the same time, the better she felt the deeper the layers of tears she could tap until finally the night would dissolve into dawn and she would stumble into bed for a couple of hours, a small margin of sleep at the edge of the day.

It was night. She had drifted away and now she was awake again: sharper, more defined. The sky was black against the window. From the half-open door came the room's only light, yellow-white light from the hall, it angled across the front of the room and cut Golda into triangles of what was seen and what was hidden. She could hear Golda's breathing, her dry breath rattling like seeds in a winter gourd, and behind that, permeating everything, was the strange humming noise of the hospital itself.

The pain was worse now, a clenched fist inside her belly. She reached for a cigarette. There was so much pain, there was almost always more pain, hurts that had not been fully explored, losses that were waiting to be registered: sons, daughters, husbands, mothers, fathers. It seemed she had spent her whole life worrying that beneath whatever surface existed was a new flood of tears and hurt. Worrying that every time she cared for someone it was somehow jinxed, that her own love was the poison that made people go bad. She swung her feet down to the floor, careful, and patiently let them search out her slippers. Then, using her hands on the bed to take the first weight, she swung outwards, shifting herself slowly until finally, breathing hard, not really hurting, she was standing at the foot of the bed, one hand on the iron stead, the other still holding her cigarette, now broken and leaking tobacco.

"What the hell," she said.

"What the hell," echoed back.

"Golda?"

"You expecting angels?" A cough from across the dark room. "You snappy city girls all staying up late. You think I don't know how to stay up late? I could stay up all night if I wanted to." And then a brief silence, followed by Golda's resumed sleep-breathing, a dry rattling contented sound.

Kitty stubbed out her cigarette, then put on the housecoat her mother had given her. She couldn't remember anything, couldn't remember anything past the point when the sun had reached her chin and she had looked up to see Ellen smoking. "I'm just as crazy as she is," Kitty said. And lit another cigarette.

Then, with a few sliding steps she was out to the green tile hall. The smoke was making her dizzy but also giddy and comfortable.

Half-way to the nursing station she met Sandra, who was leaning against the wall, watching her and smiling.

"I was coming to see you," Sandra said. She stepped beside Kitty and wrapped her arm around Kitty's waist.

"I'm hungry," Kitty said. "Thirsty. Can I get some coffee?"

"Sure. I'll get you a cup from the machine. You wait here."

The lights in all the rooms and the lounge were off. Kitty leaned against the wall, her hand automatically pressed to her side, instantly converted from soothing the growth to holding firm the bandage.

She was listening again to the hospital's noise, the mechanical chords that soaked through the whole building, the thrum of hundreds of machines in close proximity: machines to make coffee, machines to control the temperature, machines to squirt food into reluctant blood, to pump air into collapsed lungs, to shock faltering hearts into beating; and machines to retrieve it all: to cycle away waste, air, electricity—machines for everything from keeping premature babies warm and insulated, ready to be born again, to machines for keeping newly dead bodies cold and pristine, ready for the learning knives of students and the spare-parts technicians.

When Sandra came back with the coffee they went into the glass station together. Tonight there was no country music, the radio was off. Kitty was already seated gingerly, her hands burning on the sides of the steaming paper cup, when she saw in a corner, still as the night, Ellen. Sitting asleep, her head slumped to one side, her old hands folded carefully over the iron arms of her chair.

"She wouldn't leave," Sandra said. "She said she wasn't going to leave until she knew you were getting better."

"Oh Christ."

Ellen's hand in hers: cold satin, the places where the veins knotted and bulged stretched tight under the thin skin.

"They never should have let her come to visit me. Goddamn she's so crazy."

"The two of you," Sandra said. "Look at you. You sure stick together. They say country families are the strongest. You even look alike."

"She's my mother."

"There was someone else here to see you too. A man—"

"Not that—"

"No Kitty, not him. He wouldn't get by me again."

Sandra in gold. Her narrow white hands were folded together, fingers intertwined as if they could wait this way the entire night.

"Sandra."

"Yes, Kitty."

"It hurts."

"I know."

"Is it always going to hurt?"

She could feel the tears starting up and tried to hold them back, Jesus Shameless Christ, crying in front of this little girl stranger in a hospital, crying when it was already long over, too late. The hum of the hospital was breaking apart. She could hear the elevator clanking, the sound of footsteps in the hall. She felt cold, as if she had spent the whole evening sleeping in an unlucky shadow.

When she opened her eyes and looked up Pat was standing in the door frame, leaning against it as if he were carved. His face was so bruised, that the cut from Randy's ring was like a split in the side of a ripe plum.

"Hi."

His voice sounded like an old waterlogged piece of wood thunking to the floor. He slouched forward and almost fell. Then straightened himself up.

And just as Kitty began to feel pity for him welling up in her, she realized he was drunk.

Drunk? He was so inebriated, so soaked in beer and cheap rye that Kitty realized he was not only drunk, but was as drunk as a man can be and still be standing. And, to further the fact, he only appeared to be standing. He was actually stiffened-out drunk, and it was only by chance that he had deposited himself upright.

But even if his posture had been convincing, which it wasn't, the stiff way he worked his jaws preparatory to speaking would have told her how drunk he was: the kind of blind, soaking, disgusting, excuseless drunk that could leave him lying twenty hours on her bed. The kind of drunk that brought out what she hated, what she needed to be protected from.

Down one side of his face ran the cut that Randy had given him with the ring. Where it started, at the corner of the left eye, it had broken open and clotted again, leaving an arrowhead scab on his cheek. His mouth was cut and bruised where it hadn't been before, and there was plaster lining a new cut above one eyebrow.

"What happened?"

"Things," said Pat. "Different things." He paused for a moment, trying to push his eyebrows into sobriety. He might have been trying to remember important questions. Even quests: such as his own which had started off so elaborately, with a dream of his own boy's soul breaking free, and ended so badly, with a nightmare of his own prison, of his own ribs being kicked in and the revenge being taken on him. Pat might have been trying to remember this, but finally he settled for the obvious.

"Anyway," he said, "I have some questions to do with this licence."

Somehow he managed to draw it out of his pocket. It was crumpled and stained with beer. "What I wanted to know exactly was if there was going to be a wedding to follow after this or if, you know, we just wasted ten dollars on this piece of paper. Not that it matters. I mean I've gone forty-nine years without getting married and I don't know why I should be getting married now."

Kitty tried to shove her feet deeper into her paper slippers. On the table were Sandra's cigarettes. When she had one lit and the smoke sucked deep into her lungs, she felt her blood slow down, trying to ready herself for this.

"It's late," Sandra said.

"That's okay."

"People are very quiet at night."

"Quiet," Pat said. "There's only one place more quiet than here and that's where they go after. Present company excepted if you know what I mean."

"People come to the hospital to get cured," Sandra said. "Not to die." Her voice was like dry gold. "Mrs. Malone is receiving the very best of care."

"You betcha," said Pat. "You know just this very night I says to myself: Pat, you know you should be thankful they've taken Kitty in under their big downy wing in the downy-town hospital."

"I'll have to ask you to leave."

"*I'll have to ask you to leave*," mimicked Pat, wiggling his hips as he spoke.

"If you don't leave nicely, I'll have to call the police."

"*I'll have to call the police*," piped Pat in a falsetto. " *We're in the downy-down-town of the town and the gown; and if I don't eat my fleas you're gonna call the police.*" All this while standing at the door, his legs crossed over themselves, like Sandra's, one foot held tentatively forward, like her clubfoot, his voice as high and pure as he could make it.

"That's very good," Sandra said. She clapped her hands. "You should come back on the weekend. They love to make rhymes in the children's wing on Sundays."

"My rhymes," said Pat, "are not suitable for the pink pure

minds of city babies. I am the goddamn fucking bard of Salem, and I don't strut my goddamn god-gobbling wares in the maternity ward of this smelly atheistic grave of a hospital." He was holding the wedding licence before him, curled into a scroll, and was edging towards Kitty as he spoke, making her nervous, waving it at her as if it was the Ten Commandments.

"I mean," Pat said, except that he was not saying, he was shouting, "what in the hell do you intend to do about this thing?" He was so drunk his face was purple. He was so drunk he couldn't hear anything but the sound of his own voice. He was so drunk Kitty wanted to be cured, to be out of this hospital and at her own house where she could stand up and walk towards him with his eternally gnawing gut and kick him out of her house, out of her sight, out of her consciousness.

"Go away," Kitty whispered.

"Don't tell me," Pat shouted. He was standing over her, waving the licence like a club.

"I'll have to ask you to leave," Sandra said again. She was on her feet now, beside him, diminutive and golden and one hand on his arm.

"Don't tell me."

And then her other hand flashed forward. Kitty could see Pat twist towards her, his arm caught by Sandra, pinned by the needle. He was so surprised he only stood there. And then, his face gradually draining from purple to deadly white, crumpled to the floor.

"There there," Sandra crooned. She was kneeling beside him. "Don't you worry lover. Don't you worry now."

Sandra's golden mantra, the squeak of Pat's shoes as they slid along the tile floor, Kitty's quick intake then slow-breathing release: all of these Ellen had heard. And through the wet window of tears pressed between eyelids and cheeks she had taken in the whole scene: poor beaten-purple Pat skunking into the room with his stinky temper and babbly tongue, Sandra sneaking up on him like a golden snake, striking him to the ground.

As for Kitty, Ellen didn't have to look directly at her to know how she was, strung between anger and resigned amusement.

Kitty was exactly as usual, charmed and disgusted; and although Doctor Connors, that stupid round-faced squirt of a doctor, hadn't been able to find any baby in her, at least he hadn't killed her. She wouldn't be dying in the hospital, not Kitty, she'd be going home soon enough.

"You'll be all right?" Sadie had kept asking. "You sure you'll be all right?"

"Christ yes," Ellen insisted. "You'd think I was a little kid who shouldn't be let out." And stood up for them, walked around the kitchen and sat down. Hardly puffing. Just to prove she still had it in her. Christ yes. And though she let Mark help her skate-walk out to the car, she was strong enough to turn and wave to Sadie before climbing in. Good-bye, she was saying; Good-bye you skinny-shanked fish-eyed bitch and I hope you're happy with the goddamned house you tore right out of me. Had the crust to make me sit in my own kitchen without moving for twenty years. Now you can sit your own bony arse in that wicker chair and see how you like it.

She heard their voices.

Pat was slumped against the wall and Sandra had resumed her conversation with Kitty.

Her eyes rested on a thin river of tears; it was a comfortable, almost happy way for them to be: her eyes relaxed and swimming, her skin feeling moist and young.

She had left the house, just as she had needed to, and she was now thinking again of her father's wonderful and cryptic last good-bye.

What he had said was, "Them Indians sure know how to die."

In the old days she had remembered him saying this, but thought nothing of it, thought only that he meant Indians were no good for living.

But now, sitting in the clean white shadows of a Kingston General Hospital nursing station, she let there be a different meaning to his words.

Because there was a way to die, a high highway, a whole beautiful surge of dying that was built into a person, an inner fantastic flower that took a whole lifetime to seed and grow and then burst into violent exploding bloom just at that very moment you slid off that old barn roof and into the one long final free fall; and now at the end of this long night and day it seemed she had spent the last twenty years getting ready to know this; the knowledge had been growing beneath the surface of her mind, waiting to be released, growing with beautiful wildweed berserk speed, racing through her cells in a crazy undammed rush, just waiting to be discovered, to burst out and take her sliding off the roof and up to heaven in one last great long-stemmed rosy-petalled leap.

The moon was sliding down the old barn roof; the wonderful secret of her dying had rushed through her so completely that she was now happily afloat in the sensation of her own expiring, every breath, every last sweet breath feeling as sweet as the silver shining moon.

And not only was she dying, but she had realized something else—that she, Ellen Malone, eighty-two years old and an old wrinkled-skin bag of shit, was headed straight for heaven.

Heaven Now.

Beautiful, eternal, blood-clearing heaven was up there somewhere and she knew by the silver rush of her blood through her veins, by the clear feeling of every last countdown detail that this dying rush, this last slide off the edge was leading not down but up, not into the snide snaky vacuum of doubt but into the blue undeniable sky that the prophets had visited and that the aftershave-swallowing ministers bragged about without knowing. But she knew it, knew it as certain as she knew her own name, knew that her father's words about the Indians, all that long-worded stuttering stuff she had read in the Bible, the whole last wasted decades of her life were coalescing into one last beautiful upwards swan dive that would lead her into that perfect oasis, straight into heaven as sure as Moses led the Jews out of the desert.

She wanted to sing.

"I'm me," she wanted to sing. "Me, just pure perfect Ellen Malone me and I'm dying high, flying like a goddamn bird, raising my soul up into heaven like a cloud in the sky, goddamn I'm going to heaven and you don't know how it is, you poor arse, no you don't."

It was a gift.

Some people, like Stanley Kincaid and Henry Malone, they just died by accident; their lives were smashed and crashed into oblivion like chickens run over by a bulldozer, their bodies destroyed before their souls knew how to survive without.

A gift: and it had been so long, almost a whole lifetime, since she had run into a gift like this: an easy joyous overflowing in the centre of her being, a sure knowledge that came from the inside and couldn't be deflected by others—that it was making her cry.

She didn't want them to see her tears, know she was conscious, be forced to deal with them or worse explain that the only thing that had made her happy in the whole time since her husband's death was the prospect of her own. Not that she could see why she had missed the stupid bugger, Henry Malone, so dumb he couldn't tell the hole in his sock from the holes in his ears; and if there were mornings enough she had woken up missing him, there were equally the number of mornings she had said to herself, good riddance. But it was true, anyway, so good-bye Henry, or maybe hello, because if *she* was going to heaven maybe he would be there too, why not, the whole stupid world was probably going.

"Ellen."

No, don't talk, go away.

"Ellen."

She squinched her eyes tighter, trying to suppress the tears.

"What's wrong, Ellen. You feeling sick?"

"I'm okay," she finally whispered.

"Ellen, what's wrong?"

She looked at Kitty. Who was leaning forward, concerned, her housecoat open so Ellen could see how her own very youngest daughter was getting old too, the skin on her throat growing rough and bumpy, the folds in her neck V-ing down to the cleavage between her breasts.

"I'm okay," Ellen said. "I am being raised up to heaven."

"What?"

"You heard me, Kitty. The Good Lord is taking your poor old mother away."

"Jesus."

"My soul is rising up in the sky like the angel Gabriel in his fiery chair."

"Ellen, you want a cigarette?"

"I should have taken you to church more. I should have set a better example."

"It's okay. Here."

The cigarette felt fat and round in her fingers: distant.

She leaned forward to Kitty's match. Then sucked in the smoke, trying to fill her lungs, trying to force a whole heaven-wafting cloud into her lungs. They should have gone to church the whole time, the whole family there every Sunday, preparing for this.

"I just come down here," Ellen said. "I wanted to see you." She rolled the tip of her cigarette on the ashtray Kitty held for her, surprised to see half its length had already burned away. "You can't hang on too long, you know. But you can't give up too early, no." She was looking at Kitty and thinking that she, like Mark Frank on the drive down, was paying her no special attention, seemed to have no knowledge that this occasion was unique and final. The goddamn fools were thinking she was going out ranting; after all these years of gaming they couldn't tell the real beef from the baloney.

"I'm serious, child. Do you know I'm telling the truth now?" She looked at Kitty, waiting for her answer. "Do you know? My soul has lifted and I feel myself spread out across the whole sky. I am a whole cloud covering the whole earth and I feel the whole sun shining down on me alone. Kitty, that is God's truth.

"It is shining down on me."

"Hey," croaked Pat, "Hallelujah."

Ellen looked over to where Pat was sitting on the floor, his foolish grin spread over his drunken face. And behind him now appeared a grey limping shadow! Charlie her firstborn; Charlie who understood.

"Oh Charlie," Ellen greeted him. "Hallelujah." She was almost shouting as she said it, she realized it had been years since she shouted. "Hallelujah. HALLELUJAH!" The sound of her own voice filled her skull, walloped around in her brain like a giant fish leaping to the surface. "HALLELUJAH CHARLIE. HALLELUJAH."

"Hallelujah," Pat groaned. "Halle-fuckin-lujah." He had changed from his stiffen-out drunk to his jellyfish stage. He struggled to get up and then collapsed again.

"I'm going to heaven," Ellen whispered. "I'm going to heaven and it feels so good."

"Oh Lord," sang Pat, "em-brace me." He had his arms spread out wide, ready to be crucified. "Hallelujah."

"Shut up," Sandra screeched. "Get out of this place." She was descending on him, waving the needle like a knife; and as Ellen sat in her chair she saw the four of them converge: Pat, his hands now covering his face, Charlie, his cane raised uselessly in the air, Sandra swooping down on Pat like a great golden bird, and Kitty, one hand to her side and the other tugging at Sandra.

"No," Kitty was pleading. "No, please don't."

"I can't help it," Ellen whimpered. "I can't help it." For one last time she sensed them all: Kitty, Charlie, Pat—they were all reaching out to each other, their love a beautiful golden net; and then the room jolted and the air was so bright and liquid she could hardly see anyone, they were all changing now, turning into each other and then there were only bright and shimmering shapes moving like burning shadows in the air.

And then she was in the forest again, folded into the dark groves and mysterious trees, in the deep wind-rushing forest, God's breath blowing clear her veins, in the forest, her own soul gleaming like a full moon from her belly as she tumbled dark and shapeless through the rush of her dying.

Ten

These mornings the mist on the lake was being invaded by new life. The slow turning from spring to summer had warmed the surface of the water, making dense swarms of insects near the shore. And the leaves and foliage that two weeks ago had been a tense fragile green were now racing towards their adolescent flush; their colours ghosted through the mist; their thick clean smell lifted Mark Frank upright in the seat of his old wooden rowboat.

The sun was only a few fingers above the horizon, still enlarged and veiled in its rising, but for Mark Frank the day was already well advanced.

On Wednesday, the day before, Mark had delivered Ellen Malone to the hospital. First taking her to see Charlie, then Kitty. From whose room he had backed out, not wanting to see her so sick and embarrassed at having brought this off-key singing telegram; backed all the way to the elevator and then hurried home as fast as Charlie Malone's truck would take him.

Now Wednesday was gone and Thursday had arrived.

Six small gifts had already come to Mark Frank at his watery hotel.

He had secured each one by the gill to a steel stringer and now they hung from an oarlock, swimming slowly in the water as the boat turned on the glass-calm lake, propelled only by Mark's stray motions as he methodically casted and reeled in, sweeping the marshy bottom with his lures.

He knew this lake so well, he knew its hidden places better than his own dreams. Where others would see only its calm surface, the mist rising quickly above it, the shallow pretty shadows of trees dancing on the edge, Mark Frank saw mud and weeds, long silvery fish glistening in their secret places, waiting on him as he waited on them; because he had fished this lake for so many generations now, for so many cycles of fish, it was he who was expected; he was their grim reaper, their predator, the Genghis Khan who time and time again swept down from their watery sky conquering nations and wiping out whole dynasties. And in his own seasons, in summers when drought or broken beaver dams made the lake freakishly low, in winters when he fished by drilling holes through the ice, Mark Frank had one way or another plumbed and mapped almost all there was of it; from the marshy shores, where tiny gulleys channeled between the reeds, to the deep still places scattered through the lake where the soft mud bottom suddenly gave way to plunging rocky springs, thirty and forty feet down, deep cold springs that kept the small lake cool the whole summer long, deep cold springs where the big fish liked to spend the hottest days, circling the cool columns of rising water.

The sun had mounted the horizon and Mark Frank knew his fishing time was over, but still he persisted. This morning he had found himself struggling, not against the fish but himself: first setting the hook so viciously that three times he had jerked the rod back only to find the metal had ripped right through and let the fish escape; then, the times he kept the fish, reeling in with crazy speed, not remembering to protect his catch from its pain. Only when he actually had the fish in his hand, wriggling and frightened, would he momentarily return to himself. Then he would squeeze firmly and gently extract the iron, trying not to tear further while murmuring in a low voice, apologizing to this completely innocent fish for making it be the one to feel his hurt.

Thursday he had woken while it was still dark.

No slow summer seeping into wakefulness, the way he liked it.

No lazy morning in the dark that let him gradually doze into consciousness, the possibility of the lake gradually filling his mind until it drove him down to the kitchen and the stove for coffee.

This morning it had been abrupt. He had found himself sitting straight up, smoking a cigarette and staring out the window, his skin clogged with sweat.

Before going to sleep he had been writing in his diary:

He said he had been dreaming of himself as a boy and that things now didn't seem real to him. I said "What does seem real?"

He had no answer for that one. Where is he these days? I sent him to get Randy Blair and when he was leaving and gone I was afraid for him.

Pat, you crazy bugger, Pat what's happening to you? You used to know better than this.

We had a pact. We cut our arms and let our blood mix. Once in our mother's belly and once in the open air. There were years we hardly had to talk. Everything was open. Everything seen.

You were afraid, Pat, you crazy bugger you were scared when you left.

And now he woke up with his brother's fear in his own heart, pounding wildly, so even as he looked out the window, trying to make out whatever outlines the moon would allow, his heart was jumping in his chest, making his thick shoulders and arms tremble.

"Christly night," he said. He swung slowly out of bed to push the window open. Intermingled with the sounds of insects and the wind in the new leaves he was sure he could hear the echo of a running motor. And remembered how it was in the old days, when they were young and so attuned to each other he could sense Pat's coming home before it happened, and would find himself awake, comforted, the familiar step slowly working its way towards the house.

After waiting and realizing that the motor's echo he had heard was only his own wish, he had gone downstairs to boil water for coffee. And then, steaming cup in hand, naked light shining down, Mark Frank tried to make himself want some breakfast before fishing. But he wasn't hungry, couldn't imagine his usual half-dozen slices of toast and jam to get himself going, felt only the muscles of his stomach tightening with the night's tension. Even his fifteenth tin of apricots sat unopened on the counter. And where his skin had been clogged it now poured sweat, drenching the undershirt he wore all year round and the flannel shirt on top of it, running so fast he could feel pools of it uncomfortably gathered in the hollows of his armpits, running in narrow rivers down the insides of his arms, and irritating his thighs where the stiff crusted folds of his old brown corduroys dug in and chafed his skin.

On the table, left where he had finished with it the night before, was his diary. His various and painstaking entries had now grown so lengthy that the orange scribbler was almost half-filled. The pages he had written on bulged with being used, so the written half was ballooned to twice the size of the pages that were still snappy and clean. He was reminded of his school days when through the year dirt and pencil marks accumulated to make his notebooks swollen and raggedy, more often than not further puffed by water absorbed during unexpected rain or brief periods spend in puddles. And thinking of this he suddenly remembered the first time he had tried vaulting the rail fence near the edge of the marsh, one day in May. He had run up to it, the smooth motion of grabbing the rail and neatly swinging his body over it already anticipated in his mind thousands of times. Somehow he had forgotten to lift one foot. There was a long, slow arcing tip. He ended up flat on his face in the mud, his leather school bag twisted and firmly planted on the back of his neck. And remembered raising up his head, the cold mud soaked instantly into his shirt and pants, raising up his head and seeing the bright sun grow brighter in his eyes, laughing at the way the day had finally torn and ruined his clothes, soaked him in itself.

He stripped off his shirt and undershirt and started to towel himself dry. Though it was June the night air was still cool, and now that he stood naked and shivering in the kitchen, he began to be hungry. His chest and belly were covered with frizzy orange-grey hair that billowed on waves of muscle and fat; and Mark saw, flickering in the tiny intermissions of this present, his body as it had been: the schoolboy's white skin stretched over his barreled ribs, his stomach wide and bulging like a soccer ball; then he was back again into the memory of himself in the mud, his neck twisting and lifting his head to the sun, to the whole amazing panoramically wide two-eyed world.

Along the south side of the lake was a shallow bay, really only an indentation, where the bank was so steep that the cedar trees along it had never been logged. Here, mingled with the occasional poplar and oak, their roots gnarled over boulders and fallen logs, the cedars grew sturdy and tall. And in their shade was the place where Mark Frank parked his rowboat.

The fish were in a water-soaked plastic bag. Cleaned already, their guts had been thrown to one side and were being surveyed by a raccoon who had learned to breakfast off these expeditions. All of the mist had melted away; only faint traces of the cool dawn lingered in this grove.

Mark Frank breathed it in, trying to find in the air the smell of the cedars. He still felt shaky and anxious. Whatever had intruded on his sleep kept insisting itself on him; but although he had thought about it from the time he had found himself standing in the kitchen, looking down at his stupid grizzly chest and not knowing who he was, thought about it uninterruptedly his whole waking day, he had not yet solved the problem: he didn't know if it was his own fear of losing Pat, or Pat's fear of Randy that was unnerving him this way.

He climbed the hill and started to walk through the bush. He had the bread-bag of fish knotted to his belt and they bounced comfortingly against his thigh as he walked, promising tender golden fillets to be devoured with swabs of catsup, home-fried potatoes, and more cups of boiled coffee. The morning sun burned on his scalp and neck; but the heat didn't soothe him, couldn't get through the surface of his feelings, and the whole way home he was increasingly uneasy, wondering what was awaiting him there, hoping it would be only Pat, back from the city and in one piece.

Twice, in his final approach to the house, there were times he thought he caught glints of the old black Ford. But it wasn't there. Its usual parking place—a patch of grass blackened by gas fumes and oil drippings—stood as empty as it had for the past few days, green tufts starting to spring up through the dirt.

He found himself standing above this empty space and looking down at it, something about it so unsatisfactory, so unacceptable, that the sight of it made him fuzzy-headed. "Christ," he said. The sweat was coming off him again, soaking his skin for the third time since waking. And walking back to the kitchen he still didn't know what he feared most: Pat's absence or the sudden knowledge that, after all these years, they had been truly joined, Siamesed.

By the time the daylight had passed and all the sky was black save for one final red-blue narrow rim around the horizon, Mark was more than sick of listening for the sound of his own motor. The whole day it had haunted him, arousing echoes of fear, anticipation, even relief; and he had imagined it through every other noise from the bubbling sound of the bass frying in the iron skillet to the hiss of the welding torch against the reluctant axle of an old pick-up. Every time, equally hopeful, and equally angry at himself for believing, he would stop whatever he was doing to look in the direction of the driveway, confident he would see the black glossy Ford, abused but intact, rolling slowly down from the highway.

While walking to the widow Kincaid's he was still completely optimistic. With each approaching car he concentrated so intently, so wishfully, that its sound was easily twisted to the memory of his own. And, even after all these disappointments, he was sure that the widow would know something; as he turned up her short driveway he reminded himself again that she had a telephone, access to all the news.

When he went inside the widow was sitting at her kitchen table, her face red and shiny with crying.

"What's wrong?"

"Mark Frank, I didn't hear you knocking."

Her hair, which was usually brushed back and pinned into a

neat and lacquered bun, hung loose and grey around her shoulders. That, and her flushed skin, made her suddenly seem younger and Mark, on his way to sliding into his habitual seat, was so startled he kept standing in the doorway, staring at her, not sure now whether she was upset or if something strange and rejuvenating had happened.

"I just walked in," Mark said.

Violet Kincaid was sitting at her kitchen table, teapot and empty cup in front of her. There was only one light on in the room, a lamp above the old sideboard Stanley Kincaid had bought for her one year at the department store, and in its glow the pine table was rich and warm.

"You want some tea?" Violet asked.

"Sure. I was just passing by." He stepped slowly into the room; the warmth of the colours, Violet's radiant eyes slowly sinking into him, loosed the tension he had felt all day. But wary too, guilty and nervous because everytime he let himself be enclosed by this house, this sanctuary, he remembered his best friend Stanley Kincaid, the man who had husbanded this woman and called her, to him, "a cold bitch, an ice cube dressed in a dumpling."

"I was thinking of you," said Violet. "I was hoping you might come by."

Mark, pulling up a chair opposite her, found himself blushing. The one year they had spent so much time together seemed now like his childhood to him, a fondly remembered but impossible attempt to be shaped into a more tidy self; and although he still liked to visit the widow Kincaid, he didn't like to remember that once he had asked her to marry him, first inquiring of Pat whether she could get married without some special divorce from her dead husband. When she said yes, he had panicked and had to withdraw. But he didn't have the courage to tell her; he had communicated his decision by hiding in his house and stopping his visits for a few months.

So now it was unusually brave of him to persist in the face of her admission that she had been thinking of him, an honesty that was really far beyond the rules of their game, and to ask again: "Violet, you look upset. Has anything happened?"

"Just one thing," said Violet. "Ellen Malone died today, at the hospital in town."

"I knew she was up to something. I drove her in but she said she wasn't coming back." And relieved that Violet's tears had nothing to do with him, Mark turned to how Ellen had walked out of her own house, no one helping her, and driven off with him, not looking back once.

That crazy old Ellen Malone, she had fooled everyone. Sitting in the car she had stunk like an old brood mare, grinning her crazy head off as if she had a ticket to heaven.

"Don't you think it's sad?"

"Nope."

She set the cup and saucer in front of him and Mark Frank poured the tea happily, still thinking about how perfect her revenge had been, how glad she must have felt to have finally escaped the house and Charlie's wife.

"You're mean," Violet said. "Sometimes I don't like you too much."

She was sitting opposite him now, her thick grey hair hooding her face, shadowing her flushed cheeks and bright eyes. She seemed so young tonight. Grief had made her more open than he had ever seen her; more open than when they first discovered each other's warm night comforts, more than as a girl when he had watched Stanley Kincaid chase her across the county. He reached out for her, stretched his thick arms across the table. Then looked at himself, arms swollen with muscle and covered in grease and fish-slop, hands stubby and misshapen, nails hammered into weird fishlike configurations, rimmed with grease.

"I'm sorry," Violet said. "But it's the truth."

From the moment he had woken up, uncomfortable and sweating, through this entire long and untrustworthy day, he had been waiting for the moment when somehow he would be able to relax, when everything would go quiet and empty.

It was quiet now.

There was the widow's breathing and his own. A quiet wind brushing against the walls of the house. Night birds calling.

His hands were still out on the table. He looked at them, watched them for a moment, posing clumsily against the dark wood, then started to draw them back.

"Well," said the widow. "They say she died the night before last. In the very middle of the night. She was sitting in the nursing station talking to Kitty and she died. Right in front of Kitty and Pat and Charlie, talking the whole time. Kitty said Pat was so drunk and obnoxious that no one even knew Ellen was dying until the nurse punched him out. And then she was dead. One moment she was going on, talking crazy like always, and the next she was stopped. At first they thought she was just distracted—you know Ellen—but then she was quiet so long the nurse took her pulse. If it was Kitty it probably would have taken her till morning to realize."

"Ahh, well," Mark said. Despite everything, despite knowing Pat was back and, since he was drinking again, back to normal, he could feel the beginnings of tears. Tears in his real eye. Tears in his glass one too; though they were only half-felt it was his glass eye that cried more. When he cried it produced copious tears that ran in a straight falling stream down his left cheek and gathered where his jaw met his neck.

"She was the last of her kind," Violet said.

And Mark could see how glad she was to have finally gotten him softened up. Now she would go on to proclaim that old crazy Ellen Malone was the original beaver, that she had single-handedly settled the whole goddamn country, chewing down trees for logs, stripping the bark right off them with her false teeth.

"She was a wonderful woman," Violet sighed.

Her eyes shimmered. In the soft light they were the colour of brass and copper flaring in the heat of the torch. He had his hands around hers now, squeezing them; and she had folded her fists inside his palms, passive as stones, cold and round. Only her eyes were alive, pupils black and enlarged in the night, irises pulsing with grief, purple sunset colours spoking through them as now, silent, she stared at him.

There was the widow's breathing and his own.

He remembered the night he had come to tell her about Stanley Kincaid. She had cried then too, but it was no soft open storm like this; it was a violent gristly kind of crying, sorrow and relief and saved-up anger all mixed and knotted together so what finally came out was a horrible choking noise. He had held her and she had cried and choked and coughed; thinking she was hurting herself or sick he had slapped her on the shoulders only to have her pull away and slap him back, her nails raking his cheek so deep that even at the funeral people had remarked on his face: That must have been some cat.

"Kitty and Pat are getting married," the widow said. "As soon as Kitty gets out of the hospital."

He was lying in her bed.

Her bed was soft, with a thick down-filled mattress that sagged in the middle so the two of them, neither exactly feathery, were forced together. He was curled up, his knees drawn towards his chest. Against the whole length of his shins, and against the exposed parts of his belly and chest, was pressed the widow's broad back. He had one arm around her, his hand buried between her breasts, and through his fingers he could feel the rhythms of her breath.

Her sleeping breath. Because when they did this, made love together, she always finished fast, her face invisible in the dark she insisted on, her voice low and hoarse like a man's. And when the gravel of her loving voice stopped she would immediately pass out. She fell into her private dreams so quickly he felt left behind: stranded in the middle of the fleshy-branched river they had become.

In the first stage of her sleep he would be deserted, but as the hours wore on some undercurrent of her would remember they had joined. Then she would turn. Her hands, in her dreams, roamed over him, soft and accepting, to stroke and entice his skin so slow and loving he would sometimes revive and slide into her again, drawn into the midst of her marvellous need to be unconscious.

But now it was late in the night and the widow's turning to him was already come and gone. He was twice spent but not asleep; and he was beginning to sink not into his dream world, but into the thought that he had been awake for twenty-four hours now. The earth had turned its whole fat circle round since he had been woken up by fear but even as he lay trying to comfort himself in the widow's soft back his exhaustion was only temporary, a deceptive layer covering yet more fear.

He shifted himself and peered over the widow's shoulder to the window. Through the screen he could hear the soft night wind, the restless hissing of new leaves, the sharp rising spring calls of whippoorwills. No sign of dawn yet. "An ice cube dressed in a dumpling," Stanley Kincaid used to say. Mark now had an arm free, balled his hand into a fist and ran it down the widow's back and buried it in the soft flesh at the base of her spine. Cold, no; he himself wouldn't say she was exactly cold. And yet despite her non-coldness, despite her actual almost scalding heat, he didn't feel comforted. In fact he was already beginning to sweat with fear again.

He was looking at the screened window, trying to convince himself that either dawn was coming, and therefore it was time to get up and begin the slow walk to his house, his breakfast, and then the lake; or that it was indeed night and would be for a long time, that it was night and he could still sleep if, by staring at the hazy purple night sky he could hypnotize himself with boredom, with fatigue, and fall into the deep sleep his body was beginning to ache for.

Instead he found a new thought had entered his mind. It was sitting in the middle of his mind in such a persistent way that for a moment he was reminded of Pat and his obsession with his goddamn shrinking brain; but then he returned to the thought itself, which was that once it had been Stanley Kincaid who lay here, lay in the sagging bed not yet stained by Mark's sweat and semen. Once this weighted valley had been occupied by Stanley Kincaid. He had woken up in the middle of his own nights. He had stared over this self-same broad back out the window and wondered how, with his machines that needed repairs he couldn't afford, he was going to get the seeds in or the crops out. He had stared over this soft but younger back and perhaps loved this brief and only silence he would know; because in his life, married and with two daughters, there were only these few late-night hours that went unclaimed, only a few quiet times he was not either bending his body to sweat out what little the fields could give, or drinking and hoping for a frenzied fucking that would create such a swirl of distraction he could believe for a moment that was all that existed. Crazy fucking Stanley Kincaid who never fucked anyone but only lied and bragged and lied some more, lied about women who wouldn't look at him except to laugh, lied about those who didn't exist, crazy frenzied fucking Stanley Kincaid who twice a week peed against the wall of the Salem liquor store and never even discovered his own wife.

He was so taken with the thought of Stanley Kincaid, with the thought of his own undeserving body lying in the depression made by Stanley's, of his pushing at Stanley's wife, that for a moment he thought he himself was Stanley Kincaid. That he himself had been married to the widow all those years, had watched two daughters being born, had lived a life of duty and frenzy that ended in the rock outcropping that jutted out into the road near the old Catholic church. Ended in the wall of rock they had dynamited to make the road and that had since taken more than one life, a big rocky hand swatting down any strays too drunk or forgetful to make the whole curve. He could see himself in the car. He was sitting in Stanley Kincaid's clothes and driving with his foot on the floor burning hell out of the old engine and shouting at Henry Malone when it came up. He could see the headlights sweep it, brand it yellow before it branded them; and with one arm he was uselessly turning the wheel while with the other he was fending back Henry Malone, trying to reach past him for the door handle, absurdly trying to reach it so he could open the door and push him out. Still reaching when the car began to accordion and the steering column jumped for his chest.

And with the sound of the engine so loud it was roaring in his ears, filling the whole car, he realized that he was seeing with not one eye but two, and was so startled he woke up. To hear, still, the sound of the engine; and forcing open his eyes, still aimed straight at the window, he saw two yellow headlights sweeping slowly up the road, past the Kincaid house towards his own.

He sat up. The sudden motion made him dizzy and, searching for the floor with his feet, he could feel the need for sleep spidering through him.

"Mark?"

"I got to go."

The widow was turned around, her eyes flowing in the beginning light. She put her hand on his back, rubbed it in slow circles; it felt good but it felt awful too; it was so necessary and deep that it made him feel a hundred, a thousand years old; and for the first time in his life he felt not only sore or drunk or fatigued, but simple ordinary age, as if with the death of Ellen Malone a whole new generation had suddenly lowered itself onto his shoulders, inserted itself between him and everything he did: now he was the oldest; he and Pat and the widow.

They were the ones who had survived and it was their world now.

By the time he got outside, the unbearable ache in his bones had begun to dissolve. It was now his insides that hurt, that whole swollen and indefinable area of guts and organs he knew nothing about—a vague no man's land that only made him uncomfortable. Like dreams that were best left alone.

The light had started to come up and he could see the spring grass reaching for it, sexy bright blades covered with dew and thirsting for the sun. It was only June but the grass had already outstripped the competing weeds. Now, still on the edge of spring, it was entering its own fast prime, its own period of quick lush growth where every minute of sunshine, every drop of rain was fuel to its race.

When the widow's house was around the corner and out of sight, he stopped to roll himself a cigarette. Sitting on her bed, letting her hands work into his back, he had wanted to collapse. A strange and unknown feeling had come over him; he had wanted to lie down in her protection, in the circle of her warm arms and warm confident breath. He could have slept forever. And though there had been dozens, even hundreds of times he had pushed his body against its own fatigue, forced himself to keep going, it had always been with the sense that there was something in reserve, that beneath his own tiredness, his own boredom, was an inexhaustible reserve, a well of being that could never be used up.

With the cigarette made he began to walk again, slow and

shuffling, feeling in his very centre like a man too old to be alone. Every motion cut across his nerves, scraped and grated.

The rising light was inventing new hills. It painted dark trees on the horizon. It blew texture into the grey strip of road, scattering it with gravel, showing long jagged cracks where the frost had ripped it apart.

"I ain't dead yet," he said to himself, and heard in his voice something unexpected: a tone of regret. His own will was pushing his body along; and then, suddenly reminding himself of one of those bags of baloney at the sales barn, he grinned, stretched almost cocky remembering his quick need of the widow, the fine proud way she had drawn him into her, made him explode until his head rang with it.

He stopped, filled his hands with dew from the wet grass and rubbed it briskly into his face. Then he took out his glass eye. wiped it clean on the wet lemon blades, put it back in place. He could still, on his hands, smell the widow's smell. And the sight of his own old hands, twisted and scarred out of recognition, yet still soaked by sex and desire, was so ridiculous and happy that for a moment he forgot everything—his need for sleep, the deep early colours of the morning, the places where his body pulled and tore against itself—and felt only the sublime and secret victory he had won.

He, with his maleness, had snuck into the cave, and then, despite all dangers and seduction, escaped to tell the tale.

And now as he walked he began to think it wasn't age or lack of sleep that had made him feel badly, but Pat's absence. What had been in the back of his mind ever since Pat had departed with his money and knife now came forward: Randy's strength, the quick flare of his temper, and the easy way he had felled Charlie in the bar. And he remembered the recent day when Randy had been down in the welding pit with him, his young arm so smooth with muscle he had caught himself staring at the velvet skin and graceful swimming movement as if it were a woman's.

"Stupid bastard," he muttered. Ever since Kitty had come back from the city, dragging Randy like a live and reluctant suitcase, he had watched Randy prepare for this time, watched his hate for Pat grow from a child's resentment of someone new to a feeling so strong it had to be hidden.

The morning wind had started now. Across the yellow-green shadows of fields he could feel it picking up, a cool northerly wind that had already swept the lake; and he could imagine what the water would be like, waved and stippled in this night-morning light, the fish beginning to circle in the water, beginning to be hungry. The small fish would be eagerly kissing the surface, waiting for the soft falling bodies of insects, while the older ones still dozed lazily at the mud bottom, twitching against the reeds to give rhythm to their dreams.

"You'll be coming back tonight?" the widow had asked. As if Pat and Kitty's capitulation was to be a signal for their own.

"All right. If I can." And only then had turned to her, looked at her face in the night that still held the room. No longer afraid of her, of her witchery, of the dead husband that inhabited this same space. Then he had stood up and drawn his clothes on slowly, twice saved from falling over by grabbing the maple dresser. And carefully taken himself down the stairs, his knees threatening to buckle at every step. He had sat down in the kitchen again to lace his boots; above he had heard the bed creak as she rolled over in it. That sound of her body's weight was still in his mind, a close loving sound, a sound of comfort meant for him alone.

As he turned down his drive the sky seemed suddenly bleached by the encroaching sun. He could see his house, two hundred yards away, rising like a white rock out of the mist. Beside it, blurred and indistinct, so unclear he had first to wipe his seeing eye and then, squinting, patiently walk half the distance before he could convince himself it was real, was the old black Ford Pat had driven to Toronto.

"You dumb son of a bitch," Mark yelled joyously. "You goddamn stupid idiot."

Eleven

The days passed.

They started misty blue, rising up from the dark fields and the edges of the sky. They grew slowly into long warm afternoons, hours of warm even heat that coaxed out every sprout in the garden, convinced every last frozen winter seed that life was safe again. And they faded finally into deep explosive colours, early summer evenings gently sucking up the warmth to protect it from the cool nights and to save it for the next new day to be released.

Slowly Lynn saw her deserted world grow populated again.

Charlie came back from the hospital first. He was still wearing a cast but with the help of a cane he could walk. The first day he stomped restlessly around the house, short-tempered and mean with Sadie. After that he was out in the barn again, carrying on as if nothing had happened. When his leg hurt, he took aspirins and drank beer.

Then came Ellen. She was wearing a wooden coffin with brass trim. Lynn went with Charlie and Mark to watch her arrive at the funeral parlour. Charlie had wanted her at the house, waiting for the funeral in the living room, where everyone could see her. "What the hell," he said. "She lived here, didn't she?" "She did," Sadie agreed. "But she doesn't." Lynn was in the viewing room when the undertaker opened the casket to show the wonderful work he had done with Ellen. Lynn could hardly recognize her. She had never seen Ellen lying down. Ellen never lay down and she should have been buried sitting up, in her chair. They had applied so much make-up, and cut and sprayed her hair so carefully, that Ellen looked like a television grandmother. She looked so nice and acceptable she might have been quietly whisked away while puttering in the kitchen, whispering to a favourite kitten and baking cookies for the grandchildren.

Kitty, it was said, would be coming back soon. One night Lynn heard Charlie and Sadie talking about it. Sadie argued they should bury Ellen right away, without waiting for Kitty, that the body would be falling apart before it was in the ground. "Don't worry," Charlie told her, "they've got her on ice."

And that same night Lynn heard another secret too. She heard that Kitty and Pat had gotten married: that one day Pat had gone to the hospital during visiting hours and taken Kitty to City Hall where they were married by a justice. For some reason she imagined Ellen present at the ceremony, lying in the City Hall office on her bed of crushed ice, cursing silently while the justice read out of his black book.

Finally Kitty herself actually returned. Pat drove her to Charlie and Sadie's house and Kitty climbed out shakily, walked slowly to the kitchen door, was reaching for it when Lynn popped out, gave her a wild welcome embrace.

"Lynn!"

She saw her mother's face go papery white. And then recover.

She watched Kitty as she went straight upstairs and put herself to bed in Lynn's room.

"You don't mind?" she asked Lynn.

"You stay here," Lynn said. "I'll guard you."

The day for the funeral came. Everyone had waited so long for this funeral, it was worse than Christmas. Ellen had waited so long that the undertaker said they would have to bury her with the coffin closed. Even the ice hadn't been able to save her.

This failure of the ice Lynn heard about the night before the funeral, while listening at the top of the stairs, which was her favourite post. The failure didn't surprise her. If Ellen had thought ice would keep her together, she would have packed herself in it while she was still alive.

That night Lynn dreamed that she left the house and walked straight north. North through the whole farm and past all the farms she knew or even knew about until she came to the highway. Above the highway, she had heard, there were no more farms, only bush. She dreamed that she walked through the bush, through the thick forested places where Charlie said wolves and blackflies came from, until she came to a river.

It was a cold flowing river, an ice river that couldn't save anyone. She sat by its shore and after a long while, when she wasn't afraid of it anymore, she took off her shoes and dipped her toes in the cool water. And then she began to walk, following its sandy banks north to the place where no one lived.

In the morning she woke up first. Sadie had dragged an extra cot into Lynn's room, and Lynn was sleeping on it, her mother in her own bed. She looked across the room. Kitty was curled asleep, the blankets folded in a warm cave around her.

On another early morning like this Lynn might have gone over to Mark's, tried to get him to take her fishing. But today she wanted to stay and take care of Kitty. She had forgotten about the funeral; she was thinking about her dream, and she was thinking about Randy. Something about her dream reminded her of him, she wondered if she had gone looking for him; and then she remembered Randy was supposed to be living in Toronto now, the place where all the people lived.

One night, while everyone was still away, Sadie had kept her up late and told her things about Randy. Still sitting at the dinner table while the sun was down, letting her drink two cups of coffee, Sadie had told her that Randy had driven over Charlie in the truck.

"In the truck?" Lynn asked. Not understanding.

"In the parking lot of the No-Tell Motel. He drove right over him while Charlie was lying on the ground."

"Randy did that?"

"I always told Charlie to lay off that boy. There was something wasn't right with him."

"There was something wrong with him was what there was," Lynn said, trying to sound adult. She was so horrified at the thought of Randy actually driving over Charlie, aiming at him the way he always aimed at groundhogs on the road, that she wanted to giggle.

"Don't talk about your brother like that," Sadie said. "It's bad luck to think bad of your own family."

Remembering this Lynn got nervous and looked across the room to Kitty. She had shifted positions and was now lying facing Lynn. For a moment Lynn thought she was looking at her, was looking at her and knowing she was thinking bad thoughts about Randy. And then she saw that Kitty was still sleeping. She got up, crossed the room, knelt beside her mother's bed. Kitty's eyes were closed but Lynn could see her eyes moving behind her closed eyelids. Frightened Lynn put her arms around her mother. She felt Kitty shudder, as if she were already packed in ice and remembering her life.

Charlie, Sadie, and Lynn had gone ahead, and now Kitty was alone in her mother's house. She was sitting in the parlour, which had been her mother's favourite room, sitting on the old couch with the faded willows overhanging a turquoise threadbare stream. This stream, Ellen had told her, this stream she had watched while Kitty was being born. And now Ellen was dead and Kitty herself was not going to bear any more children.

She stood up and went into the kitchen for a glass of water. The table had been broadened by its extra leaves, and pushed back to cover the whole wall opposite the wood stove. On top of the table, neatly arranged, were trays of plastic-wrapped cookies and sandwiches. And fronting these, like a utopia of bowling pins awaiting The Biggest Bowler Of Them All, were twenty-four bottles of ten-dollar rye. The refrigerator bulged with three turkeys and two hams and in the barn refrigerator were six cases of beer. Just an emergency ration, Charlie had said, because with the insurance money he had bought not only the visible rye, proudly lined up on the maple table—despite Sadie's objections—but also more esoterically hidden supplies which he refused even to discuss. "After all," he had pointed out defensively, "it's not just a funeral, it's Kitty's wedding party too."

It was now noon, and she had insisted on this short time alone. Ever since she had been let out of the hospital it seemed she hadn't quite been able to catch her breath, not simply because she was busy, or nervous with all the arrangements, or even because she and Pat had finally gotten married, but because her actual breathing had gone wrong; as if to protect herself from pain she was cutting herself off before the air got in deep enough to help.

She had come in for a glass of water and that intent had carried her to the kitchen sink. But now she found herself standing beside the sink and looking not for a glass but at her own reflection in the old mirror there. She saw herself looking drawn, so worried she hardly would have recognized herself, new networks of tiny lines on her face where the life had drawn back from the surface. Her eyes, always wide, now seemed askew, liquid ovals in a face that was all screwed up around them, and suddenly she saw she had become one of those old and crazy women she had always imagined, a crazy old woman with her insides choked sterile and her face bone-dry twisted around her crazy eyes. She was trying to cry, needing to find at least the liquid of her own tears, when she heard the door open.

And then the footsteps, at first hesitant, then firm.

"Randy."

"I come for my stuff."

"Randy."

"Dad's waiting in the car, outside."

"Ellen died."

"I know. I thought everyone would be at the funeral." He was standing near the hallway, in the alcove created by the black wood stove, standing beside Ellen's wicker chair with one hand on its back, as if calling her to witness what he had endured.

"I'm sorry," he said. Then turned and went upstairs, his boots falling with familiar weight on the steps, tromping each one down, the way he had walked since he was two years old, then tromping along the long hallway to the flowered wallpaper room.

Aware now of the sound of an idling motor, Kitty stepped out to the porch. Sitting in his big steel-blue salesman's car, his thick pink arm jutting out the window, was Randy Blair Senior. He was wearing sunglasses and though she stood and looked at him, he didn't remove the glasses, didn't even wave at her.

She sat down on a chair on the porch, sighing as she did, and pushed her shoes off.

Now Randy Senior had turned his head towards her, was pushing back his glasses and peering at her curiously, as if his round baby's eyes couldn't quite recognize her. She could feel the dried tears on her cheeks, a thin fragile surface that cracked as she tried to smile at Randy, and was suddenly reminded of the day he had gotten her pregnant, the stiff glazed surface of her thighs. He was out of the car and walking towards her. In one hand, between thumb and forefinger, he held his sunglasses, rotating them as he walked. He was wearing a white patterned short-sleeved shirt, a tourist's shirt, and grey flannel slacks. His arms were pink already; soon, she knew, they would be a solid mass of freckles; because he didn't tan, not Randy Blair, only freckled and peeled, his soft skin too delicate for sun, for wind, for anything but city sheets and soft cotton clothes.

"I came with the boy," Randy said.

In the hospital he had looked fat and shapeless, hopelessly tired, his hair fallen out and his eyes faded. Now he seemed powerful, even sinister.

"You look okay," he said. "I wanted to make sure you were all right." He smiled at her and put his sunglasses on. In the hospital, when he had visited, she had felt sorry for him, had mixed up the old and the new Randy, had felt sorry for the way she had left him, for the aged wounded baby in him that had presented itself to her in a raincoat and baggy suit; but now she was meeting a stranger, abrasive and distant.

"I'm all right," Kitty said. She stood up, ignoring the pain. She was going to stand up in front of him.

"Last time you could hardly hold your tongue." He was crowding her, forcing her close to the railing of the old porch.

"That's right," she said. "I didn't mean to hurt you." She could feel her dress brushing the wood and had now reversed the balance of her feet, promised herself that if the rail pressed into her she would start swinging.

"I guess you didn't." He paused. The hair he used to slick back proudly was now almost gone on top, fallen away to reveal the high-domed skull sweeping down to his sunglasses like a giant bony muscle. "I guess you were going to give me an apology."

"No."

"Maybe you should."

"Maybe you should fuck right off. Maybe you should take your stupid body off these steps and down into your fat-assed car before someone around here loses their Christly temper with you."

And then the screen door opened and their son was standing between them, his arms filled with two cardboard boxes of random clothes and tools, his old rifle strapped over his shoulder.

"I'll be going now."

The three of them stood on the porch, uncomfortably shifting around. If Mark Frank had come along he could have shouted and sworn at them. He could have called them goddamn stupid idiots and asked them what they were doing.

They wouldn't have known. For the first time since Kitty's birthday at Union Station they were a family again.

On their first attempt, in Toronto, they had lasted almost two years.

On this attempt they made it for less than five minutes.

They stood on the porch and they shifted uncomfortably. Randy, who might have heard his parents' conversation, looked back and forth between them. This was what he had.

"Well," Kitty said. "You better kiss your old mother good-bye." And she watched while Randy loaded the boxes, but not the rifle, into his father's arms, watched while Randy Senior turned away from her, pretending nothing had happened, and made his way down the steps towards the car, watched while her son hesitated before finally stepping forward, wrapping her into him.

"I'm sorry. I didn't mean it to be this way."

She could feel his heart echoing wildly in his chest, confused and furiously young, and wanted to keep her arms closed tight around him, hold him until he broke and cried so she could finally give him whatever he had been missing this terrible and unending childhood. But when his embrace loosened she stepped back, her arms folded across her chest. She was desperately waiting for the right words to come to her, some final benediction of love, forgiveness, wholeness. But could think of nothing, came up without anything but a smile. "You be well," she mumbled. "And don't forget to come home when you want to."

She watched him turn, walk down the steps, and join his father, who, after burning up half the lawn getting turned around, waved laconically, looked at her through his city sunglasses one last time, and started down the driveway.

Her mind blank, perfectly clear, she sat down on the chair and put her bare feet up on the railing. Then, after a while, when she had caught her breath, she went into the house again, into the parlour, and looked once more at the old couch that had been Ellen's favourite, at the faded willow tree and the threadbare blue stream that fed it.

She stood in the centre of the room, her hands folded across her stomach in a new gesture that was already becoming a habit, one palm resting on the bandage she still wore. Beneath the bandage was an incision as wide as a mouth: a place where they had reached in to carve up one ovary and choke off the tubes. Now the wound was throbbing. With her eyes fixed on Ellen's birthing couch it seemed, for just one moment, that the old stream might become something more than itself, might leap out in a great watery roar to meet her pulsing wound; might, carrying the fertility that had passed to herself from her mother and would now fall to Lynn, leap right out through the whole room, sweep out all the dust, old memories and signal events, and become just pure liquid force.

After she had gone upstairs and changed into her clothes for the funeral she went into Randy's room and saw that he had neither emptied nor cleaned it, only taken a few random belongings from the dressers and shelves. The cupboard was still jammed with old winter jackets and boots; on the floor were heaped shirts and trousers of assorted sizes and colours—old discarded Randys that she hadn't seen for years. Closing the door she noticed that the bedroom walls were still blooming with the same flowers that had been conceived on the day Charlie brought Sadie home, and she had decided to redecorate the house.

"We'll have to be tidying this up," Kitty said aloud. Her voice sounded like Ellen's used to, and for the second time that day she inspected herself in the mirror, this time using the tall and narrow five and dime special Randy had nailed up to his cupboard door.

The woman she saw was amazingly proper, even formal. The suit bought years ago in Kingston still fit her; her legs in their nylons stuck out trim and tanned. She looked to herself, in her pale-blue synthetic white-threaded suit, with its matching white-veiled blue hat, altogether cured; and though the girdle she wore chafed at her hips and pressed uncomfortably against her bandaged stomach, she couldn't help turning sideways to examine the line of her own figure, to see how astounding it was that despite everything, once suited and veiled, she could have been the same person she was ten years ago.

The veil was a special effect. It had come with the hat and now she wore it awkwardly pinned over her forehead, a compromise between ruining her vision and keeping in tone with the funeral. The veil was the first she had worn since the day of her wedding with Randy Blair, when she had pinned it the same way, for the same reason.

Randy Blair.

What would he have said if it was he who was sitting on the porch of his dead mother's house and she who had arrived in a goddamn idling car, dressed like a tourist and looking for a fight? Or pretending not to look? Because, now that she remembered, one of the reasons she had left him was because he was selectively blind. Save for that once-a-month Sunday when in an excess of guilt and showmanship he could clean the house, make the meals, parade Randy Junior around on his shoulders, he never saw the mess in the apartment when he came home and wanted his belly filled with dinner and beer, never saw his son when he needed anything from a bottle of milk to his diapers changed.

She had worn the veil on the day of her wedding, and on the day she decided to leave, after a screaming fight that lasted the whole night, she had seen it come falling unused out of a dresser drawer as she packed. Spitefully she had tossed it towards the toilet, never looking back to see where it landed; like her son she had taken what she needed and left the rest.

She took off her hat and stepped towards the mirror, in the same motion unpinning her hair and shaking it down to her shoulders. It was wispy and the blond was already turning white from the spring sun. Now the nervous way she had seen herself in the kitchen came back, the old woman superimposed on the youthful blue silhouette. She looked like women she sometimes saw in movies, women she saw in drive-in movies who were going to go crazy.

"That's all I need," she said. "Can you imagine me, crazy?" She went to step away but wanted to inspect herself, to keep her whole body confined to the narrow space the narrow mirror could reflect. For a moment she thought of taking off all her clothes to look at herself, naked. She had never done that, never. Even that day in the No-Tell Motel with Pat, when there was a big bureau above the mirror and she could see herself all the way down to her knees, she hadn't done it, had avoided the sight of herself as she walked to the bathroom where again she had avoided the mirror as she stepped into the shower.

She was looking at herself in the mirror and she felt nervous, as if she were drunk but not exactly, nervous confined to the small space of her reflection, nervous to see herself so formal and rejuvenated, nervous to discover she was the person she had been hiding somewhere in her mind, the woman who goes crazy, loses track, suddenly discovers there is nothing to contain her.

She wanted to take off all her clothes, was on the verge of stripping, on the verge of seeing herself naked when the fear came on her, as strong as it had been twenty years ago, welling up so fast it bumped her from the inside like a hand slapping at her naked heart.

"Ellen, Jesus Ellen." She was still in Randy's room, trapped by his mirror and her own blue vision of herself when she heard

Pat's car making its slow way up the drive.

Pat, she hardly recognized. He was dressed in a dark suit he had gotten somewhere, a black sack of a suit that hung loose on his bones and made him look a scarecrow. The bandage on his face from Randy's ring had come off. The new scar was thin and red, an elegant fish-hook scar that ran from his cleanshaven jaw up to his cheekbone and the downward border of his eye. That eye, when he had come back from Toronto to visit her at the hospital, had been swollen shut. Now it was half-open, surrounded by a bruise of iridescent yellows and greens. It looked like a patch of grass recovering from an unexpected acid bath.

"You want a drink?"

"Not yet," Pat said.

They were standing in the kitchen, in front of the absurd shining array of Ellen's life insurance rye. Each was wearing the ten dollar gold ring they had bought one another for the wedding and, standing in front of Ellen's legacy, Kitty caught Pat looking at her hand just as she was looking at his. She laughed nervously and moved towards him, suddenly wondering what it would have been like had she and Pat lived together from the beginning, worn proper clothes and lived in town like other people did.

"I think I will," Kitty said. "Just a touch." She stepped to the counter and took one of the bottles, twisted off the cap and drank straight from the narrow mouth, swallowing once, twice, three times, forcing the rye down, trying to concentrate on the burning in her stomach, trying to convince herself that it was forcing down the rising panic, the image of herself in Randy's mirror. And then, holding the bottle, she saw her hand was shaking, shaking as she tried with her other hand to screw the top back on. It shook at first with a slow and regular rhythm.

And then it betrayed her. There was a quick uncontrollable spasm, and then a thin squirt of rye trailing through the air as the bottle dropped and shattered on the floor.

Immediately Pat's arms were around her and she was clinging to him, squeezing and shaking and trying to cry, her tears choking deep in her gut, cramping with every wave and making her stomach convulse like a child's.

"Look at me," Kitty said. "I'm going to ruin my suit." And then she started to laugh: at her own stupid tears, at the puzzled look on Pat's face, at the sight of them both dressed up like never before in their lives just for crazy Ellen's funeral, at the fact that they in their once-in-ten-years suits and once-in-ten-years shined shoes were standing in a spreading pool of rye, wasting what most of the time they would walk miles to taste.

When they got to the cemetery it seemed that the whole town had already arrived. There were so many waves of black suits and summer dresses that as they walked towards the grave where everyone was already gathered, it was impossible to see the centre of the action: neither the coffin, nor the minister, nor even Sadie or Charlie or Lynn.

They picked their way slowly along the gravel side of the road. Kitty, in her high-heeled shoes, felt a girl again, the girl who had worn heels for the first time at her father's funeral, the girl who had cried so long and hard Charlie had had to take her away from the service. But at least this day she was dry: her skin felt dry and her tear ducts felt dry and she felt dry from the back of her throat, which needed another drink, to the very pit of her gut: dry of tears, dry from lack of proper drink, dry as if in the hospital they had emptied out every last drop of her, a well that could no longer run.

She had, she noticed, one hand pressed into her side where the growth used to be; she took it away and crossed her arms as they walked, holding close to Pat for comfort, seeking the purchase of his hand on her elbow, his long body keeping slow to her pace, brushing against her with every step. As she walked she lowered her eyes, avoiding the red, well-meaning faces that stared out from their funeral best, watching only the green trampled grass as Pat led her to the centre, to the grave where she finally looked up and saw Charlie standing opposite her, one arm around Sadie and the other around Lynn, grinning like a maniac, ecstatic and triumphant, grinning and winking at her as if his whole rubbery small-featured face had gone right out of control.

"Ain't this something? The whole goddamn town is here. She finally got them all right where she wanted them, in the cemetery, and she's gonna sneak up behind and give them all the one good boot in the arse they deserve, one good boot in the arse and they'll be under the ground and she'll be out like a jack-in-the-box laughing her fool head off."

"Shushup Charlie." This from Sadie.

Without thinking Kitty had slipped out of her tight high-heeled shoes and let her nyloned feet dig deep in the new earth they had thrown up from the grave. She could feel it cooling her soles, feel the damp earth trying to seep between her toes, to surround and nourish them, to surround and seduce and draw them down. She looked to the bottom of the grave. There, sitting in the rich black earth like The City Of Gold risen from hell, was Ellen's coffin: the black satiny paint and the ornate brasswork sparkled in the June sun. The minister's voice began to drone, the townspeople sighed and sang as he instructed, but Kitty only saw Ellen again as she had last been at the hospital, gleefully proclaiming that she was dying, pounding her fists on the steel arms of the nursing-station chair, singing Hallelujah, Hallelujah-Oh.

She felt Pat's arm tighten and she nestled to his warmth. She had worked her feet right into the earth. They were soaked and happy right up to her ankles; cold too, the ground down there was still cold from winter. It seemed forever since she had just lain on the ground, let the sun warm her skin and the earth soak into her until she lost track of herself and fell into the trees and the sky. And now she felt the first trickle of her tears, opened her eyes and saw Charlie, saw the sun too, facing her, burning hot on her chest and helping the empty spaces open up so when she closed her eyes again the voices were blown right away. She could feel nothing but the wind, the spring air blowing through her, Ellen's soul thick with hers, loving her, loving her.

Pat's arm around her. His corded muscles bit into her side, holding her up while he dragged her back from the grave. And now she looked down and saw Lynn was at her feet, kneeling, trying to force her high-heeled shoes onto her dirty nylons; they were wet and coated with black earth up past her ankles.

"Look at me," Kitty said. Lynn's face turned up to hers,

puzzled. "I took my shoes off. You know how it is."

Lynn grinned, her face bony and open; a curious amalgam of herself and Pat, not exactly a compromise or a mix, but both of them put in one place; but where she saw Pat, scarred and protecting himself, and herself nervous and turned-in, the frightened boundless crazy in Randy's mirror, Lynn was still untouched, still opening to the world.

"Let's wait," Kitty said. "Let the others get home first." The grave had been heaped high; on top of the black coffin with its ornate brass trim, a coffin so fancy and so false Ellen could never even have dreamed it, there was now a mound of fresh black earth, a long humped mound decorated with pots of flowers, wreaths, even a bouquet of daisies and brown-eyed susans.

Around her waist was Pat's arm and in her hand was Lynn's, smaller and curled up tiny, like a sleeping butterfly she used to call it, but her fingers were more like caterpillars, curled warm and so young they felt boneless, curled into her palm so trusting she couldn't help being reminded of Randy, couldn't help comparing this side of her that now peacefully centred Pat and Lynn, to the image of herself standing on the porch, feeling sick and turned-in, trying at the same time to forgive her son and defend herself against his father; and for a moment the panic started to rise and she saw herself again in Randy's mirror, the woman-in-blue, the woman in the movie, narrow and uncontained. In the movie the glass cracked; the image split in two. Right now that was all she was: one woman split in two by these two men, by her children by them, by her own conflicting feelings.

"I was thinking," said Pat, "we might walk back to those lilacs."

She felt far away from herself. She was a swooping bird looking down at herself, as if she and Ellen had mixed and now Ellen was trying to force her up too, take her up in the air; the canny old bitch, she always wanted her way, take her up in the air so she'd have company in heaven, desert the blue-dressed woman she saw walking beneath her, the middle-aged woman with the white-blond hair holding onto a young girl with one hand, and supporting and being supported by a skinny long-legged drunk on the other; she saw the three of them walking and her sense of herself was snapping back and forth, erratically crackling from the eyes of the walking woman to the bird's eye view. So that one moment she was above them all, circling, watching the three-some on their stumbling way, and the next she was back in the grove where they were walking, the purple-flowered edge exuding a smell so sweet and heavy it could knock her to her knees.

Lynn, beside her, was not aware of the details. But she knew Kitty's arm felt dangerously like the chicken she had one day held on top of the grader – in the moment before it toppled to the ground in its mysterious suicide.

Grabbing hold of Kitty's arm Lynn pushed up with all her strength.

"What are you doing?"

"Keeping you up."

She looked to Kitty's face. Ever since she had come back from the hospital Kitty had been almost impossible to recognize, her face dissolving into so many lines and worries it seemed she was trying to turn into someone else. At her feet, by the grave, she had wanted to shove Kitty's shoes on so firmly they could never come off, glue them to her feet in a promise that she would stay together, keep being her mother.

"You go ahead. We're just going to sit down here."

Kitty let go Lynn's hand and watched her sprint away towards the edge of the cemetery, to the hill overlooking the tracks that the body-train used to ride. At least that's what they used to call the train carrying caskets of the dead from town; and now Kitty remembered that at nights when she was a child and a strange wind was heard sometimes Ellen would laugh and say that was the body-train, carrying new bodies to feed the hungry cemetery.

"I don't feel so good."

"You want a drink?"

"What have you got?"

"Just this." From his pocket Pat drew out one of the kitchen bottles of rye, unscrewed the top, and handed it to her. "I just thought you might be wanting something," he said.

She swallowed: just once, small and careful.

"I got to sit down," Kitty said. "I feel so awful." She stepped forward and then saw, a few paces away, a tombstone with a worn and comfortable top. "They said never step on a grave but they didn't say anything about not sitting on the stone."

She kicked off her shoes and held her hand out for the bottle again.

"Who is it?"

"My father," Pat said. "You got your arse on his head."

"Don't be profane."

She had the bottle in her hand, but she didn't want any. She was already starting to cry.

She lifted the bottle to her mouth but stopped the rye with her tongue, let it burn momentarily and then handed it back. She was wet now, she didn't need anything to remind her, anything to be reminded of; she was crying, she had her face in her hands and she was crying; she had her feet dug into the grass and she was sitting on Terry Frank's gravestone, and then slowly she lowered herself down so she was on her knees, she felt the damp growing up her legs, then lowered her head until it was on the cool spring grass, the pulse of the earth cool and easy on her face, welcoming her slowly, letting her weight find its own way.

"Ellen, Jesus Christ, Ellen you were such an idiot."

The wind came up again and she was filled with the smell of grass and earth, the sweet dying fragrance of the lilacs, but this time she was alone, she could feel only herself, no Ellen, no mother mixing love and sorrow, no bird up in the sky to fly away with, no one at all but her own cried-out self. She got up slowly, shook her head and saw her strange blue suit, her nylons black to the ankle and with runs up both calves.

The afternoon was beginning to darken. Gradually the sun was sinking in the sky, turning the horizon a deep misty blue. Kitty brushed herself off, forced her wet feet into the shoes, and started walking back towards the gates of the cemetery. Lynn, who had been down at the tracks, had returned with handfuls of daisies and dandelions, a few blossom-loaded twigs from an old and crippled apple tree. All of these, stems first, Kitty watched her push into the fresh earth of Ellen's grave.

Theirs was the only car left. While Pat carefully turned it

around, Kitty tried to straighten her hair in the rearview mirror. The skin that had seemed so dry and fragile earlier in the day looked normal now. Once again she could look at her own face without really seeing it; and caught herself as she was pushing her hair back from her forehead, shifting her eyes away from her own image.

As they drove the reddening sun was multiplied by the tin roofs of barns and houses, dotting the hilly landscape. And as they followed the winding road, the cool grass smelled sweet and thick even through the fumes of Mark Frank's battered but mobile black Ford coupe. Already the grass was knee-high; in a couple of weeks it would be up to the waist and they would start taking it off, mowing and baling and piling up supplies for winter in the midst of this first burst of summer.

She felt curiously peaceful. Cried out and clear she watched the patchy fields and stroked Lynn's hands.

Kitty was sitting in Ellen's wicker chair, looking up at the antique clock with its black barbed arrows, joined both together and soberly pointing straight up to heaven. Midnight, and the glass in her hand had turned empty. Midnight, and the party had started to disperse, voices from the yard and house thinning into almost distinguishable words, stories and declarations gradually winding down, mixed with the sound of engines starting, curses, as the cars, crowded randomly into the driveway while it was still light, now manoeuvred from fence to manure pile in the effort to get out.

She pushed herself up and went to the counter. The first instalment of Ellen's insurance policy had disappeared within an hour, the whole township drinking down the rye as if prohibition had been declared; but then Charlie, the perfect host for once, had, cast and all, limped down the rickety steps to the basement that Ellen's own grandfather had dug by hand a hundred and twenty years ago. From it, hidden in the cast-iron belly of the monstrous wood furnace, Charlie had withdrawn the second instalment of Ellen's insurance policy, a second case of twenty-four bottles of rye. And when that too was ingested, this task carrying the party well into the evening, Charlie was again equal to the situation.

Once more he dragged his cast down the stairs; once more he reached blind into the iron belly; and once more the prize was his. Like a warrior returning from battlefields stained and honourable, Charlie limped up the stairs dragging with him the third case of rye. This case, only half-empty, still held forth.

From one of the bottles on the table Kitty poured herself a drink. With Charlie trying to besot everyone within fifty miles, Sadie had countered with food; the walls of the parlour were lined with white-linened card tables covered in turkeys, hams, trays of quartered crustless sandwiches, a half-dozen cut glass bowls filled with salads. To this food, which she had last seen several hours ago when it was still relatively virgin, Kitty now felt drawn. And swallowing the first sip of her drink, crossed her arms carefully over her belly and began the complicated walk to the parlour.

Every few steps she stopped and exchanged greetings with someone. For the first couple of hours, the party had tried to be a funeral, and at least the façade of solemnity had been observed. Every single person, from crones as old as Ellen and hobbling worse than she ever had, to children so young they tripped when they curtsied, had come up to extend their sympathy. But now the funeral had long since evolved into the wedding, and the party had changed into a gathering indistinguishable from the late hours of all other weddings—or, for that matter, the late hours of all other funerals, church socials, Christmas and Thanksgiving dinners: a large porridgy drunk where everyone was finally left with the need to reconcile the good time that was gradually going downhill with the hangover that was gradually building. The only difference between this mixed party and the other, more purely happy occasions, was that there was no dancing; though Charlie had at one point tried to start the record player Sadie had pulled out the plug.

And in fact this, of all nights, belonged to Sadie; because although it was both Ellen's funeral and Kitty and Pat's marriage party, it was most of all the night when Sadie had finally wrested the house from the Malones, living and dead, and taken it for her own. Near the beginning of the evening she had been restrained. "We'll miss her here," she said of Ellen. Then she got more elaborate: "That was the place she like to sit. I always knew I'd find her there, in the morning. Charlie always said they'd have to bury her in that chair. Now it's here and she's gone." By the middle of the party, Sadie had told her story of the chair to all the neighbours. Her normally sallow cheeks glowed, her black eyes were so bright people even remembered *her* wedding, the strange slim bride she'd been; and, as if feeling that way again, Sadie, when she stopped telling the story of Ellen's chair, began to tell of her decorating plans. "That couch where you're sitting. I've always hated it, you know. Charlie. Charlie! I hope you're going to take that to the dump next week."

In the hallway below the stairs, Kitty, as she made her way towards the parlour, bumped into Sadie. "Well," Sadie said. "I never thought I'd see the day." Now, at midnight, her whole face was on fire. The house was hot with liquor and people. Sadie had taken off her shawl and was wearing a black sleeveless dress that emphasized her bony shoulders and long arms. These she threw around Kitty. Then stepped back.

"Married again. I never thought you'd have him."

"Sadie, you dumb clown, of course—"

"Never mind," Sadie whispered. "It's all over now." And in a gesture absolutely new, gave Kitty a queenly smile and swept by her to the front porch.

When Kitty finally got to the parlour, she found only Mark Frank. He was sitting on the maligned birthing couch, his glass eye turned backwards so only the white showed.

"How you doing?" he asked.

"Hungry." She looked around the room. The supper, so carefully laid out by Sadie and the neighbours, looked as if someone had let the pigs in. "You got your eye inside out," she said.

"I was thinking."

Kitty found a clean paper plate and began to fill it with celery and radishes. "What were you thinking?"

"I was thinking," Mark said, "if you'll excuse me, that old Ellen should have been here."

"She liked a party."

"They should have had her in a corner, you know, standing in that shiny casket of hers, just like she was alive."

Kitty found a chicken wing and began chewing on it.

"What do you think?" Mark asked.

"It would have been nice. Charlie wanted her but Sadie wouldn't let her in the house after she was dead. You know how she is about Ellen."

Now that she had started, she couldn't remember when she had last eaten. She tore some turkey from one of the carcasses and made herself a sandwich with the turkey, some of the white crustless bread, and tomatoes picked from the remains of a salad. And when she had finished half the sandwich and had a few sips of rye to wash it down, she sat beside Mark on the birthing couch and looked with him at the corner where Ellen should have stood. Because she agreed with Mark. Ellen should have been there.

Not from any pious need to remember her while they guzzled her insurance booze. And certainly not from any wish Ellen would have had to see them all stumbling around making fools of themselves—she'd seen that hundreds of times anyway.

Ellen should have been there because Kitty wanted Ellen to be at this wedding, dead or alive. She wanted Ellen to see that after twenty years of messing around and being divided she had somehow tried to settle the whole entire mess she'd made, tried to put Randy Blair behind her and start to make whatever life she could with Pat. At least she was trying.

And the second reason she should have been there was that Kitty didn't want to spend the next twenty years morbidly thinking about Ellen's dying. She wanted it to be over with. If Ellen had been there, if Ellen had been stood up in the corner with her jaws wired shut and her eyes propped open, there would have been absolutely no doubt that she was dead. The sight of Ellen with her mouth finally and unremittingly closed would have been so terrifying that Kitty knew she would have gotten absolutely drunk: not tight, not wobbly, not passing-into-sleep drunk; but wildly, uncontrollably, tears-and-tantrums drunk.

"Well," Mark said. "I guess we're relatives now."

"I guess."

Despite the fact that she had known Mark almost her whole life, she had never, especially since starting with Pat, exactly been comfortable with him.

"I sure like that girl of yours. Lynn."

"She likes you," Kitty said. She was slightly drunk, but not drunk enough for this sudden sentimental meeting. "You've been good to her."

"Don't say," said Mark. He winked his backwards eye at her. "I mean, what the hell."

"What the hell," Kitty agreed.

They sat awkwardly on the couch, looking at the empty corner where Ellen should have been, until finally Kitty stood, put her hand on Mark's shoulder, then went upstairs.

Searching from room to room she found Lynn asleep in her clothes on top of a pile of coats. Kitty threw the coats outside the door, closed it, then lay down beside Lynn, cradling around her. The pain where they'd operated had come back; she could feel the ache where the knife had been, the muscles stretched and sore in her belly and groin. Lynn was whispering in her sleep and Kitty put her hand gently on Lynn's neck, rubbed it slowly while her dream passed and her breathing deepened. From below and outside she could hear the party's final noises. Sadie, now hysterically drunk, was singing Auld Lang Syne. Every few seconds the walls and ceilings were raked by the headlights of a departing car. And then she too was pulled into sleep; she could feel herself drifting off, dozing to the sound of tires in mud, Sadie's wavering voice, the slamming of doors, Lynn's breathing, her own crying which had started again. Until she lost consciousness to the feel of her own slippery skin, swimming eyes closed and soothed by her own unresisted tears.

Lynn was dreaming of the place where no one went. She felt Kitty's body spooned to hers, the wet flow of Kitty's tears. In her dream she let Kitty's tears melt into the river. She was walking north. She wasn't looking for Randy, or Kitty, or even Mark. She was past the place where the wolves and black flies come from, past the places where anyone lived.

She stretched into Kitty and settled deeper into sleep.

Twelve

While Kitty and Lynn fitted into the jigsaw of their dreams, Pat Frank and Mark sat out on the porch with Charlie Malone, helping him kill one last bottle of rye while Charlie slipped from a state of cheerful drunkenness into a kind of hazy half-sleeping drinking, smoking, and inane conversation.

"I'm going to sleep right here," Charlie Malone said. "I'm not dragging that goddamn thing up the stairs again."

He was settled in Ellen's wicker chair, which they had brought out from the kitchen, and he had both his legs—one in the new slimmed-down walking cast they had given him and one naked in the blue serge trouser it had been married in—propped up on the porch railing. To accompany his words he tapped his cast with the rubber-tipped hospital cane.

"Look at that," he said. "That's township history."

On the fresh plaster of Paris, which only one day ago had been newly white, was a hieroglyphic mass of squiggles and dots, the accumulated signatures of exactly two hundred and thirty-eight guests. Some of these signatures were lessons in themselves. Others went along with explanatory mottoes like "Get Well Quick," and "This'll Teach You," and "Don't Use This To Kick The Outhouse Down."

"That was good," Pat said. "You did it right."

"You sure? I never had to throw a wedding and a funeral in the same party."

"It was perfect. Ellen would've approved." He had the rye and was tossing the bottle from hand to hand.

"Some wedding," Charlie said. "Some funeral. Some wedding party. I think your esteemed wife has passed herself out upstairs."

"At least my wife went upstairs to pass out," Pat said. Sadie, still glowing, was curled asleep in a corner of the porch.

"Too bad Ellen couldn't be here." Charlie sucked his knuckles reflectively. "She would have liked it."

"I'll pick Kitty up in the morning."

Charlie was still sucking his knuckles and mumbling about Ellen when Pat turned and started walking down the drive to where he had parked his brother's car.

He was not drunk; nor was he exactly sober. He was in that rare and rational zone he sometimes found, a narrow and calculating state that drinking a lot over many hours sometimes brought him to, a feeling that he was enclosed in a slightly varnished replica of himself, a model Pat Frank that could do everything with precise accuracy, so long as it could move slowly.

Which condition was fine with Pat, because in addition to this need for slowness he had accumulated over the evening, he was also tied in place by a five-inch strip of adhesive bandage that circled his ribs where the shoes of Kitty's son and his father had done their dance. But it was not only his drinking and his ribs that slowed him. Picking himself up from the ashcans and green garbage bags that littered the alley behind Randy Blair Senior's apartment building he had known something irretrievable had happened. Although it was not the first time in his life he had lost a fight, or even the worst beating he had taken, this one had crossed a new line. For this there would be no revenge.

Even as he wiped the dirt and blood off his pants he knew he wouldn't be going upstairs, pounding on their door; nor would he be lying in wait. Even while he was carefully fingering his

face, which felt like the inside of a bruised doughnut, and gratefully finding that his loosened teeth were still in place, he knew
that he would let them get away with it, that what he had taken
from his own father he was giving to young Randy. And that
what Randy's father had given him was only his reply to the
theft of Kitty, the damage to his child.

He had sat on top of one of the tin-lidded cans and rolled
himself a cigarette. Every time he moved he could feel his ribs
trying to grind themselves together. The smoke stilled his blood.
But when the first cigarette was finished his breath was still shallow and hurting, so he had to start a second and then slowly—so
slowly he had time to give up the pledge he had made, and instead to promise never to let himself be this sober again—he
walked down the drive to the street, and down the quiet street to
a brighter noisier one. In a few minutes he had found himself a
dark and comforting tavern. It was only when he went into the
bathroom, where the fluorescent lights burned yellow-white and
he saw his hands shaking, that he thought of looking up, looking
into a mirror to see what they had done to his face; and saw the
long jagged scar, Randy's ring scar like a hook coming down
from his eye to his jaw. Both that eye and the other were swelling.
They sat like purple eggs on top of his cavernous face. The un-
scarred cheek was bruised. There was blood dried from one nos-
tril. He washed and slapped water and spat into the sink until he
felt almost normal, until the bleeding from his mouth had diluted
from crimson to pink.

"You okay?"

"Sure."

He straightened up from the sink to face the cop. And then it
was as if a whole ocean had sprung loose in him; it was only as he
closed his eyes and pitched forward that he realized what was
happening, that he was fainting, swooning like a goddamn
woman in the middle of this strange city.

He was sitting at the wheel of Mark's car. In his half-drunk varnished clarity he was very carefully threading the key into the
ignition switch.

"You can drive?" Mark was asking him.

"I'm okay." Miraculously the key jiggled into the slot. Without pausing he started the car, savouring the roar of the engine as it caught; and then, feeling stronger, he began turning the steering wheel, wrestling the heavy Ford around in the narrow Malone drive. Beside him, in the light of the dash, Mark bulked like a heavyset gnome; hunched forward, huge shoulders and back rounded like the smooth ancient rocks that stuck out of the fields, he was breathing so deep and heavy Pat could hear him straining through the sound of the tires whining in the mud. And when he was finally turned around and on track, and the car was lurching its way towards the highway, Pat noticed Mark was slumped against the door.

"Anything wrong?"

"Nope."

"Feeling sick?"

"Maybe you could stop."

Even as the car was still rocking Mark was out the door and on the ground, bringing up Ellen Malone's insurance policy in heaves so long and horrible-sounding that Pat, despite the fact it was his own brother, his own *twin*, gunned the motor to mask the noise.

"That's better," Mark said when he climbed back into the car. He was stamping his feet on the floor and rubbing his hands together. "Can't take the real stuff after that horsepiss you bring back from town."

"Ingrate."

"A person could die of drinking," Mark said. "Did you ever think of that? I was lying in the widow Kincaid's bed the other night and I was thinking that if a person drank like you they'd be dead."

"I feel fine." They had come to the end of the drive now and were poised at the edge of the highway. The headlights, yellow and weak, cast uncertain pools of light on the bush opposite the road, illuminated only a few leaves and branches before fading. Pat shifted into first and eased the big car up onto the pavement. At some point on the way home from Toronto the loaded up grease and oil Mark used to placate the bagged-out cylinders and head had burned away; now the motor operated with a raspy clinkety-clink that made it sound like an old bucket of bolts shaking itself to death. In first gear the noise reminded him of Mark's bedsprings as he rocked himself to sleep on the Pillow Kincaid, but in third it was a vaguely danceable beat, and Pat found himself snapping his fingers to the loose clanking of the pistons.

"Sounds awful," Mark observed.

"Makes me want to sing."

They were rocketing along at thirty miles per hour, which had become its new top velocity.

"I don't know," Mark said. "We might better have taken Charlie's truck. If we wanted to get home without walking."

"Don't scare it."

But it was too late. There was a muted mechanical sigh, like the sound of an iron throat being cleared, a distinct warning cough, then a muffled explosion. Pat instinctively grabbed at the wheel, jammed his foot onto the brake, and tried to calm the fishtailing car. Then he saw a smoky, hallucinatory object: a red glowing piece of metal emerged from the hood like a burning nose, poked briefly in the air, then flew upwards, narrowly missing the windshield and leaving a smoking hole behind it.

"Jesus-by-Jesus Christly Christ. I told you something was wrong."

"You was right."

They climbed out of the car. The headlights, already weak, dimmed further and glowed like two orange cat's eyes.

"That was my best engine," Mark said. He kicked at the front grille. "My best fucking engine and my going-to-town car."

"I'm sorry."

"I send you to Toronto in my best car to get Randy Blair and you come back half-dead and the car gutted out like someone stuck a fist up its ass."

He kicked at the car again, this time shattering one of the orange lights.

"What the fuck is going on?" he shouted. "Just tell me what the fuck is going on around here." He kicked out the second light.

"All right," Pat said. "Now don't get upset."

"I'm not upset."

Now that the headlights were gone, the night began to melt. As they moved about the car Pat could see the checks on Mark's plaid shirt, faint red and blue squares coming out from the v where his suit jacket hung open. The road, which had been an indistinct grey when they were driving on it, now resolved into potholes and gravel, a grainy corrugated surface that faded away from them like a long wrinkled snake. He reached into his pocket for tobacco but then, breathing deep and feeling the lining of his throat raw from the dozens of cigarettes already rolled and consumed during this long day, changed his mind. Mark had calmed and was now sitting on the hood of the old Ford, his back propped up on the windshield.

"What happened to you? You never came back empty before."

"I don't know," Pat said. The memory he couldn't stand, the memory he had but wished he could forget, was not that of finding himself in the alley, beat-up and so sober that every muscle in his body felt as if it had aged a million years, nor even that of himself curled up like a scared baby on Randy Blair's unmessable carpet, trying to get away from their city shoes. What he wanted to forget was the *grateful* way he had felt, his pants pissed with fear and his face bleeding from places he couldn't locate, when for a moment he had regained consciousness and felt them carrying him down the back stairs of their Toronto apartment, *gratefully* felt them carrying him down to be thrown out on the street like some old piece of garbage, so helpless and ruined they couldn't be bothered killing him, couldn't be bothered worrying about what he might do in return.

"I guess we better get walking," Pat said.

He watched Mark slide slowly down from the hood of his broken car. Taped, limping from a knee that had somewhere gotten banged up, his throat too sore to receive smoke, his belly unwilling to accept one more drink, Pat felt so bad he didn't know how he was going to walk the two miles home, didn't know what he was going to do about his open hurting chest or the open hurting question Mark had given him, still unanswered, still waiting like an unpaid debt to his brother's hulking body.

"I guess I'm getting old," Pat said. "Losing the old killer instinct."

It had been a matter of imagination: of focussing, of imagining his hand reaching down for the knife, pushing it open, of seeing in his mind the metal of the knife against the flesh of Randy's throat, opening the blood of Kitty's son.

"Too old to fight," Pat said.

He slapped Mark on the shoulder, felt his own hand stopped dead against Mark's bone and muscle: unbroken, unyielding, his brother's body would shuffle and grunt its whole way to eternity.

They were walking home. The light was beginning to grow and with the promise of day the sky was shifted from absolute black to a dark, lucent blue. Pat could see the pitted road, the face of his brother which in this light looked blue-grey and cast from heavy steel, and vaguely, where the horizon was close, the ragged edge of evergreens and maples.

The road they were walking on, paved in a forgotten era of political patronage, ran west. It started at the town of Salem, the actual moment of paving in fact commencing just at the place where the Salem Garage And General Repair marked the town's old boundary, went west past various farms to the graveyard, passed the turnoff to the Malone place, continued to an old and long abandoned church which was kitty-corner to another Malone place, that of old Joe Malone which he had gained by marriage to Katherine Beckwith, and which, with its two silos and long sloping fields traversed by drainage ditches, was so uncharacteristically prosperous that Joe and Charlie's relationship, though they were first cousins, was itself drained away to a hostile neutrality, wound from there through swampier sections and around two beaver ponds the tourists called lakes and built cottages on to live among the black flies, to a long bushy stretch which was ended by a new series of farms including that of the widow Kincaid. It was only about a mile west of there that Mark Frank's car had broken down.

After another mile they came to a place in the road, invisible to anyone in this light, and indeed to a stranger in full daylight, where the rail fencing was actually a gate: a modest gate of cedar rails so eaten away by weather and time that they resembled wooden licorice twists. Beyond this gate, which they had as children called the arch of the mysterious ancestor, was an old and unused wagon trail which cut north to the lake that used to back the Frank property and where, every summer morning that he was able, Mark Frank still went fishing.

At the hidden arch the brothers, like schoolboys pausing out of habit, stopped and surveyed the small cedar-lined tunnel. Without further consultation they swung over the fence, moving their bodies with a weird slow-motion agility that had nothing to do with the shuffling half-drunken way they had been walking. Once in the bush, this unexpected grace continued. Where on the road they had been stumbling and bumping into one another, they now moved quietly, each step balanced and absorbed in the soft earth, every dip or twist in the path, every branch anticipated and known, built into the flow of their motion as if this path, these trees and bushes and the ground they grew out of were part of their own bodies.

In a few hundred yards the bush ended and they came out into a field: hillocked and rocky, dotted with junipers and the spiky forms of young waist-high evergreens.

It was now over a hundred years since this field had been cleared, by some ancestral relation long buried and forgotten. Then, having discovered he had broken his back and half-killed his oxen only to release useless swamp, he had allowed the trees to grow back in: first pine, which had been already logged-off for pulp, and then cedar in what was left of the soil.

Through this disaster of sweat and good intentions the Frank brothers walked until, following separate paths through the maze of prickly junipers and mounds of fieldstones, they arrived at the focus of this whole field, the point towards which the twisted cedar rails, the useless Herculean effort of clearing, the long needlecovered path had all been directed: the house of the mysterious ancestor.

This house was no obvious mansion.

It was a flat grassy area, interrupted by a perfectly rectangular hole. The hole had been filled to the surface with melon-sized rocks.

Although they had often discussed the house, had virtually seen it rising up like a medieval castle to dominate the surrounding landscape, they had in fact no idea whether it had been made of log, clapboard, or old shingles and tarpaper; whether it had been multi-turreted and immense or a mere squatter's shack; whether the windows had been graced by real glass or just coloured paper to keep out the bugs and the cold.

Not only was the house left entirely to the imagination of the beholder; but the name of the ingenious builder was also entirely unknown.

Even when they were boys the name of the mysterious ancestor had been entirely unknown.

And the work of this failed Ozymandias had been long burned, survived only by the small basement filled in with rocks to protect cattle from falling. Announcing what had once been the lawn was a row of apple trees, each original and ancient one surrounded by the twining branches of its own progeny, each one a mass of tangled limbs so thick that the large and sweet apples they had once produced had now multiplied into an annual host of tiny bitter fruit that mounded at the trees' base. Beyond the row of apple trees was a small ditch. At this time of year it was already dry, its bottom only damp from the spring runoff, but when they had been boys the ditch had been a small stream, wet the whole year round, and then they had imagined that a century before, when this place was still forest, and discovered by the man who cleared it, that the small stream was deeper and larger, a river filled with suckers and trout. And they imagined that in this unthinkably old time when the land was still populated by pagan trees and red Indians that the mysterious ancestor had somehow arrived in the midst of this forest, seen the river wind in its own natural clearing, and dreamed of becoming prosperous, of building a house and living in a river-glade where he would pass his summer evenings listening to the sound of moving water.

From the old house-site, whose inscrutable moral they had tried their whole lives to decipher, the brothers moved across the remaining open space of the field to a path that began to lead downhill towards the lake. Here the scrubby bush gave way to a stretch where oak and maple competed for the rich ground. In this place there was no light at all, only small patches of dark blue sky and stars where the forest canopy had been temporarily broken by wind or lightning. As they walked they could hear not only their own breathing, which had grown deep and practised with this practised walk, but the breaking and crackling of last year's leaves.

There had been a time when they wondered how leaves could survive whole winters, how it was their tiny skeletons could be snowed on for six months and then be rained on two months more, and yet revive enough to crackle and break.

No such questions any longer existed. Like the stone-filled basement any hypothetical reasons for the nature of things had long ago been overwhelmed by the force of their existence, by the force of all these mysterious things that grew familiar because they happened without fail, season after season, beginning, growing, dying with such finality that explanations seemed only something invented in the wooden school they had long ago attended.

And which had long ago burned down.

At that time in their lives, when they were still trying to understand, they had often avoided chores and their father by taking this long way home from school. The maple forest was then much younger. The memory of it – trees straight, competing underbrush and poplars cleared away, twin maple sugar shacks battened against the weather and surrounded by neatly corded wood – was so strong that Pat Frank seldom saw the bush as it was now, only thought that these lightning and rot-scarred trees that grew twisted and lumpy, leaving dead branches, whole trunks laying across ground that had once been carpeted only with leaves and grass, were just a visual aberration, a temporary blurring of the eyesight that would give way, as soon as someone had a few spare weeks, to the neatly tended bush it was supposed to be.

Tonight, though every inch of the path was known to his shoes, and knew them, Pat's perception was different. In the now-rising light he saw the bursts of spring leaves and the twisted remains of the maple forest anew, as if with each second of dawn it was growing again, painted into the clear morning air with no past at all, no previous image; painted into the clear morning air so new and clean he could suddenly smell the deep valley of oxygen rushing between the trunks. He turned and looked behind him: to the east the sky was showing a faint wash of pink, and the upper reaches of leaves were turning a bright and tender green with the first touch of sun.

He was trembling. He could feel his heart beating faster, dizzy, stuttering and trying to open up, but this time it was not pouring out love. It was not burning with love, or need, or hate, or regret: just open, dizzily neutral. On the brink of falling over he stood and trembled, not daring even to move his hands towards his cigarettes; froze and gradually felt the day begin to suck into him: at first wispy and faint, then in a rushing torrent that pounded in his chest and rose up his spine until it washed right through his skull, the sun lighting up and beaming through his eyes. For a moment he saw it blinding white and bursting with pure waves of life, life translucent waiting to be formed. And then he blinked and it was gone, the forest returned dark and enclosing, the few glowing patches of sky still dotted with stars.

When they got to the lake the surface of the water was stippled with tiny points of silver light.

"We should go swimming," Mark said.

In the old days Mark had always been the one for fishing and swimming, his round boy's body taking like a seal to any water there was; but now he seemed to Pat more like an old rock-bear, grizzled and toughened until there was nothing he wasn't immune to.

"Sure," Pat said. He took off his shoes and socks, wiggled his feet into the cold sand, and reached into his pocket for the tobacco. "You go first." Breaking into his mind, short-circuiting whatever he saw or thought, was still the moment in the forest. And in the spaces between the wind's brushing against the water, Mark's puffing as he twisted out of his suit, Pat could still hear a faint buzzing in his own brain, scalding hot and pouring out sweat as if the pores had been blown open from the inside.

He took off his tie, opened his shirtfront to the morning air. Mark was naked already, standing at the shore, arching his back and rubbing his wide hairy belly as if he had just woken up from twelve hours of sleep. With his stubby penis and long lopsided testicles he looked too vulnerable, too delicate to be exposed to something so neutral as air. And then, as Pat watched, Mark waded in slowly, his arms held high out of the water, waving at crazy angles as he tried to protect his feet from the sharp stones. And then with a grunt and a splash he was in, great sprays of silver beads marking his entrance.

While he smoked Pat took off his jacket, loosened the belt of his trousers, trying to get himself accustomed to the cold, the idea of this season's first swim. Already Mark was stroking rhythmically towards the centre of the lake. Pat's varnished coating had been dissolved by the moment in the forest; with its passing had come the beginnings of a hangover, his first since the night Lynn had asked him if Kitty was going to die.

The clouds were gathering at the back of his neck, the bony place where one of his spine's knuckles was swollen big as a baby's fist, and he could feel them starting to move upwards, clouds seeking out his brain, his poor idiotic shrunken brain. He pictured it grey and tightly drawn into itself. It was trying to hang on to its outer edges, keep control of those hopelessly dry cells that died and gathered as dust in his mind's empty corners, pieces of his memory and life dropping off like so much dead skin.

Mark was now far past the centre of the lake. Looking out Pat could barely see him, only the ripple of his wake and the dark dot that was his head. It seemed to Pat, just now, as he watched his brother swim into the darkness, that these past few weeks had been both the best and the worst that he had ever known, that somehow, at forty-nine, he had just lost his innocence. And then, with a force he could feel on his lungs, everything opened up once more. He was blinded, drawn back into himself, into the tight bright place in his mind that was still sitting drunk in Lynn's room waiting sad and hopeful for spring to slide into summer, his chest filled with the sweet heavy smell of lilacs. He stood up and coughed. His eyes were misted over, wouldn't focus properly. When he finally had them rubbed clear Mark had turned around, was swimming towards him with slow, rolling, powerful strokes. Only his heels broke the water; they made a noise like an idling engine and left a trail of tiny white bubbles. Occasionally he submerged and swam along underwater. When he surfaced he was always in the right place, along the original straight line.

Later Mark would enter it in his diary. The next day, when Pat and Kitty had gone to Kingston and he was left alone with his barnyard traffic jam of broken cars and his bulging orange scribbler, he would say how it was:

> *I had come in and was putting on my clothes when he started taking off his. They used to tell us we were identical twins. Not only did we come out of the exact same place, me first, but we looked so alike for two years they could hardly tell us apart. Since then we haven't been identical but I didn't know until last night how different we'd got.*
>
> *He is skinny like a picture from the war. His ribs show except where they are covered in white doctor's tape, and he has no belly, shanks like a starving horse. His back shows the knobs of his spine sticking out like a long row of swollen knuckles, his knobbly knees stick out and his shins are so sharp that if he could twist them high enough he could shave with them.*
>
> *All over he was bruises and scabs where that Randy Blair put it to him. Like he said, he's too old to fight.*

He also told the diary how Pat had gotten married to Kitty Malone. Saying that news he felt, right then, sitting at the kitchen table and filling the goddamn scribbler with words he hardly knew how to spell, that something lonely had happened to him, that he was alone in a way he never had been since he slid out a few moments before the brother who had warmed him for the nine months of their quick-changing existence. Felt alone in a way that was new since then, an empty sad feeling that made him want to be young again, two-eyed, capable of living his life in a different way, surrounding himself with flesh of his own making; an empty sad feeling like the one he had had watching Pat go into the lake slowly, paddle around near the shore the way he always had, then come out so wet and bedraggled he looked worse than a skunked dog.

And, himself warm and comfortable, seated naked on a log and letting the wind blow him dry, he had watched Pat stand helplessly shivering on the gravel, shivering so his splayed knees banged together like driftwood and his arms threatened to shake right out of their sockets as he rubbed himself with his shirt, climbed still dripping and shaking back into his suit.

"I was thinking," Pat said.

"You were."

"I guess we'll be living at Kitty's house. At least until she gets mad and kicks me out."

"That's all right," Mark said. "Don't worry about coming back. I ain't expecting too many boarders." He took his eye out, washed it in the lake, then set it back in, making sure it was facing forward. Then took the tobacco Pat offered and, still naked and sitting on the log, rolled himself a cigarette. "Nothing wrong with settling down," Mark said. "I was thinking of it myself."

"Anyone in particular?"

"Not really." He grinned at Pat. "Well," he said, "to tell the truth—if I was going to get married after all this time I might choose someone with a little more weight. If you know who I mean."

Thirteen

"I was thinking about music," Pat Frank said. "I was thinking about those old heart-sopping songs they used to have on the radio when we had just met and we would drive one of Mark's old cars down to the lake and lie on the grass while the radio played. Do you remember that?"

"I never listened to the music," Kitty said. "I was always wanting you too much. Didn't you want me? You were so goddamn old and lecherous, you probably thought I was Rita what's-her-face, that fat waitress you were engaged to from Belleville."

"Never."

"What was her last name?"

"Don't remember."

It was night, the second night after Ellen Malone's funeral, and they were sitting in the kitchen of Kitty's grandfather's retirement house. There was one light on, a naked light bulb hanging from the ceiling, and on the table were the remains of supper, a teapot covered in a furry wool cozy, and one last package of tailor-made cigarettes from the carton they had bought on the day of their wedding. Now Pat reached for that package. The motion stretched the muscles of his back. He flexed them tentatively, then drew in a deep breath. That morning he had unwound the doctor's tape, tearing off his chest and back, it seemed, more hair than his head had known for two decades, and now when he breathed deep there was a small grinding on the inside of the short rib below his heart, a broken edge he imagined getting frayed and sharper until it worked its way inside.

"You should wait for the doctor," Kitty had said.

But he wasn't waiting for the doctor, for any doctor, because at the hospital in Toronto they'd x-rayed him and shown him a shadow on his lung, a dust cloud as ominous as any he'd ever imagined in his skull, and it wasn't something he wanted to know more about.

"Do you cough?"

"Sometimes."

"Blood?"

"I ain't that curious to look."

They had made him spit, so they could examine it under a microscope; and they had filled their needles with samples of his blood. After two days, when they had bled and probed and turned him practically inside out, he had stood up, looked out the window with his hands behind his back to keep the Johnny-coat covering his ass, and decided there was only one way he was going to leave that place on foot. And that was out the back door.

"Laughton was her name," Kitty said. "Rita Laughton. You brought her home to show her off to Charlie once. She looked like a nurse in her white waitress clothes. She looked like she wanted to pop right out of her clothes to get at you. God I was jealous. Charlie used to tease me about her all the time. Whenever you didn't come around for a few days he'd say you were off with Rita, poking holes in her doughnut."

They were sitting at the kitchen table. Beside the sink was an ironing board and, hanging from it in creased and dazzling splendour, were Pat's green khaki workpants and shirt. It was Kitty who had done the washing, by hand in the sink, but it was Pat who had ironed, insisting that this final touch, this *coop de grass*, was man's work.

"I never liked her," Pat said. "I was only lonely."

"Lonely! Didn't you see me?"

"Jailbait," Pat grinned. "My daddy always told me to stay away from young girls and broken-down cars."

Beside the furry-domed teapot was a bottle of rye. That bottle Pat now reached for, his hand sliding across the table with such practised unconscious ease that for a moment even *he* didn't know he was reaching for it; and then, having it secure and comfortable filling the palm of his big hand, he tipped it gently into his cup, watching the alcohol swirl on the copper surface of the tea.

It was late evening.

While Kitty had made supper and he had carefully ironed his pants and shirt, the sky outside had gradually gone through its twilight rainbow, changing from a light blue fading afternoon to an assortment of deeper colours, finally painting itself a hollow lustrous blue streaked with scarlet clouds that built the rim of the sky into a velvet setting for the first stars. And now those first stars had changed and rotated, been joined by thousands and millions of others. But through the kitchen window Pat Frank saw neither the last traces of day nor the brilliant night whiteness of stars, but only the reflection of the kitchen, an odd angled replication of himself sitting at the table, comfortably adding rye to his tea as if this was the habit it had taken him a lifetime to perfect, as if this was a well-earned cocktail to celebrate a whole era of hard work and family life.

In the morning it would be time to go back to work at the Salem Garage And General Repair. They were expecting him at eight o'clock; by noon he would be dead on his feet and counting the hours until closing. In the two weeks away he had forgotten what it was like to be working, to have his time measured out on the greasy white card they kept for him in the office. The few months of the job seemed to have lasted forever. How it had started was an absolute mystery: one perfectly normal wet March day, while in Salem to visit the liquor store, he had found himself in the office of the Garage, his hands in his pockets and his tongue stammering as he asked if they needed any help.

"It's only natural," Mark had commented, when Pat told him what he'd done. "Every few years a man wants a job."

But he hadn't been prepared for the complex swirl of new engines he had never seen, ancient vehicles he had long ago forgotten, all streaming to the garage in a choked confusion of complications and emergencies, each one demanding complete and instant service. Even during those rare times when his body fatigue was pushed aside, when he knew exactly what he was doing and was in the exact centre of doing exactly what he knew, there was a feeling that the world was growing bigger while he was growing smaller, that an infinity of sadistic engineers and careless drivers were ceaselessly inventing new and impossible problems while his own mind was losing ground, cells dropping off at the edges, dust building up where there should be experience, the grey fluid resilience of his brain turning sullen and rubbery just at the time he needed it most.

He was dreaming. And then the dream broke free and he was only sleeping, sleeping and not sleeping, not sleeping and lying on his back breathing slowly of the night air and gradually remembering his dream, roaming slowly through its great elaborate castle as if it were new.

He had been dreaming he was in a castle, a boy-prince imprisoned in his own stone castle. It had a thousand rooms he knew of, ten thousand more he'd never seen, whole unexplored wings that spoked out from the central hub and a dizzying wall that surrounded the tips of the spokes in a ragged moated circle.

He was lying on his back and discovered that resting on his left palm was Kitty's hand, hot and still with sleep. His right hand was folded over his chest, protecting the place where his rib hurt. But now it didn't hurt; it was too hot, even humming as the bones knitted together in the heat of his sleep. He was stuck inside his body, a prisoner to its every need, its every whim for a bottle or a fight or a piss in the middle of the night.

He was dreaming himself into a castle, into the dreams he had had when he was a boy. It was still early in the summer, a summer for which the whole spring was now past and he had wasted that whole spring trying to dream himself into his own boy's dreams, because he couldn't think ahead, even lying with his new wife's hand folding like a mole in his own he couldn't think as much as one year into the future, could only escape into the past, into the memory of himself as a boy: looking forward.

His boy-self *had* looked forward: looked to each day as if it were unknown, woken up each morning and looked around to see what was changed and what was the same. If Mark was still there, still breathing, if Terry Frank was downstairs drunk or sober, if outside it would be rain or sun. And though then too he had had the dream of a castle, had the dream of himself as a boy-prince lost in the exquisitely huge and elaborate castle that ended in a high wall looking down to nowhere, at that time he had loved his own prison, because it was rich and complex, because he was sure it was a place he would finally leave.

He was awake now, fully awake, staring at the dark rectangle where the night angled in the uncurtained window of Kitty's bedroom. In his mind was the memory of his dream, and the thoughts of his prisons now and then, but more than his dreams or his thoughts there was an uncomfortable feeling, the feeling of his whole brain being filled with the complicated cloud of everything he was trying to figure out, a complicated cloud that was itself like his castle, all compartmented away from itself, a world of its own that branched out in all directions and then ended in a pile of its own rubble. It was too much, too intricate, a grey aching maze with no escape.

He closed his eyes and tried to drift back to sleep. Instead he saw Terry Frank sitting on his summer bench with a bottle in his hand and his empty face looking at him as if he had just appeared out of the ground like a surprise tree. And wondered now, suddenly feeling pity, if the old man had short-circuited in some way, had found his old drunk head so full and aching with the dark impenetrable mystery of everything that he had decided finally that it was too much, not worth the bother, had decided he would just step out for a while, Goodbye Charlie to the whole tangled mess and maybe he'd have another try some other time. Goodbye Charlie to what he couldn't think, to what he couldn't feel, to his sons he didn't really want, to the farm he was too lazy to keep. And why not? Who in this world was ever going to figure anything out? Who was going to be a boy without looking forward? Or grow old without looking back? Why not just step right out, look at that great big yellow sun crazily splashing itself over the green green grass? Look at that yellow sun burning itself to oblivion just to push the green grass up every summer, shining its heart out for grass that six months later would cripple and freeze, drive itself back into the earth. Jesus, who ever heard of anything so crazy as the same seasons happening over and over again forever?

He pushed himself up in the bed and sat with his back propped against the wall, his legs crossed. It was strange to be sitting like this, he hadn't sat this way for years, decades, since he was still living in his father's house and had sat up to interrupt nightmares. A person can't think when they have no blood in their brain to think with, Terry Frank had explained to his sons; it's like when your foot goes to sleep. That had been a good one, he and Mark had thought; it's like when your foot goes to sleep—and had told each other that was what was wrong with their father, the circulation to his brain and heart had been cut off and he was just buzzing away for a while, waiting to fall off the end of the world.

To sit up he had let go of Kitty's hand. Now it sought him out, inspecting, in its sleep, his crossed legs, trying to translate them into his ordinary prone body, settling finally at his right foot which it grasped contentedly. They were married now, officially and legally joined by the best offices of the Kingston City Hall. Forty-nine years old, the oldest never-wed bachelor in the whole township aside from his twin brother, and he had gone down without a murmur, not once protesting as the clerk rushed through the service, pronounced them wed, then indulged his curiosity in a long stare that surveyed both their faces for some clue as to why, unencumbered by friends, family, or the likelihood of pregnancy, they would have sealed themselves to each other at this late date.

"Of course," Pat had explained to Kitty, as they were having a drink at the Italian Palazzeria they had chosen for their wedding feast, "with these shiners I could pass for a younger man. I mean young enough to marry a squirt like you." They had ordered spaghetti, and it was Pat's first experiment with eating this particular dish. To begin with he had followed Kitty's advice, and tried winding the stringy pasta onto his soup spoon with his fork. But then, observing the lady at the next table, he just took up his knife and cut it into pieces. "A person can't eat dinner with a spoon," he said. "If you don't mind my manners."

"Manners," Kitty said. "There's no point you worrying about your manners." For this occasion she was wearing a blouse with crinkles up the front and a fuzzy white cardigan sweater—both very tight and both loaned to her by Sandra. And in Sandra's clothes she looked like one of those prim and polished city ladies who sometimes came to the Salem Garage And General Repair and said their car was "acting funny."

"My car acts funny too," he would reply.

At the restaurant they had a drink before dinner and then ordered a bottle of wine. Kitty had chosen the brand; it was a foreign wine that the Salem liquor store didn't bother to stock. It came in a straw basket, like onions, and tasted sour for the first two glasses.

"You used to drink this kind of stuff in Toronto?"

"For God's sake," Kitty said. "Don't act like a hick."

He had flushed sharply, a jolt just like in the old days when such a remark was a prelude to a series of increasingly nasty comments to which, finally, he would reply either by losing his temper and escalating from sarcasm to pure obscenity, or simply withdrawing, doing his own Goodbye Charlie, stepping back to see exactly what she wanted to work herself into.

"Goddamn sharp-tongued bitch," he thought. The memory of her in the restaurant, trying to make him wind yards of spaghetti onto a dirty soup spoon, being superior in her sprayed hair and Sandra's clothes about a bottle of foreign wine that wasn't fit to water the garden, started to goad him; and sitting with his back digging uncomfortably into the wall and his knees starting to hurt from keeping his legs crossed he realized there was nothing so mysterious about the dull ache in his head, the fact that he couldn't sleep: he was only angry: angry at this woman for trying to lead him away from himself, angry at himself for being so desperate to escape that he didn't know who he was any more, didn't know anything about himself except that once he had been a boy who wanted to be a man, and that now he was a man, an aging man past his prime with one rib cracked, his hair lost, a new wife, and no better dream than that of being a boy again.

He straightened out his legs, then swung out of bed, stood up on the worn carpet of Kitty's bedroom and stretched, trying to make himself comfortable again. Kitty was murmuring in her sleep but, still angry, he shut her voice out. Summer had come quickly and this night was warm and humid, even close. Close, yes, he hated it when the air was so close it filled up his chest and made it tight, clogged his skin so it couldn't breathe. That was the way it was in cities; air so close a person couldn't breathe, close and thick with poisons that filled the lungs and blood. A person wouldn't have to smoke or drink in the city, it all came free, just a few glasses of foreign wine were enough to slow a person down in the city. Even the No-Tell Motel was turning into the city.

Pat stood in the centre of the room. Coming through the window was a diffuse glow that made it possible to see the outline of the bed, Kitty shifting again in her sleep, the dresser and the dull grey sheen of the mirror. There was not enough light there, however, to see his own reflection. Not that he was curious; he was only going for his tobacco and papers which, after stubbing his toe on one of Kitty's shoes, he finally located by patting his hands over the shadowed surface.

Night, it was the middle of the night, and it seemed to him he had been sleeping so poorly these past few months, waking up so often in the dark, that he had at least learned one thing—to roll cigarettes without looking. By the flare of the match he saw that Kitty's eyes were open.

"What's wrong?"

"Nothing," Pat said. "Couldn't sleep." He put his hand out to reassure her, rubbed slow circles at the top of her back.

"You all right?"

"Just up for a moment. You go back to sleep." The sheet had worked down and his hand was on her naked skin, smooth and silky, warm from sleep and soft to his touch. It wasn't an old thing with them but new, a trick he had learned from those nights he stayed over when Lynn was home and she couldn't sleep and would call for him. And for a few minutes he would sit beside her on the bed, feeling close to this child who was his and not his, feeling her thin child's skin glide like a kitten's on her perfect bones.

Kitty was breathing deeper now, asleep again, and to keep things the same, to keep her from waking up, he tapped the ash on the floor. Lynn was like that too; once he had talked and rubbed her back to sleep he had to stay sitting on her bed mumbling nonsense to her until her sleep was deep enough and she forgot him and moved away. Lynn: he tried not to think about her. She had a place in him he could go for weeks and months without finding. Even seeing her he would sometimes stay numbed from her, smile and nod as if she had popped out of nowhere and had nothing to do with him.

Now that Ellen had died and he had moved into Kitty's maybe things would be different; maybe Lynn would stay with them and he would see her every day when he came back from the Garage, see her every day for enough days and weeks and months that they could grow together, the old wounds open and heal again. The possibility that he would be living with not only Kitty but Lynn woke him up completely, and he felt his hand on Kitty's back grow tentative and confused.

"Pat, what's wrong?"

"I was thinking."

"What?"

"I was thinking about Lynn. About whether she could stay down with us."

He could feel Kitty's back grow tense under his own tensed hand, and he lifted it away as she twisted under the sheet.

"I don't know. Christ, Pat, it's the middle of the night."

He got up from the bed and crossed the floor to the dresser. Uselessly, because what he wanted was a drink and there was nothing there, so once up he kept going, into the kitchen. There he opened the refrigerator door and found a cold beer he had hidden in the vegetable compartment. As he took the first swallow he thought that now he was living with Kitty, not Mark, he would have to stop hiding his liquor. Which reminded him that only a couple of weeks ago, just before Kitty told him about the operation, he had found a bottle of Mark's sherry hidden with the old pots. To surprise him he had drunk half the sherry and then re-filled the bottle with the cheap vodka stocked by the Salem liquor store. One of these days Mark would reach up for his sherry he was so proud of hiding and would get more than he expected.

"Pat. What are you doing?"

"Just walking around."

"Come back to bed."

He moved slowly through the hall, the can of beer in one hand and the remains of his cigarette in the other.

"You really want Lynn here?"

"Yes."

"Okay."

Had they not just gotten married, had Kitty not been slowed down by her operation and Ellen's death, had Pat not been recently beaten by his own hero's dream and more recently soothed by his renegade beer, it would have been the perfect night for a fight. Warm and summery, a sliver of moon in the clear sky, it would have been a perfect night for them to take offence at each other, for Pat to drink brandy instead of beer until his head hurt, his throat started to go raw, and his legs itched for a long summer's night walk.

In the end Pat could have stormed out of the house Kitty's grandfather built—a mere retirement cottage in *his* mind—no place for scenes of spite and passion. And in the end Kitty could have gone out and sat on her grandfather's porch. Calm and serene, perhaps smoking a cigarette, she could have finally relaxed from the task of alternately fighting and appeasing Pat's drunken self-hate, relaxed from the sound of his drunken shouting and her own not exactly silent barbs, and listened instead to the peaceful fadeaway of Pat's self-righteous stomping through the bush and then, when it had finally melted into the night, the rising dawn-sounds of birds and wind.

But Kitty Malone had changed. She was reaching for Pat Frank in the night. She could feel the echo of the old panic welling up in her, but stronger yet was the need to touch him and be close. The fear slipped away. In the deep centre of this watershed night, of this very night which was near the end of June and was the shortest night of the year, Pat and Kitty finally wanted to stay together more than they wanted to push themselves apart.

As Pat slid into bed, he felt Kitty nestle against him, draw him around her, take his hand and press it in hers, take his fingers and touch them to the cheap gold ring he had bought her, take his fingers to her mouth and silently kiss the tips, one by one, sucking and kissing the tip of each finger until his whole hand was warm and buzzing, and then she took it and folded it between her breasts, sighing as she closed him into her.

He woke to her moving his hand again, guiding it from between her breasts and slowly, speculatively, drawing it down her stomach, brushing it past the oblong pad of bandage and gauze, and putting it to rest on her abdomen, the way she did when she had an ache. For a moment it rested there. Then she began to move it down again: across the bristly mound where they had shaved her, down between her warm thighs.

He pulled her close. Everywhere his fingers moved they could feel the sharp stubs of her hair. With the grain she was like a baby; against it she felt like a newly cut field. She wriggled around him. Sleeping, lazy, he could feel his need of her starting up, darting through him like fish scattering in shallow water.

"Pat," she said.

She reached down and suddenly he was inside, stiff and trembling, afraid to move because this was the first time since her operation, the first time for so long he was afraid that if he moved he would burst, the first time since they were married, too, and now reminded him of the very first time of all, twenty years ago when he had been so stiff it had hurt.

"Pat." She arched her back and he breathed deeply, the sudden intake of air calming him. She stretched and he cupped his hand under her chin, on her stretched throat where the staccato tremors started, waved out from deep inside her, deep where they had touched her, so deep he was afraid she was going to hurt herself, so deep he was afraid her stitches would burst open.

He could feel himself waver.

"Pat."

He had his hand on her chest and her heart was beating so violently he thought it was his own. He clung to her as she began to churn around him, and then the bumpy rhythm of her heart sped further, his fear flattened out and dissolved.

"Pat."

The room was pink with the beginning light. For this moment her eyes were calm, deep blue, and resting easily in his. For this moment he felt close to her, open, unafraid.

"You all right?"

"I don't know." She reached down and her hand came back bloody. He threw off the covers.

"That's all there is," Kitty said. "Just a few drops."

This morning their skin was sweet pink and brown. Sweet summer warm, the air brushed across them.

"Look at us," Pat said. He was sitting up in bed, looking at the stripe across his belly where the bandage had been, looking at the bony set of his own chest, at the way his long corded arms hung from his shoulders; and he was seeing Kitty too, lying flat on her back with her belly gently dipping like sand hammered smooth by the sea, her legs Vee-d apart from each other, the soles of her feet pressed together as if she were praying to the morning in some newly invented ritual. He saw himself and he saw Kitty and for a moment he didn't know who was who, who was observing and who was being watched. And then it was like in the forest: the room opened up and he was aware only of the warm morning air, of the rush of his own breathing.

"Pat. What are you thinking?"

"I don't know." He stood up, elated but also fatigued, so exhausted that even as he stretched he could feel the sweetness that more sleep would be, could feel the total need of his body to collapse and be spared the day of work at the Salem Garage. He stepped across the room and looked out the window. In the weedy green field lay a low glowing mist, and through it shone the bright white rays of the rising sun, traversing the whole world in great angled blocks. "Look at that," Pat said.

They were sitting on the porch of Kitty's grandfather's retirement house. It was seven o'clock in the morning and the sun was already over the edge of the trees, burning away the last traces of mist and heating patches of earth where the dogs could sleep away the morning.

Pat was shaved and wearing his newly ironed uniform, the green creased khaki draped like metal over his angular bones. In one hand he held a cup of coffee, in the other a cigarette.

"I guess I'll be coming home tonight," Pat said. "After work."

"You might as well. You live here now."

She watched Pat's face as it hesitated, tried to keep its composure, then finally gave way and grinned at her.

"Family life," Pat said. "It's the latest thing." He finished his coffee, gave her a wink from one swollen eye, and began the long walk down the drive towards the highway.

Kitty watched him as he wound his way out of the yard and blurred into the encroaching maple bush, the dark green of his clothes gradually swallowed and finally completely hidden by the new lighter green of exploding leaves. There was everything to do: it was weeks since the garden had been weeded; she wanted to talk to Sadie about Lynn; the whole house needed to be cleaned. But for now it was enough to roll another cigarette and step carefully off the rickety wooden porch to the warm summer ground. The dogs stood up and swarmed around her. There would be other seasons but now, one more time, she was standing straight, ready to live out the warm endless summer ahead.